My NEXT Husband Will Be NORMAL

A St. John Adventure

by Rae Ellen Lee

DISCLAIMER

In the pages ahead, you'll read how a warm climate and a long-held secret melted one person's most fundamental notions. Yet this curious tale is only my skewed take on things. For if Tom and I were called to trial as witnesses of a car crash, the jury would sit, jaws dropped, as we each swore to a different number of cars and people, location involved, even the day of the week the wreck happened. Also, a few names have been changed for reasons of privacy. In one case, I'm hoping a name change might short-circuit an attempt on my life.

And *please* be forewarned. I may not have reacted to certain events the way you *think* you would have. This book is also not a psychological treatise on how best to operate when paradise turns out to have pitfalls. But if you enjoy reading a quirky, true relationship drama, humorously told—set on a tiny but extraordinary Caribbean island– then this book is for you.

P-book: ISBN 978-0-9619328-5-5
E-book: ISBN 978-0-9619328-4-8

Design and production, Kate Weisel, weiselcreative.com
Cover images from iStockphoto.com

GREAT BLUE GRAPHICS

As I did for the first memoir,
I Only Cuss When I'm Sailing
(first published as *If* The Shoe *Fits*)
I dedicate this book to Thomas N. Lee
1943 – 2007 (when he became Rebekah Jane)
who, shortly after we married,
said, "I'll feed you and give you something to write about,"
and kept his promise in spectacular ways.

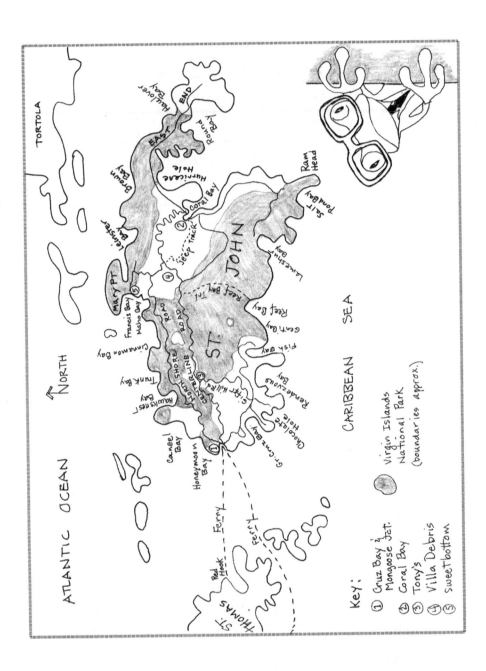

Also by Rae Ellen Lee

Powder Monkey Tales — A Portrait in Stories
(as told by Wesley Moore alias Post Hole Augerson)

I Only Cuss When I'm Sailing
(first published as *If* The Shoe *Fits*)

The Bluebird House

Contents

BIMBO MUSIC

A Prologue

The wind screams. Whitecaps froth and spit off the tops of mountainous waves.

"We're okay, Baby!" Tom shouts. "The boat won't tip all the way over."

It's what he always tells me. But this time we're sailing in the Strait of Juan de Fuca. This is different. This is big trouble. And, once again, he's forgotten that my real name is Rae Ellen.

A sudden *crack,* like a gunshot, announces a new crisis. A pulley on the starboard side has snapped loose from the deck. Now the forward sail, the jib sheet, flails wildly in the gale-force blow.

"Grab the helm," the Viking captain yells.

A feeling of dread sweeps over me like a rogue wave. But I don't have a choice. Tom must rummage in the gear locker for the needed part and some tools, so I take charge of steering the boat. I hang on, gripping the wheel at ten o'clock and two o'clock, as we bash through an armada of buttes and pinnacles toward Vancouver Island. I glance at the depth meter and let out a guttural moan. The meter reads a depth of only 36 feet. The numbers are spiraling downward, 35 … 34 … 32. Vancouver Island looms ahead.

"Come about!" Tom barks.

I spin the wheel, turning the boat away from the island, the rocks, and the shallow bottom. It's what any sane person would do.

"Why are you turning that way? The wind is from the west." The Viking is not happy with me.

"The wind is from everywhere," I mumble, spinning the wheel again. Of course a real sailor would *know* to turn the boat 180 degrees in the opposite direction, to come about. But it's too late now. We have to jibe, which means I must turn the boat in a nearly complete circle. So I cuss *The Shoe* around—first *sideways* to the attacking wind and waves, now head-on *into* purgatory, then *through* the blast to the other side. But just as we reach the proper orientation, the end of the boom catches in the line used to trim the sail.

Tom scurries to untangle the mess. "Now get us back on course!"

"What course?" I scream. "We've been zigzagging all over the Strait. We've been in and out of Canada six times."

"Parallel to land," he states loudly yet calmly, clearly baffled at my ignorance. "We gotta sail east to get home."

Well, of course. And to think I once lived a normal life on land, before agreeing to this crazy sailboat idea. "It's a no-brainer, really," Tom had said, "since the wind *is* free and we *are* broke." If you don't study the notion in any depth, it almost makes sense. And I am open-minded. Why not get a boat, fix it up, learn to sail, and then boldly set off for St. John in the U.S. Virgin Islands? Because that *is* our goal, our chosen destination. "We'll live on the boat," Tom said. So I finally relented, in a tiny *well, all right* voice with my fingers crossed behind my back.

And now, I've had about all the free wind I can take. At the exact second Tom completes the fix on the broken thing, I abandon the helm to him and descend the steep companionway steps to cower below-deck in privacy. My drop into the bowels of the boat is hampered by eight layers of clothing. I'm like an overstuffed chair. When I finally step onto the galley floor, the muffins I'd baked earlier lie strewn among the coffee grounds and guts from our aluminum drip coffee pot. I flex my knees to absorb the rock and roll motion of the boat, and let go of the overhead grab rail. Squatting, I brush the debris off the muffins and store them in the oven, where they'll be safe. Because while the boat thrashes wildly, the stove is gimbaled to stay level. The boat shudders violently. When I stand up so I can hold onto the grab rails, I get a head rush.

Everything above deck—the halyards, sails, and lines I'm not allowed to call ropes—are all slamming and clanging against the mast, the boom, even the hull. Certain of a frigid, watery death, I squeeze my eyes shut and pray that the end will come suddenly, like when they knock you out with those drugs before a colonoscopy.

"Whales!" Tom shouts from the cockpit.

My eyes jerk open. He must mean our old friends, the Orcas.

"Hurry!" he yells down the companionway. "They're heading straight toward us."

Grabbing my camera, I crawl back up into the cockpit and hook my safety leash onto the binnacle post. Four black fins about eight feet high plow toward us on a collision course. But I'm fearless in my hope for a perfect photo. Will they surface and arc? Only their fins are visible as they travel like torpedoes toward us through the steep waves and spray. Each whale is two or three times the size of *The Shoe*. I snap a couple pictures.

"They will turn, won't they?" I yell to be heard over the din.

In answer, the orcas dive under *The Shoe*, one at a time, and surface a few boat lengths behind us.

The wind rages and gusts. "Here, take the helm. It's time to haul in the jib."

I jam my camera into my North Face jacket pocket and grip the helm. On the deck in front of me, Tom drops the sail and lashes it down.

"Now, heave to," he shouts. "I'll tie the third reef in the main sail."

I would rather go through childbirth again. But I know what to do. In the chaos of flying lines, spraying water, and wildly flapping sails, I turn the wheel and stall out the boat. Which means the broad side of the boat now faces the screaming wind, and we're tilted over at about 45 degrees. The wind shoves at us without mercy. Finally Tom has reduced the size of the main sail so it will catch less wind; however, as soon as he takes the helm from me and turns the boat to regain headway, a different piece of hardware snaps off the bow.

"Take the helm again! Quick!" Tom shouts. "And when I tell you, turn the boat directly into the wind."

I do as I must. He leaps onto the deck and makes his way toward the bow to fix the mystery item. His knees on his long legs are flexed to give him a lower center of gravity and absorb the boat's wild motion. But the fool isn't holding onto the grab rails affixed to the side of the deck.

"Hang on!" I yell, like his mother, interrupting his further instructions to me. But I'm quite sure he says, "Don't be bashful. Make the boat do what you want. You're the boss."

So I steer the *Titanic* while cussing, moaning, and shivering in the cold. Confronting death head on, I turn the boat into the wind with grave determination and gun the engine. At least we have an engine, and it's actually running. We bash upward into a monster wave, drop suddenly down into the valley of the shadow of death, slam steeply up again, and now, as if a rug is pulled out from under us, back down we go. Tom squats at the bow, untethered in the 50 knot gusts and spray. While I ponder the real possibility that he'll be washed overboard, a wave crashes into the boat and I'm pitched off sideways like a rag doll. Determined to save our lives, I maintain my death grip on the wheel, and strain my right arm as my left kneecap and thigh smack against the top edge of a storage locker.

Why are we out here? Why am I doing this? Sure, the weather was fine this morning in that nice little cove in the shelter of Vancouver Island's Barkley Sound. While eating cereal in the cockpit, I'd listened like a good little first mate as Tom talked about the elemental beauty of sails—as if he was talking about the first stone wheels, or the discovery of electricity. And I had thought, *wow*, I want to write about the physics of sails, discover who they really are, maybe write a story from the viewpoint of a spinnaker. And now to get back to Bellingham we have to use those sails, which is fine, except for the weather. My anger at being in this dangerous situation feels flat, level, open on the sides, and as vast as the ocean.

Tom fixes the problem on deck and saunters back toward the cockpit to take over the helm.

"Those waves are at least fifteen feet high," I groan, cowering above the companionway steps, underneath the dodger.

"No," Tom says. "They're only about ten feet high."

But I can tell you this: right now the height of the waves is *about* 15 feet and they are steep, close together, and life-threatening. More ominous than the size of the waves is the deafening roar of the unrelenting wind.

Tom turns the boat south toward Port Angeles. I stand below-deck now, knees flexed, hands monkey-fisted on the two overhead grab rails. I glare out the port window at the receding waves as *The Shoe* wallows in the troughs between the waves. As soon as we are lifted up to the top of a wave, we surf down the other side. Tom is having the time of his life. Every few seconds he looks over his shoulder and *up* at the tops of the waves rolling toward us.

"Boy, did you see that one?" he shouts, laughing with glee at a departing rogue wave. "This is exactly the kind of experience we need before sailing to St. John."

I hate him. Tomorrow I'll take a helicopter or a float plane from Port Angeles to Bellingham. Surely they take credit cards. I will not endure this nightmare one more day.

Finally, at dusk we arrive at the Port Angeles city dock. Our faces are wind-burned red and mine is fixed in a grimace I fear is permanent. I limp slowly along the dock. As usual, we're holding hands. Some habits are hard to break.

We find a restaurant at Harbor Mall that serves drinks. Tom orders clam chowder and I get a chef salad served on a glass platter shaped like a big round fish. We each sip a mug of beer. Sixties tunes are playing loudly overhead. I think, at least I'm not hearing Jimmy Buffet. If you're around sailboats, you can hardly escape him.

"You know how I feel about sailing," I growl. "It's stupid and dangerous."

"How can you say that?" Tom says, wearing his incredulous face again. "Sailing is beautiful. And the boat will take care of us. It knows what to do."

"I want answers," I say, speaking each word with emphasis. "You're the captain. Why didn't we reduce the sails sooner?"

"Well, I had prayed for wind but when it came, I kept thinking it wouldn't get any worse." He shrugs, takes a bite of clam chowder and says, "This is really good."

"We want different things," I say, glaring at him. "You need someone pelagic, someone who studies sea birds for a living, or maybe one of those oceanographers. At least find someone who grew up sailing, someone who thinks it's an acceptable way to die."

"But I want to be with you."

"That doesn't make any sense." I'm on a rant and this time I'm determined to be heard. "I've tried hard these last couple years to like sailing and feel safe. You know that. And no matter what the weather is doing, I have to go sailing because the boat is where we live."

"Yeah," Tom shrugs and pauses, like he's giving thought to what I just said. "The fetch *is* definitely long in the Strait, with no obstacles to slow the wind. That's probably what happened. I'll bet that wind got started way over there in Kyoto."

"You son-of-a-bitch! You can sail all by yourself to fucking Kyoto." Tom's lack of acknowledgment of my feelings is all too familiar. But this time I'm not getting back on the boat. In fact, I'm going to sleep here in the restaurant where it's nice and warm and smells good, not like mold. And in the morning, after the helicopter trip to Bellingham, I'll catch a flight to Montana. That's it. I'm going back to Montana.

Another 1960s song is playing overhead now, something about following your man wherever he goes, that deep, deep oceans and very high mountain ranges are no match for your love, are no obstacles at all in holding you back from tagging along with him.

I can't believe my ears. No wonder I've been leading this reckless sailing life, so often on the edge of death. That's the kind of music I grew up listening to—bimbo music. I begin to laugh, louder and louder. I'm hysterical. I shriek with laughter. People's forks are paused mid-air while they stare at me. Suddenly, I stop laughing and begin to sob uncontrollably. I howl. Tears stream down my face and splash onto my half-eaten salad on the glass fish platter.

Tom touches my hand. "It's okay, Baby."

This is so absurd that I begin to laugh again, and I can't quit, except to shout, "Stop calling me Baby!" Everyone in the restaurant is quiet now. And I'm embarrassed. I mop at my face with my dirty napkin.

The song surrounds us again, a repeating refrain about loving him and, by God, following him no matter what, no matter where, like what can you do if he's your destiny? I want to yell, *Get your own life!*

The song is so foolish that I shake my head and can't quit. A piece of food, maybe lettuce, is stuck on my right cheek. I can feel it there, but I don't care.

Slowly, painfully, I slide out my side of the booth and we walk through the restaurant. I'm limping slightly and my arm hurts. I hold my head high, but I know my face is a hideous sight, so I drop my head down and watch my boots take one step and then another. Tom opens the door for me. We walk silently along the waterfront, hand in hand, back to *The Shoe*. I don't know how or when, but I will exit this hazardous lifestyle. I picture myself on an airplane. I am warm and dry, and I'm holding a drink featuring rum. Is that a Jimmy Buffet song I hear? The plane is en route to the U.S. Virgin Islands, and soon I'll be lying on the beach in the sunshine, resting up from the last few years. I picture warm sand between my toes, the ocean sparkling like opals on fire. A green turtle surfaces. Pelicans fly overhead, waiting, watching for the right moment to dive for a fish.

Some people have a baby to save a marriage. But we're too old. Maybe all we need is to get back to St. John, where we can live out our lives as beach potatoes. I'll be watching for a way to get us there, and it will not be on a sailboat.

WHY ST. JOHN?
AND WHY DOESN'T THE ISLAND FLOAT AWAY?

The first time we visited St. John we said we were doing research for a novel. When we left Helena, Montana, that day in late November, 1996, it was minus 10 degrees Fahrenheit. The moment we stepped off that airplane into the warm, moist, 80-degree F air, we were goners. The next thing you know, we were no longer wearing underwear. And we were drooling slightly out of both sides of our mouths.

By the end of our ten-day visit, during which time we forgot to do book research, we found ourselves pondering life's big questions: how could such a small piece of land sustain so many feral cats, goats, safari taxis, bananaquit birds, roosters, and massage therapists?

Life's big questions remain a mystery, but I have uncovered some facts and made some observations.

For instance, the number of visitors to St. John during the last 20 years has ranged from 700,000 to 1 million a year, many of them doctors and lawyers and such. If your personal physician or legal advisor was among them, he or she probably experienced "vacation brain," the way we did. This syndrome is caused by the cells' reaction to the sudden change of climate, especially when said cells have been working overtime to keep the host body alive in a frosty climate. After encountering a big red rooster wandering out of an open shop door, visitors from The City have been known to say, "Oh … I didn't know you had peacocks here." Or, standing knee-deep in the ocean, he or she might look puzzled and blurt, "Where are we in relation to sea level?" It's true. Perfectly intelligent human beings, including those who claim status as the valedictorian of their high school graduating class, have asked, "So, what keeps these islands from floating away?" The *Tradewinds* newspaper police log once reported that a visitor renting a villa at Peter Bay, where the millionaires stay, called to report a dinosaur on his deck. Don't let this happen to you. Those prehistoric-looking creatures are iguanas, and they're quite harmless unless you're wearing *I'm Not Really a Waitress Red* toenail polish.

The 2010 census registered a population of 4,170 (plus or minus) assorted human beings on St. John, including Fred the Dread, Boiler Al, and Hermon Smith, characters you'll meet if you hang out on the island for a while.

There are many reasons people come to live on this nipple of land in the Caribbean. Some of those reasons are, obviously, weather related. I've read that if you are a person of character, you're not so apt to be needy when it comes to climate. But why not be somewhere consistently warm and moist and welcoming? Why not live where gentle rains caress your body, and tree frogs and other strange noises tickle your ears in the night? Why not be surrounded by a turquoise sea as warm as bath water to swim in, among green turtles and bright blue fishes, and lie on warm sand the color of honey?

According to a quote by Captain Phil of the s/v *The Wayward Sailor* in an article in *Tradewinds* by Allison Smith, "Some people are looking for their destiny, some are looking for their truth, and others are just looking for a parking space." Others manage to engineer their own witness relocation program, although I enjoy substituting *witless* for witness. On our second visit to the island, in January 2001, Tom and I rented a car one day, and gave a Bordeaux Mountain resident a ride. He told us that police still come looking for people on the island by their alias or nickname, and that you don't always get to know someone's real name until after they die. Then you might learn they're on the FBI's Ten Most Wanted list. Occasionally, the secret that someone is hiding from the rest of us is the same secret he's hiding from himself.

This very special island could have ended up as one of the many neighboring British Virgin Islands, except the United States purchased St. John, St. Thomas, and St. Croix (the three U.S. Virgin Islands) from Denmark in 1917. The Danes had planted sugar cane, tobacco, and cotton, and at one time there were over 100 plantations on St. John, worked with slaves brought from Africa. The island is now divided into estates named after those plantations, including Enighed (which, properly pronounced, sounds like the whinnying of a horse), Glucksburg, Zootenval, Calabash Boom, Fish Bay, and Hard Labor. After the purchase in 1917, the island was ruled by a governor appointed by the U.S. Navy until 1931, when the Department of Interior assumed control. Now an unincorporated U.S. territory, residents cannot vote for President of the United States, although they receive other benefits of citizenship, including the right to serve in the military and, of course, pay taxes.

In 1950, Laurence Rockefeller purchased more than half the island and developed Caneel Bay Resort. When he and like-minded friends donated acreage to the U.S. Government as public park land, Congress formed the Virgin Islands National Park (VINP). Now about two-thirds of the island is public land, and vast stretches of its terrain are lush, green, and laced with hiking trails. The other one-third of the island is dotted with shackteaus, unfinished houses that look like concrete bunkers with rebar sticking up, and villas, many with stunning ocean views.

Cruz Bay, located at the west end of the island, is the main harbor town. Coral Bay, a smaller concentration of buildings and services, is near the east end and enjoys a more rural atmosphere with an enduring population of hippies.

The average annual precipitation ranges from 43 to 55 inches, compared to Seattle's 38 inches and New York City's 47 inches, keeping in mind that snow is also precipitation. Winter temperatures range from 77 to 84 degrees, although it can get down to a chilly 70 degrees on 1,277 ft. high Bordeaux Mountain. Summer temperatures range from 82 to 90 F, but when the trade winds stop blowing in September and October, it can feel like a sauna.

Hurricane season begins June 1 and ends November 30, and hurricanes do hit the islands. There was Hugo in 1989. And the big one,

Marilyn, in 1995, after which the name Marilyn no longer reminded anyone of a luscious blond trying to keep her skirt from blowing up around her ears. Everyone has a Hurricane Marilyn story, and you will hear conversations in which a resident will say, "Hmmm, let's see, was that before Marilyn, or after?" Other hurricanes have come over St. John in recent years without leaving major wreckage in their wakes: Georges in 1998, and Jose and Lenny in 1999.

Geographically, the island is located 1,075 miles southeast of Miami. The Atlantic Ocean sloshes up on the north and east shores of the island, the Caribbean Sea on the west and south. And although a certain air of lunacy and mischief prevails, the island does not fall within that vast area of unexplained disappearances and phenomena called The Bermuda Triangle.

At approximately 19 square miles in area, St. John is roughly the same size as Manhattan; however, this island is surrounded by sandy beaches and water the mystical color of rare and precious sapphire. And, yes, formed as it was from volcanic activity, the island goes all the way to the bottom, which keeps it from floating away.

That first visit to St. John, in 1996, wrecked us like a hurricane. Vulnerable travel virgins that we were, the island felt other-worldly, mysterious, and oh-so romantic. Sometime during that visit, we crossed over the line separating us from voodoo and the super-natural in ways we couldn't understand. We sobbed on the ferry when we left. And tears stung our sunburned faces on our flight back to the mainland. By the time we landed back home in snowy Helena, Montana, we'd made up our minds: one way or another, we would live on this tiny speck of land in the Caribbean.

OUR *LITTLE* SHACKTEAU *IN PARADISE*

*I*t's been two and one-half years since that fateful sailing trip in the Strait of Juan de Fuca and the evening I heard that bimbo music, and nearly five years since our first visit to St. John. But here we are, on a March day in 2001. A safari taxi, one of those full-sized pick-up trucks with bench seats and a canopy, drops us off next to a sign tacked on a tree that states, SNOW EMERGENCY ROUTE. Nearby is an abandoned vehicle with a vintage license plate on it that reads *American Paradise.* We have finally arrived, and we did not get here by sailboat.

A middle-aged guy in shorts, T-shirt, flip-flops, and uncombed thinning brown hair materializes, as if out of nowhere. Our new landlord introduces himself and leads us to a tiny shack downhill from the driveway. "I call this the pool cabin," he says, proudly. "My father stays in it when he's on island."

This is no cabin. This is a chicken coop, complete with dried chicken shit on the porch. We'd only glimpsed the place at some distance during our January visit a couple months ago, while driving around in the rental car. I'd made arrangements to rent the place by phone. It's funny how things can look so much grander far away, especially when that's what you want to see.

Now as we step onto the creaky, postage stamp of a front porch, we see how miniscule the place really is—maybe 8 ft. x 12 ft. Bahama shutters that open up and out like eyelashes, are, in this case, made of warped plywood. Sticks prop them up, exposing two small torn and rusty window screens.

The rickety old wood door scrapes across the plywood floor as we open it. I groan. In the dim light my eyes make out a huge rubber dinghy, fully inflated, leaning against one wall.

"You'll be storing that dinghy somewhere else, right?" Tom says.

"Nowhere else to keep it," the landlord laughs. "That's where it lives."

This problem is nothing compared to what reveals itself as my eyes adjust to the darkness. The place is filthy. Are those more dried chicken droppings on the floor? A futon mattress on a platform occupies much of the shack. The mattress is gritty and gray, except for the stains of all sizes and colors. A board resting on two stumps creates a shelf along the wall near the door. On this board, which serves as the kitchen counter, are a few unwashed dishes along with a one-burner hotplate and its frayed cord. On the floor underneath the board is an apartment-sized refrigerator, its door resting ajar. And what do you know? There's a chest of drawers. After years on a sailboat without this piece of furniture, I've lusted after one of these. Except on this unit, all five drawers are pulled out at rakish angles.

I'm in a state of disbelief. Tom must be, too, because he stands trance-like and stares dumbly, his mouth hanging open. I notice his knees are flexed, as if he's on the boat, as if a lower center of gravity will help absorb the shock.

Our landlord carries the moment. "I'll go string a utility cord from the main house so you'll have electricity to run the hotplate and refrigerator."

After he leaves I gawk at the mattress, backing up as if it might attack me. I bump into Tom and almost knock him down. My jaw hangs open, and when I find the wherewithal to form words, it's as if they're coming from some distance. "I wonder why he calls this the pool cabin?"

Tom, who usually has an answer to everything even if he has to make it up, grunts, "Huh."

"This is unbelievable," I say. "I can't sleep on that."

"Maybe we can take it outside on the porch and whomp the dirt and dust off it," Tom offers. Leaning near the door is a broom, with its business end frayed almost beyond recognition. He reaches for it in slow motion, as if he's in a vertical coma.

I lift up one corner of the mattress. Wood slats lie unevenly spaced on top of a piece of weathered plywood. Millions of tiny ants and dozens of cockroaches have set up camp between the slats. Now disturbed, these creatures are milling around in the dirt mixed with insect droppings and the corpses of dead cockroaches. They, too, seem dazed and confused.

"They're happy where they are," Tom says. "We'd better not try to sweep them. If we stir them up, they'll scatter all over hell."

"I'm not staying here," I announce, dropping the mattress onto the insects, sending up a cloud of dust and disintegrated beetle dung.

But we both know there's no choice. Even if we could find a vacancy elsewhere on the island, we have no extra money for it. This place is cheap, almost too cheap to be true, an important virtue in short-term housing for people in our tax bracket. After living on the sailboat for four years, I'd spent hours fantasizing about this step up on the housing ladder.

Of course, our new slumlord already has our deposit and first month's rent, required in advance of our arrival. His demeanor is that of a middle-aged ten-year-old, but surely he can't be oblivious to filth. He has to know this place is unfit for human habitation, and in a snake-oil salesman kind of way, he also has to know *he's got us.*

Tom sweeps off the mattress and we make the bed, careful not to rile the teeming varmints underneath. Resigned to my fate, I resolve to honor their squatters' rights. If they'll be nice little bugs, certainly we can all co-exist in peace.

Next we investigate the mini refrigerator. Before coming here by safari taxi, we'd purchased groceries at Starfish Market to supplement the boxes of Rice-A-Roni and cans of chicken we'd brought. Now we need to keep the perishables from rotting. The refrigerator is lined with bits of decayed food and dried scum, and the door doesn't latch. Tom leaves to find water, and brings back the utility cord and a quart of water in a cooking pot with no handle.

"The Governor says to go easy on the water. It's expensive."

"The Governor?"

"Yes. It's nicer than what I'd like to call him."

After washing the grime off the inside of the refrigerator, we install our foodstuffs. May the clear plastic grocery bags be sufficiently prophylactic. Tom searches around outdoors and finds a rock big enough to hold the refrigerator door closed. Then I make sandwiches while Tom washes out the dresser drawers, a task which requires several more trips to the big house for water.

It's common for people in shock not to speak. I've seen it on TV. Tom and I now point, grunt, and use glances to communicate. After we eat our sandwiches, I sniff an armpit and tilt my head toward the big house, where the shower and toilet amenities are located. Other tenants occupy rooms in the big house, and The Governor lives on the top floor in the penthouse apartment. Silently, we sort through our luggage for clean underwear and towels.

Even before stepping into the bathroom, we catch a whiff of sewer. Soon enough we see that the toilet is full. I leave to stand outdoors in the fresh air while Tom attempts to flush the toilet. Nothing happens, because there's no water in the tank. He stomps past me and finds a bucket lying on the ground around the side of the house, which he uses to pour water into the tank so he can flush away the evidence.

Tom comes back outdoors. "It's gone. Let's try the shower."

When we lived on the boat we often showered together. We'd walk the equivalent of several blocks along the dock in cold, piercing wind to the bath house. But once inside, the stall was always clean and warm. We could feed a dollar into the meter and count on a hot shower with strong water pressure. Now only cold water dribbles and spits from the shower head, and it's a good thing we wore our flip-flops because the shower floor is scummy. Worse than that, it doesn't drain.

At least the cold water restores us to a more conscious state.

"Welcome to Glacial Lake Missoula," Tom says.

"Or… maybe this is the pool he was talking about."

Back in the shack, Tom lines up our morning coffee fix. He places a filter in our dented aluminum drip coffee pot, left over from our backpacking days in Montana and the sailboat years. Our gallon of drinking water from the market sits next to a clean cooking pot. And next to that is a bag of Seattle's Best Sumatra coffee, ground for drip. We're all set for morning. We must be at The Canvas Factory in Mongoose Junction by 8:00 a.m. After leaving this hell-hole, we'll walk and hitch-hike into Cruz Bay, where we'll buy a business located in one of the Caribbean's most elegant shopping destinations.

Horizontal at last, we lay side by side in the dark, covered by a sheet, lined up perpendicular to the slats under our mattress. The only barriers between us and the soiled futon mattress are the mattress pad and fitted sheet we brought.

Speaking up to be heard over the frog chorus in the nearby trees, Tom says, "Looks like our landlord banged this shack together out of scraps he found after Hurricane Marilyn. The pieces of rusted metal roof are totally mismatched, and the plywood and boards are all different thicknesses and sizes."

"Hurricane archeology. It's kind of resourceful," I say. "And I wouldn't mind at all, if the place wasn't so filthy-dirty."

"I know," he says, already drifting off.

Just once I'd like to fall asleep first, but I never do. I concentrate on my breathing, which is so boring that it usually does the trick, but not tonight. So I review my life. Not all of it, mind you. Only the last six weeks, since our January 2001 fly-in to find a way to live here, which meant find a way to earn money. In that six weeks, we not only cobbled together a down payment for a lot at Fish Bay—the last, flattest, cheapest half-acre lot on the island, where we hope to build a house someday—but also for The Canvas Factory. These two "investments" took most of our money from the sale of some property I owned in Montana. During the last six weeks we also lavished even more time and money on the sailboat. Then we got it appraised, applied for an equity loan on the old bucket, and listed it for sale. Now look where we are—in a bug-ridden shanty that's no bigger than the living area of the sailboat.

As I start to fade, I can almost hear the clanging ropes against the sailboat masts at Squalicum Harbor—the halyard chorus. This thought somehow reminds me of the ants and beetles underneath us.

When I remove my ear plugs to listen more closely for the scratching of the bugs, the landlord's dog starts barking, and several more dogs in the neighborhood join the serenade. No matter. Lots of people in the world would be grateful for living conditions this good. Besides, being thoroughly warm makes me feel amiable. If I were a cube of butter, I would start to liquefy.

WALKING THE FOOT (or WTF?)

It's raining this morning as we set off walking up the road less grav-
eled. I'm carrying the umbrella; Tom is hiding under his Army National Guard rain poncho. Water runs off us in braided streams, like
spring runoff in Montana.

We walk along the Gifft Hill Road past the island's garbage dump
and ascend the steep hill up to Tony's, a concession stand selling
drinks and snacks at the junction with the Centerline Road. In front
of Tony's, Tom points left toward our destination. That's how you
hitchhike on the island. And since the cars going our direction are
driving in the left lane, it's easy for them to pull over to pick us up.
Soon a newer pickup truck stops and we crawl into the back and drop
our butts onto a bag of cement. I am mortified. On the day I become
a business owner in an upscale shopping complex, my entire bottom
is wet, and in this moist climate, I'll have diaper rash by the end of the
day. Tom's poncho is long enough for him to sit on, so at least he'll
have a dry hinder.

When we arrive, Cynthia and Jim, the current owners of The Canvas
Factory, are waiting for us in front of the shop. We shake hands before
following them to the attorney's office. Mongoose Junction, where the
shop is located, is a complex of several two-story buildings designed
to look like the original Danish sugar plantation estates. The thick
walls are built of colorful rocks, conch shells, and chunks of coral
that look like brains. We walk past R & I Patton Goldsmithing, The
Fabric Mill, and The Clothing Studio, where artists paint on cotton
beach wear. Arching overhead are tall leafy trees with orchids growing on their trunks. We step onto a courtyard next to a shop named
Bamboula, with African textiles and drums in the window, before
climbing a flight of concrete steps to a collection of offices. And before

you know it, papers are signed and money changes hands. No smiling, no banter, no foreplay.

In January, we'd met with Glen Speer, the designer, builder, and part-owner of Mongoose Junction. He told us The Canvas Factory was one of the founding businesses in the Junction, and that the shop has been owned and operated by Jim and Cynthia for over 20 years. Mongoose Junction is one of the main shopping destinations in the Caribbean. Dozens of shops sell items both practical and sublime. There's food, clothing, art, gear and gifts, all with an international flavor.

By the time our signatures are dry on the contract, we're back inside The Canvas Factory. One of the original artisan shops in the junction, we'll be making most of the items we sell. The Canvas Factory is also in a key location, on the ground floor of a building located right off the North Shore Road, the paved route that winds its way into the Virgin Islands National Park.

This is a very small operation, in a space the size and shape of a one-car garage. The display and sales area takes up the front half of the shop. Canvas bags hang from every wall and sit on shelving units. One wall is devoted to hats in cheery colors. The manufacturing area occupies the back half of the shop. A cursory glance reveals two sewing machines, a cutting table, strap material, and rolls of solid-color canvas. Separating the two different functions is a sales counter.

Training begins immediately, with a brisk yet thorough description of how the business works. We're told there are 34 bag styles and shown the materials to make them. The canvas is 100 percent cotton, thick and heavy, with every square yard weighing 18 ounces. Nine different colors of canvas, in 36" wide rolls are stored on horizontal rods. You pull a sheet of canvas off a roll onto the cutting table, where you measure and mark a pattern on it and cut out the pieces into batches for sewing. Speed is crucial. The bags are sewn on the industrial-strength, walking-foot sewing machines. Then you display and sell them. And there's the ordering of the colorful hats and caps, all sporting embroidery in island motifs exclusive to The Canvas Factory.

Back in Bellingham I couldn't find my car when I came out of the grocery store. Now I'll be learning to do all of *this*? My head spins like the little girl in *The Exorcist*. I think I'm going to faint, like I did that time I forgot to drink water for a couple days. What was I thinking? I mean, when the opportunity first presented itself, Tom and I agreed that we were a little long in the tooth to take on a factory and borrow the money to pay for it. But buying a business was a way to live on St. John. In other words, we just bought ourselves each a job.

At exactly 9:30 a.m. Cynthia opens the two arched front doors. The doors are constructed of wood and painted a coral color, with a hook on each side that fastens to the outside of the building. The second floor of the building extends out over the face of first floor, where we are. This creates an arcade that connects us with the neighboring store, Hurricane Alley, purveyor of beach wear and snorkel gear. Above us is a beauty salon.

Customers begin to wander in and out of the shop. After watching Cynthia conduct a few transactions, I step up to the sales counter and reach for their money myself, and immediately jam the credit card machine. I forgot to mention my unique electrical field that causes electronics to go haywire. Tom tells me this mysterious ability of mine has a name, the Pauli effect, after Wolfgang Pauli, a Nobel Prize-winning physicist who, upon entering a lab, would cause expensive equipment and glass beakers to implode.

In spite of interruptions by the pesky customers, I manage to sit on my wet butt and sew a small open tote in black and tan. I'm almost able to walk the foot, which is how you control the speed. However, the sewing machine appears to be past its prime, like me, and no longer sews a straight line. The thing even jumps a stitch once in a while. I end up removing and re-sewing stitches, but in spite of that Cynthia is amazed at how well I'm doing. This makes me feel wonderfully smug, approval slut that I am. Especially since Tom, a former machinist, is at the other sewing machine having lots of trouble. Since he routinely does everything better than I do, I am overjoyed.

This business is going to be a huge challenge, but unlike the sailboat adventure, I think I can succeed. Still, there's an incredible amount of work to this operation. I'm relieved we have an excellent employee, Angie, to help us, especially since Tom will leave in three weeks, and Jim and Cynthia will only stay for part-time training another two months. This thing has to work out; we don't have a Plan B.

Glen Speer stops by to see how things are going and brings us more papers to sign. He's our sugar daddy in all of this, since he's loaning us most of the money to buy it. We sign our promissory note and lease agreement. When I see in black and white how expensive every square inch of the shop is each month, I make a decision: I will be real darn nice to the customers. Glen is pleased that things are going well. When he smiles, his face lights up in a charming, bashful way.

In the afternoon, Tom and I visit the bank. To avoid a catastrophe when opening a checking account here, we brought nearly all of our remaining funds in the form of a cashier's check. Now the bank officer, a large West Indian woman named Thelma, tells us we'll have to wait six business days before we can access our money. We are dressed more or less like homeless people. It's evident to her, I suppose, that we live life on the skinny branches. But what does she want? We still have all our teeth.

I stare at her and shrug, then throw both hands out to my sides, palms up, in that gesture of drama and disbelief my ancestors had perfected, just before blurting, "Well, Jesus H. Christ!" But instead I say, "We need the money right away. That's why we brought a cashier's check."

Tom, who has better breeding, more political savvy, and is an expert at smooth-talking people to get his way, frowns at me and says, "Thelma, if there's anything at all you can do to help us in this matter, we'd really appreciate it."

So Thelma leaves to talk with the bank manager, as if we're buying a used car and our credit is bad. We wait for ten minutes, and when Thelma returns to her desk she phones our bank in Bellingham. We listen as she verifies everything: Are you a real bank? Are these suspicious-looking people really who they say they are? Did you issue this cashier's check? When Thelma hangs up the phone, she turns to us. "Here's what I can do for you. I can reduce the time you wait for the money to three business days."

"Thank you so much," Tom says, just shy of licking her shoes.

Buying a business involves dealing with all kinds of applications, all requiring money. The V.I. government requires us to apply for a business license. We can't simply assume the existing one, which the former owners had renewed year after year by paying a sizable annual fee. So I act as our secretary to complete the forms and applications. But our lives don't fit the forms.

"Just put down any old thing," Tom says. "It probably doesn't matter."

"But you're leaving for the summer. I don't want to go to jail for fraud."

I take a break from the paperwork to walk the three blocks to the post office. After crossing the street to walk on the sidewalk, I pass the vanilla-colored stucco building that is the National Park Visitors' Center. The sidewalk next passes the harbor area where barges come and go to St. Thomas and to the British Virgin Islands. Last week one of the foot ferries, the *Caribe Tide*, was arriving and one of the car barges was departing, when they collided. In broad daylight. Twenty passengers and crew on the foot ferry were injured, but no one was hurt on the car barge. Right now there's a traffic snarl because the damaged car barge is still out of commission. Next I approach Cruz Bay's central business district, more like a carnival than a downtown area. My mouth waters as I pass Uncle Joe's BBQ, and I step to the beat of the music at Cap's–the open air bar across the street that plays music from the Dominican Republic and features one dollar beers all day, every day. Finally, I cross the busy intersection to the post office. And here comes a raggedy, skeletal, toothless man walking down the middle of the street, the one who is always smiling and holding a can of beer up in the air like a trophy. His name is Lindy, and we've heard he had a run-in with some chemicals a few years ago that left him addled.

I'm sure he's harmless, but I sidestep to avoid a collision.

Two weeks ago we shipped several boxes of personal goods to ourselves c/o general delivery. While I don't expect them yet, I'll ask to see if they've arrived. That way the clerks and I can get acquainted. I wait in a long line for 15 minutes, listening to people visit. One woman says to another, "Wasn't the rain wonderful? I actually got to take a shower this morning."

Finally it's my turn at the counter. I'm standing in front of a tall West Indian woman, one whose eyes appear to be half closed. She says something fast and unintelligible, and while she isn't looking at me, I *think* she must be asking me how she can help. So I say, "I'm expecting some general delivery packages. I shipped them a few weeks ago from Washington State by parcel post."

"Oh, Baby. You got a LONG time to wait." She smiles then, more of a smirk, as she looks out the window. "You shoulda sent them packages Priority Mail. You get what you pay for."

"Thank you," I say, wondering if I will always be called Baby.

Back at the shop, Cynthia shows me how to cut out a canvas bag. She rolls a single layer of forest green canvas onto the cutting table, and selects a pattern diagram from a three-ring binder. With a 36" metal ruler and a chalk pencil, she measures and marks the canvas and then cuts it out with a pair of sharp scissors. Next she measures and cuts the zippers from a continuous chain. She puts this batch of materials for three mini bags into a clear plastic bag with a note announcing what they are. The entire procedure takes her two minutes. Now it's my turn. To cut out the three mini bags takes me over an hour. I call the activity "cutting crop."

One reason the sewing machines are difficult to operate is that you don't simply step on a pedal and go, like with a car or a regular domestic sewing machine. Instead, you have to rock your foot back and forth to walk the foot and control the sewing speed. You push a button to reverse and backstitch, and you bump the side of your right knee against a lever to lift the foot. Every single time you begin to sew, you must also hold onto both the top thread and the bobbin thread, or a hopeless tangle will ensue and require lots of cussing to straighten out. But I keep trying. And when Cynthia, who isn't one to gush, says I'm doing phenomenally well, that she can't *believe* I sewed the circle end inside a duffel on my first attempt all by myself, I am pleased beyond measure. Especially since it's 6:00 p.m. and quitting time.

Finally, after our first big day as owners of The Canvas Factory, we close the doors. It's already dark out and the tree frogs have begun to sing. We learn to "close out," and when we tally and record the total sales by credit card and cash, Cynthia announces that we had a good sales day. What a relief. We do need to earn enough money to keep the business and ourselves afloat through the coming low season.

By the time we hitchhike and walk home to our little hovel, we're both exhausted and hungry. On the hotplate, we manage to cook Rice-A-Roni with veggies and canned chicken. The hottest setting isn't very hot, so it takes three times as long as normal for it to cook. We finally eat at 8:00 p.m., to the tune of a dog-barking serenade and the crowing of roosters. They crow any time of the day or night here. Why do they crow in the first place, and why do they choose one time over another? I always wondered the same thing about cows. In Montana, you could be almost anywhere and hear a cow moo. Tom and I chew our food while sitting on the edge of the bed. Now other evening sounds chime in: donkeys bray, goats bleat, frogs sing, and once in a while we hear what sounds like the snorting of a hog.

As we lie in bed, Tom says, "It was hard for me at the shop today. I see myself as a leader, and now I'll be the one who knows the least."

"Welcome to feeling *less than*," I say. "Women often find themselves in that position. And I always felt that way when we were sailing."

But I can tell before I finish speaking that The Viking has fallen asleep.

By the time I awake at 2:00 a.m. for my nightly excursion to the toilet, Tom and I have already been asleep for five hours. I put on my robe and grab the flashlight. Before touching the door to open it, I shine the flashlight on the gauzy white nest that occupies the outside of the door, in a crack next to the window pane. Tonight I see that the tarantula living here has eight furry legs at least an inch long. So that I won't startle her, and vice-versa, I tap the window lightly. In response, she disappears inside the door.

As I step off our porch I see that lights are on in several upstairs rooms in the big house. On the step near the open doorway, a young man sits smoking pot.

"Good evening," I say, walking around him.

"Yo," he says, dreamily.

Back in bed I ponder how overwhelming the shop is. Then my mind speculates on when, exactly, we might access the money we deposited in the local bank. And will we ever have time to sit by the ocean? Finally, my thoughts seek out the tarantula living in our door. All my life I've been terrified of many things, including spiders. Confronted now with a sizable arachnid, I mostly feel curious. Maybe I'm finally evolving. Maybe it's because she's a female tarantula, which I know because of the white gauze nest. Whatever the reason, I feel nurturing toward her and her offspring, even her extended family. Even though she could so easily drop down to the floorboards, walk her furry little feet under the door without even ducking, strut herself over here to the mattress, and crawl right into our bed. But just like the insects underneath our mattress, my pet tarantula seems happy to stay on the door.

In my sociology and anthropology classes at the University of Idaho, this wasn't mentioned, but I would bet that throughout history, as Homo sapiens in trees and caves went about their knuckle-dragging business, they encountered and befriended large arachnids, like tarantulas. I want to believe they, too, kept these warm fuzzy louts, with their gentle souls, as pets.

I'm going to call her Thelma, after the bank lady in charge of our money.

LIFE'S A BEACH

(dedicated to Dennis R. Hart)

"Dot's honmade," Angie says to a short, rotund older man. His wife wants to buy a large zip tote, but he's hesitant. Possibly it's the price. "Dis is not Duffel Bag Discount," Angie says, touching the man's arm. She laughs and adds, "Ah, come on. Don't be so chip!"

The man's face lights up. He blushes and laughs with Angie, and reaches for his credit card. One more customer has fallen in love with her, at least for a little while. Lucky for us, she agreed to stay on at The Canvas Factory. Originally from the Philippines, she's fun and pretty, smart and quick, and her English is adequate, if you're paying attention. For instance, she has a charming way with vowels. She does not say long "e's," which is why the word *cheap* comes out *chip, spreadsheets* become *spreadshits*, and *beach* becomes—you guessed it—*bitch*. She pronounces the "z" sound as an "s," so zippers become *sippers*. And she operates at the speed of light as she teaches me what she calls "the technique of faster."

As many as four of us work in the tiny manufacturing area at one time. Five days a week Angie and one other person, usually Tom, are sewing; while a third person cuts crop, usually me. And either Cynthia or Jim is here training us, which requires constant monitoring on their part. In addition, since our prime location is on the street, any one of us might be telling a passerby where to find the restrooms.

Mosquitoes love the dark areas under the sewing machines and near the floors. Luckily, the shop has a mosquito-killing apparatus that looks like a tennis racket. There are batteries in the handle, and when you press the button on the handle while sweeping the racket through a cloud of mosquitoes, you could get lucky. The wires might connect with a mosquito or two, and when this happens you will hear the most delightful popping sound. You have electrocuted a mosquito, and you will feel ecstatic.

When I'm not cutting crop, I'm learning to sew a new item. But the sewing instructions are handwritten, much like nineteenth century recipes: take a pinch here, remove some feathers, turn 90 degrees, chain to the next piece, and be sure to backstitch.

The former owners say things like, "Oh, this will all become second nature to you. You'll see." God, I hope so. Maybe I'm a bit feeble to be learning so much so quickly. I try taking notes to review at home, but I'm told, "There isn't time to waste taking notes. Just watch what I do and then you do it. You have to work faster." By the end of the day, I'm exhausted, my body parts ache, and I am completely overwhelmed.

After closing the shop in the evening, Tom and I trudge the four blocks to the bus stop near the ferry dock to wait for the 7:25 p.m. bus. Seagulls flock around the dock, like they're bringing us news or gossip, or maybe the truth. We each stand gripping a dollar bill for the fare, hoping the bus is running tonight. But after waiting 15 minutes, we walk three blocks uphill to the Texaco gas station to hitchhike. Several streets converge at this important intersection, and everyone heading east on the Centerline Road must pass by. So we stand pointing, trying to look respectable, while hoping to catch a ride, any ride. If we can only get to Tony's we'll walk the remaining one and one-half miles to our shackteau.

Soon, an aging Suzuki Samurai stops for us. We climb into the back though the tiny open rear window, and sit on a spare tire. Tom hunches over so his head won't puncture the faded candy-striped canvas top. Our chauffeur, a balding man in our age group, works as a massage therapist at Caneel Bay Resort. He tells us he's living cooperatively with another massage therapist in a two-bedroom apartment on Gifft Hill. When we tell him where we're living he laughs out loud in disbelief, but we're too tired to laugh with him. Then he tells us he's leaving the island around May 1 and his roommate might be looking for someone to share the rent. If I want, he'll tell her I'm interested. "I want," I say. He drives us all the way home in the dark to our bug-ridden chicken coop.

The amenities over in the main house prove to be worse than I first thought. This evening I discover that if you lean over sideways too far while sitting on the toilet, you and the toilet can tip over into the stagnant pool in the shower stall. After recovering from that third-world event, I discover the toilet won't flush. I fill the handy bucket with water to pour into the tank to flush. This toilet and the island's bus system are similar: sometimes it works and other times it doesn't. While holding my breath and flushing the toilet I look away, and notice a suspicious brown smear on the wall.

The next day a miracle happens. Glen and his wife, Radha, visit us at the shop. They're leaving the island for ten days and need someone to house sit for them, starting in a couple days. They know this is short notice, but the person they had lined up can't do it. Would we be interested? We leave the shop in Angie's good hands and follow them across the parking lot to their home, located in the trees behind Mongoose Junction. Made of teak and stone and glass, the house is similar in design and construction to the buildings in Mongoose Junction. The place is perfect for the cover of *Architectural Digest*. It's air-conditioned and features teak furniture, bookshelves with hundreds of books, and walls sponge-painted the color of warm ochre and cinnamon. Outside, orchids and other lovely plantings grace garden areas, in addition to the native trees all around. We'll feed two parrots in a big cage in the living room, as well as several cats living in the back garden. Some of the cats are draped in the crotch of an enormous tree. We'll also feed other, more feral, felines that live below the house.

This stroke of good luck comes not a day too soon. In the evening, after finishing our dinner at the shackteau, Tom goes over to the main house to wash our dishes. He returns, fuming.

"There's no water!"

"So, no shower in the morning," I say. Without a shower every day in this climate, a person starts to smell pretty ripe.

"Days ago I gave The Governor extra money for our share of a truckload of water," Tom says. "He could have ordered it sooner, but NO! He waits until we're totally out of water. And when I tried to talk to him just now, he acted like it was no big deal. What an asshole."

On the morning we are to begin housesitting, we plod along the road, each carrying a duffel bag with clothes and some plastic grocery bags with veggies, boxes of Rice-A-Roni, and other food scraps. We look as bad off as we smell.

"Where's a shopping cart when you need one?" Tom asks.

But soon a ride comes along that takes us all the way to Cruz Bay.

Over the next few days we find it convenient and pleasant to live in such a splendid home. From the small teak dining table we look out a big window into the jungle. One tree sports a climbing vine with leaves as big as pillow cases.

Now, when the shop gets too crowded, Tom simply walks "home" and works on the laptop computer creating spreadsheets using Excel. He also sets the business up in Quickbooks, and enters old business data. He appears at the shop one afternoon, a man on a mission. At that particular moment I'm ripping out a crooked seam on an open tote so I can re-sew it, while cussing under my breath. When I look up, Tom announces, very seriously, "We need a business plan."

Angie glances his way, and returns to sewing. Cynthia, working at the cutting table, stops and focuses on Tom over the top of her reading glasses, but says nothing.

"No we don't," I say. "We need to cut crop and sew bags as fast as we can, then sell 'em. End of plan." While saying this, in a way that smells of disrespect and sarcasm, I poke a hole in my index finger with a tiny sharp scissors. Blood drips off my hand onto the sewing machine but, luckily, not onto my canvas bag.

Later while eating dinner at a real dining table, tasting food we cooked on a regular stove, we're both too tired and distressed to talk. And while I'm convinced a business plan is unnecessary, I really ought to apologize for my response to Tom's idea. But instead, I say, "I just want to go to the beach and hide my head in the sand."

"Me too," Tom agrees. "We need to be reminded why we're here. Tomorrow let's walk to Honeymoon Beach."

Neither Jim nor Cynthia will be in the shop to train us today. And Angie is accustomed to working alone, so it's no big deal if we leave early to go to the beach. But things are so hectic at the shop that we stay until 2:00 p.m. before walking to the house to put on our swim-suits. By then we're so tired we have to rest. Finally, at 4:00 p.m. we leave the house, only a couple hours before the tropical curtain will drop and darkness descends. Off we go, walking the two miles on the Lind Point Trail, joking about our new life.

"Some people retire at our age, but oh, no, not us," I banter. "Nosirree. We buy a little shop of horrors so we can work like Energizer bunnies six or seven days a week for the rest of our lives."

"But, of course, we didn't *know* we'd have to work so hard," Tom adds, "until after we signed the contract to buy the business."

"For being so darn mature," I say, "we sure are naïve."

"Now that's a foregone conclusion."

"Or a foregone delusion."

Making fun of the situation is one way to deal with this latest test of our characters. At least we're doing this *together;* we're *both* con-fronted with a situation that feels adverse. Before, when the sailboat lifestyle wasn't working, it was *me* against Tom and the sailboat. In the end, no amount of joking—on paper, in my head, or out loud—made that situation workable.

The trail trends through dry, scrubby vegetation and ropey cactus that climbs and bunches up all over itself into the shape of low foot-hills. After 20 minutes of plodding along, we dive off the Lind Point Trail down a steep unsigned path through trees toward the ocean. As we reach the sand and the sea grape bushes, we glimpse a partial view of teal water and a small beach. And then we both see it—lying splayed out on the wet sand at the shoreline—a bloated nude corpse I feel sick. Our first visit to the ocean since arriving on the island over a week ago and here's a dead man washed ashore. I grab Tom's arm. The corpse is the color of bread dough. The waves wash up over the body and back out, and at the same time, flopping first to one side and then the other, in a playful, watery massage, is his big, limp penis.

A woman sits in a dinghy not far from the body. She's topless, and displays zero alarm that a body is lying nearby. The man must be alive. Tom and I look at each other and shake our heads. What a relief. We step out of the bushes onto the beach and discover how overdressed we are. Another nude man lies on the sand farther uphill from the water's edge. At the other end of the beach are two guys frolicking naked in the water.

"I can't handle this," I say.

"Me neither," Tom says. "Honeymoon Beach is supposed to be good-sized. This must be Salomon."

No one appears to notice our arrival or departure. We make our way back up the short, steep trail to the main path and walk until we find Honeymoon Beach, where everyone is wearing beach attire. We collapse onto the blond sand and stare at the ocean and several small cays. Puffy marshmallow clouds decorate the horizon. The sound of waves washing in and out is mesmerizing as we sit in a catatonic state. Finally, I'm able to pull off my T-shirt and shorts, revealing a faded black one-piece swimsuit. Tom, already wearing his swim trunks, removes his T-shirt and we walk into the water.

I splash and swim for a while and then sit on the beach. Watching Tom amble out into the surf, I smile. Every time I go to check out his buns, there aren't any. After resting on my towel a while, catching some late afternoon sunshine, I prop myself up on my elbows to stare again at the waves as they roll gently in and out, in and out. Tom is swimming toward the boats anchored offshore. On our first visit to the island, in 1996, he swam out to a boat anchored in Salt Pond Bay on the southeast end of the island. He got an eyeful, and today I know he's hoping to see another naked woman on board one of the boats. Maybe he'll get lucky. I sit in a stupor of blissful sub-tropical warmth, and smile at the bumper sticker I saw recently on a derelict car, *SAIL NAKED. IT ADDS COLOR TO YOUR CHEEKS.*

Every now and then Tom surfaces to smile and wave. I suppose I should be jealous, but I'm not. So what if he's being a peeping Tom? With nothing to do at this exact moment, I stare at the opalescent water and palm trees, and listen to the lulling, healing, sighing wash of waves. Pelicans flap along above the water, diving headfirst like missiles into schools of unsuspecting fish. Zigzagging high overhead are the dark forms of magnificent frigate birds. How could Polynesians have wrangled and trained these wildish, prehistoric-looking birds to serve as homing pigeons? And now, just like a homing pigeon, Tom returns to shore.

He reports, "No naked women, but it was a great swim anyway."

We lie quietly on the beach, side by side on our beach towels, soaking in the late afternoon sun.

"The ocean is that color because of the way water absorbs sunlight," Tom says. "Particles in the water scatter the light, refracting rainbow colors, especially blues and greens." His voice is dreamy, as if he's speaking from a distance or he's under the influence of a powerful sedative. "The sandy bottom acts like the backing of a mirror."

"Thank you, Einstein," I whisper.

"Sure is fun lying here on the bitch."

"Even more fun," I say, "than laying out spreadshits?"

We walk slowly back toward Mongoose Junction. Just as the tree frogs begin to peep and sing, and the tropical curtain drops the darkness, we reach our temporary home. And what do you know? It's rum-thirty.

In the morning, at the small dining table, Tom says, "In terms of keeping our brains nimble as we age, we're doing exactly the right thing by getting into this business. I'm going to stay here today and work on the numbers."

Tom has done many different kinds of work and changed careers often. In addition to being a drug enforcement agent in Chicago, a commercial pilot in his home state of Minnesota, a farmer in North Dakota, and a Republican legislator in Montana, he's been maintaining a fleet of charter sailboats for San Juan Sailing in Bellingham.

He's also a precision machinist, and has crafted several items for Bill Gates' new home in Seattle, among them a fancy door handle. So why not work on spreadshits?

At the shop, sewing is one of the last things I do because so many other tasks require my attention. Besides, Angie excels at sewing and everything else she does, including sales. She also dusts the shelves and bags. Dust travels on clouds from the Sahara and settles on the North Shore Road, and when it's kicked up by vehicles, the dust drifts into the shop through the open doors.

The only places to sit in the shop are at the two sewing machines, and right now those chairs are occupied by Cynthia and Angie. So all administrative decisions and activities are happening, or not, while I'm standing at the cutting table. This executive location consists of two feet between the cutting table and the sewing machine closest to the sales counter. But all decisions are on hold at the moment because whenever Cynthia's in the shop I feel and act brain-damaged. So I'm pretending to study a cutting pattern while watching a lizard dart across the rock wall in front of me. The little creature stops, pooches out its chest and does pushups to warn me away. They run all over the walls and surfaces of the shop, hunting insects, bless their hearts. So what if they leave little turds that resemble mouse droppings everywhere? Lizards are my friends. I could watch them all day. Maybe that's my real purpose in life.

While watching the lizard, I'm puzzling over all the details that aren't written down anywhere, details I'm sure Cynthia thinks everyone but me knows. Worse than that, several rolls of canvas are getting dangerously small and we need to order more. But that would cost $1500. And even though Thelma has finally released our funds, we can't afford to spend that much. Then, too, we need to order caps. A shop on the island embroiders the caps for us and delivers them, and they're smart enough to require payment upon delivery. It would be easier to run a small country than this shop. The lizard decides I'm a threat. She leaps onto the window sill, expands her throat and does pushups again. As I ponder life and lizards, Tom is up at the house creating documents we don't need. Finally Angie announces, "You need to cut anudder botch of medium sip totes."

So I focus on botching that up, relieved to be told what to do. As I slowly figure out the pattern and cut out the totes, customers wander into the shop and need help. Actually, I love the customers. They're lots of fun, and why not? They're on vacation. And ever since a guy handed me a $100 bill the other day, I no longer mind when a customer interrupts my work.

After cutting out the medium zip tote, Angie tells me, "We need some extra-extra large cargo bogs." So I cut out one of those. With all the pieces, straps, zippers, and interruptions, this takes a couple hours. And Angie sews it up in less than an hour, stuffs it full of wadded up newsprint, puts it on display, and announces, "You bedder cut anudder one of dis bog." But dis bog is huge. It's like a flight suit for a baby elephant. And why would anyone want one? They're expensive, they're enormous and, even with the clean, lightweight newsprint we stuff in them for display, they already weigh about 20 pounds. I want to tell customers, "Don't you realize you can buy big luggage with wheels?" Besides, I'm painfully slow when marking and cutting out this complicated pattern with so many pieces. And after standing all day, my legs feel like bags of cement.

Angie's husband, Dennis, drops by the shop once in a while. He's American, and he and Angie met when they were both in New Zealand. It was Angie's first trip away from Manila, and she was visiting a brother. She didn't speak English at the time, although she understood it fairly well. Somehow they managed to communicate because not long after they met, they got married.

Dennis calls himself The Drive-By Auto Guy. On his flyer that's posted all over the island, he adds, *If I can't fix it, you don't need it— bullet holes cost extra.* His own car is an elderly, silver Toyota station wagon. By way of reverse-marketing, his car sports a shark fin welded on top and has a squealing fan belt to announce its arrival. A sign in the back window warns, MAKO SHARK – STAY BACK 30 FEET. Many of his clients drive vintage "island cars" that are rusted, dented, and burn lots of oil. When someone's vehicle dies or fails to pass inspection to get its annual registration renewed, they call Dennis.

Colleen, the massage therapist with the two-bedroom apartment, calls the shop to talk with me. I've already looked at the apartment and like it. She tells me I can move in May 1. Tom will be leaving shortly after we finish our housesitting gig, so I'll have only a couple more weeks at the chicken coop. I immediately call The Governor to give him notice, so I can get back my security deposit.

Before you know it, our housesitting gig ends and it's time to return home to our hovel on the hillside. Dennis helps us move. With all our gear and the three of us in the shark mobile, we're loaded to the gills. Dennis and Tom are in the front and I'm in the back seat underneath our belongings: duffel bags; laptop computer bursting with mysterious spreadshits; three big cardboard boxes that finally arrived from Bellingham, the contents of which are now forgotten; and several garbage bags of odds and ends.

After arriving at the chicken coop, we unload everything onto the porch. We're dazed, as if we've just fallen through a trapdoor in the universe somewhere beyond the force of gravity. Tom and I stand together waving goodbye to Dennis. We listen as the shark mobile shrieks its way back upstream past the dump and up the steep hill to Tony's. The squealing noise stops. In the momentary stillness, I picture Dennis checking for traffic before turning left onto the highway for the easy downhill swim into Cruz Bay. I have just been expelled from the mouth of a mako shark and abandoned on a remote, lonely shore.

LIABILITY INSURANCE

*T*his morning when I reach Tony's, a young man is already waiting for a ride. Tom has left for the summer and I'm alone. I ask the young man how he likes it on the island, and he tells me he's from Michigan, where it's cold, and that he likes the weather here. He builds villas and is living in one of them now. Soon two Willie Nelson look-a-likes stop in a rusty old white Samurai. It's a tight fit, but the young man and I squeeze into the tiny back seat. The two Willies live on sailboats at Coral Bay and work at construction and landscaping jobs. They sail south to Trinidad in May, before hurricane season starts. The young man says he's on his way to St. Thomas. The driver says, "Oh, so it's St. Traumas day for you." Everyone laughs.

We pass one of those partially-constructed concrete island homes, with pieces of rebar sticking up from the top of it.

"That place looks exactly the same as it did in 1996," I say. "We thought it got damaged in a hurricane."

"Might look like that forever," one Willie Nelson says. "The family just lives in the bottom floor, next to the cistern."

"They're like that all over the island," the young man says. "Until the house is finished they don't have to get the final inspection and a CO."

"A CO?" I ask.

"Yeah. A certificate of occupancy. Costs money. 'Course, finishing the place costs a lot more," the driver says, speaking up over the breezes blowing through the open windows and the roar of the engine. "And you don't pay taxes on the house until you get your CO. So, if you aren't fussy, you can live in your unfinished house and save a lot of money."

"Sure looks like heck," I say, as we pass another dwelling with rebar sticking up. Out yonder, the Caribbean Sea glitters in the morning light.

We round a big bend and there, run up into the branches of a tree below the road, is a small beat-up red pickup truck.

"That's my landlord's truck," I say, craning my neck so I can look past the driver's beard.

"Happens all the time," the other Willie says.

Bantering with these guys is great fun and reminds me of my days in the Forest Service, a geezer-rich agency if there ever was one. In those days I often found myself in a vehicle full of men driving out to the field to look at a project.

Now I tell this car full of men that we're buying The Canvas Factory, that I'm shocked at how much work it is, not to mention expensive. The driver looks at me and shrugs, "Well, if it doesn't work out, at least you bought yourself an adventure."

And the adventure continues. Every few days I call the business licensing office on St. Thomas to find out when I'll receive our license. I tell them I need it so we can use our electronic credit card machine. I'm told "soon come." Island time is a wonderful time if you're on the beach, but not if you're running a business.

Even more expensive than the application for the business license is the liability insurance we're required to carry—covering us up to a one million dollars if someone puts her head in one of our small zip totes and gets strangled in the straps. This insurance for the shop is, however, way less expensive than what Tom carries in order to maintain the fleet of charter sailboats. If you make a mistake while sewing a canvas bag, the bag won't ever sink and endanger your life. It's comforting to know we'll never be sued for malpractice.

When Tom calls, he tells me what's happening at Squalicum Harbor back in Bellingham. He and his cat, Twodot, are living on the boat until it sells, which I hope will happen any second. He says, "For a cat, Twodot does very well on a leash. You should see him. He runs along the dock like a doggone dog."

He reports that he's the senior crew member on a Wednesday evening racing team, on a big boat called *Air Power*. And at work he climbs in and out of bilges, while banging his head and elbows, just like before.

Then, in a tone of wistfulness, he says, "A little sailboat with a one-cylinder engine just putt-putted out of the harbor on its way to Mexico. They couldn't violate the *no wake* rule if they tried. You should have seen the old hemp ropes hanging down from the top of the wooden mast. Looked like crepe paper streamers on a Maypole." He sighs, and I hear envy. "I sure hope they make it."

"Well, we need you to come back down here to help *us* make it."

"I'm looking forward to working with you and Angie and to being warm again," he says. "But I did just have to renew my liability insurance."

"Oh, Lord. I hope the check clears the bank."

Jim is also the hypnotherapist on the island, and probably doesn't need liability insurance for his work. While he shows me how to sew a bag, he tells me he's helped several people. Without mentioning names, he says, "I did smoking cessations for two different women. They both quit smoking *and* ended their bad relationships." He tells me he's also used self-hypnosis to cure some of his own serious health problems, including cataracts and an ailing heart. Doctors told him he needed a new heart valve or he could die. He tells me that while he was in a meditative state, he pictured a healthy heart in great detail. He imagined holding this healthy heart lovingly in his hands, and pictured this heart in his chest doing all the work a heart does. He says he did this a couple times a day for a month or two, and when he went back to the doctor for a checkup, his heart was perfect. The doctor couldn't believe it. Jim healed his eyes the same way, making his cataracts go away.

"My back hurts," I tell him.

"Okay, try this," he says. "It's a simple self-hypnosis technique. Say a mantra over and over. You could say, *I don't have to put up with it any more. My back feels wonderful.* Just say it over and over, and believe it's true."

I tell him I might want to try hypnotherapy some time. He says there's a woman on island named Lucy who is becoming a certified hypnotherapist, and she's good.

Tonight, before going to sleep in the chicken coop, I try self-hypnosis. Why not? I don't have health insurance. Okay, here goes. "I don't have to put up with it any more. My back feels wonderful." I say this over and over, and I believe it's true. Just before falling asleep, still repeating this phrase, I feel a mild electrical current circulating slowly around my body. I really do feel it; this isn't just a dream. Unless ... Thelma? Is that you?

While I truly believe that all things are possible, in the morning my back still hurts. Besides that, when I catch a glimpse of myself in the broken wall mirror I see that in the night, a mosquito bit my left eyelid. My eye is nearly swollen shut and I am grotesque, especially since a mosquito bit the bag under my left eye the night before. And I'm out of Preparation H, which would reduce the swelling. In spite of everything, I close my eyes and feel a glimmer of hopefulness. I speak to the mirror. "I am smart and efficient at work today, and our business license arrives at the post office."

While walking toward Tony's to catch a ride, I work it. I imagine myself at the post office, holding a window envelope containing the business license.

Up at Tony's, a woman in a light blue Samurai stops to give me a ride. I climb into the passenger seat and say, "Thanks for stopping. My name's Rae Ellen, from The Canvas Factory."

"Welcome to the island," the woman says with great cheer. "I'm Lucy."

As we bounce along in her Sammy, I share with Lucy, the second hypnotherapist on the island, my new mantra and how I felt the electrical current. She encourages me to continue my efforts at self-hypnosis, and says she'll stop by the shop to see me sometime. After she drops me off at the Texaco station, I walk to the post office. I want to test this new positive thought process, and see if the business license has arrived. But when I check the mailbox I see a suspicious-looking window envelope containing a pale yellow slip. At exactly the moment I rip open the envelope, I hear a commotion and glance up to see two men carrying a woman out of the post office on a stretcher toward an ambulance. And while I truly hope the woman is all right, my attention is drawn back to the yellow slip and a non-sufficient funds charge for the $3,100 check I'd written for last year's taxes. I am so shocked and dumbfounded at receiving this NSF charge instead of the business license I expected, that I want to run after the ambulance driver, fall at his feet, grab onto one of his legs and yell, "Take me, too. Please. I'm begging you!"

IN THIS LAND OF SUN AND FUN

Mosquito netting can feel like a prison or a place of respite. This first morning at Colleen's apartment I'm feeling safe from mosquitoes, even smug as I huddle inside the net that drapes over my twin bed. I'm sipping coffee around the floating corpse of an ant, when I notice a scorpion-like creature crawling on my left arm. I scream. Coffee flies. I squash the creature in the rumpled sheets, and end up on all fours, panting and whimpering. When I look up, a bananaquit-sized cockroach is crawling up the outside of the mosquito net, looking in at me. And while a bananaquit, that adorable little yellow and black bird of the Caribbean, is only the size of a finch, that's still big for a cockroach.

Escaping the mosquito net, I shake off the experience and prepare to take my first warm shower in over a month. My joy is exquisite, the kind that follows deprivation. The feeling's not an orgasm, mind you, but it's right up there on the Richter scale. I'm ready to step into the shower, but first, in an effort to maintain good relations with my new roommate, I ask, "Do you need to use the bathroom before I take a shower?"

"No, I don't," she says, in a tone that reveals she isn't a morning person. "But remember the saying, *in this land of sun and fun, we don't flush for number one.* And we don't use much water for a shower, either."

Looks like my exquisite joy was premature, sort of like a quickie.

I already know the water rules. On islands in the Caribbean, rain gutters catch the rainfall and it flows into cisterns, or concrete rooms built under homes. The water is drawn up to the living quarters by a pump. You turn on a faucet and you get water. Except when you don't. If it doesn't rain for a long time or people are careless with water usage, they have to shell out hundreds of dollars for a tanker truck of desalinated water.

Later at the kitchen table, Colleen tells me how she started out on the island at Maho Bay Camp, where she worked up to manager status. After a few years she left to become a massage therapist. She's approaching 50, a single woman, sturdy of build like me, with a full head of auburn hair cut to shoulder length. I have ten years on her and I'm a fearless asker of inappropriate questions. For all I know, she could be a lesbian.

"So, have you found any men to date on St. John?"

"It's like this," she says. "There are eight men to every woman here."

"Lucky you," I say. "That's not bad for a gene pool."

"Well," she says, not smiling, "the odds are good, but the goods are odd."

"That's too funny." I laugh, but she doesn't join in. So I tell her about the man that once sat on me during a large group function. "The guy simply didn't notice the seat was taken. He leaped up and was so apologetic that he actually made eye contact with me and talked to me. You should have heard him. He blathered on, telling me a bizarre story about how he'd shipped a life-sized cardboard likeness of himself to his twentieth high school reunion, which was why he was at the party."

"Sound like the goods were odd at that party, too," she says, this time smiling. "Just be glad you already have a man."

I don't tell her that since Tom left, I've been so busy I keep forgetting I have a man. Instead I tell her, "One of my mother's favorite sayings was, *Men! They fool you by walking upright.*"

"Oh, that's a good one," she says, and this time she laughs out loud.

I steer clear of my more personal struggles, since we're on a small island with a method of communication that's faster than the speed of light—the coconut telegraph.

She's clearly the alpha roommate and this is fine, since I'm so experienced at deferring to others. If I were a member of a wolf pack, I'd be the one lying on my back, feet in the air, exposing my soft underbelly in a sign of surrender. That is, until one of the other wolves ordered me to get up and help them bring down an elk so we might all have dinner. After the kill, I'd hang back and eat the leftovers, the unidentifiable parts of the animal's guts that taste bitter, the parts the wolves with more gumption don't like.

My new daily schedule is simple: eat, sleep, get up, kill mosquitoes, hitchhike into town, cut canvas and sew, banter with customers, try to do what I'm told, make phone calls regarding the missing business license, and then hitchhike or catch the bus home. Repeat.

Hitchhiking is both my transportation and social life. Weekday mornings, Gifft Hill is a hitchhiker's paradise because of the private elementary school near the apartment. Parents drop their children off at school and head back toward town with an empty car, making it easy to catch a ride. On Sundays, however, trying to catch a ride is like waiting for the business license to arrive. If Colleen is going to town, I ride with her in her white Suzuki Sidekick with its ragtop and missing rear window. The car smells a little like chicken shit, not that I mind, and there's usually a chicken under the passenger seat. After shooing it out the door, flapping and cackling, I grope for an egg and usually come up empty-handed.

My first view, after leaving the apartment to catch a ride, is the Caribbean Sea. I walk along in the sunshine, passing homes with yards, some landscaped, some not, and then walk past the garbage dump. A broken down cyclone fence and a row of palm trees and shrubs help to screen the trash and wreckage, but nothing stops the smell of rot and decay in the subtropical heat. Often a collection of workers from the dump are sitting under one of the trees, shooting the breeze. I don't understand much of what they're saying as I walk past, but what I hear this morning is, "blah, blah, blah, fockin' blah, blah, blah, fockin' dog." When they see me they stop talking, mid-blah blah, and watch me walk past. I say "Good Morning," and their response is friendly but unintelligible. I contemplate my lack of facility for other languages as I pant my way up the steep hill, squeezing my cheeks together to control the sway and jiggle of my butt.

LET US PUT A LIZARD ON YOUR LUGGAGE

The vigorous use of my brain continues. If Tom is right, learning new tasks will keep my gray matter young and nimble. If I were a tree, I'd be experiencing a serious growth ring, like trees do from bursts of rain and fertilizer and hot sun. When I mention this brilliant simile to a customer wearing designer beach wear and hair spray, she says, "You know, of course, that without seasons the trees in the tropics don't *have* growth rings." And here I stand with my dandelion degree in landscape architecture.

Angie keeps me on the right track with production. Just to be on the safe side, I've made the executive decision, as CEO of The Canvas Factory, to let her be the boss. One day we run out of sales slips, so Angie sends me to an office in another building in Mongoose Junction where you can purchase business supplies. I walk across the interior plaza between the stone walls, passing shop fronts with their glass doors framed in teak. I ascend a few steps to a second smaller plaza, and climb an elegant stone stairway. I'm walking tall, dressed in an over-sized, purple, short-sleeved thrift store shirt with red cowboy boots all over it, along with a pair of faded yellow Bermuda shorts the color of Montana prairie grass. Sturdy, well-worn sandals, constructed from old rubber tires, complete my ensemble. Besides representing the best of my wardrobe options, this attire facilitates hopping in and out of Samurais and old trucks while hitchhiking.

At my destination, I open the door to see a young, slender, well-dressed blond woman sitting behind a large executive desk in a room almost as big as our shop. She looks up at me but says nothing.

"Hi. I'm Rae Ellen. My husband and I bought The Canvas Factory and we just ran out of sales slips." I stop talking, embarrassed that I look like me and she looks like a super-model, or maybe Kim Basinger without the bright red lipstick.

"So," she says, "are you a seamstress?"

"No, but I've sewed all my life and the sewing logic is the same." I don't tell her I've never once sewed something even I would be caught dead wearing. What I really want to mention are twig shutters I built for the brothel I renovated. Instead, I say, "The trick is learning to use a walking-foot sewing machine. The clutch is a key component, making it something like a piece of farm equipment." I tell her this, but here's the deal: a walking-foot sewing machine doesn't *have* a clutch, at least not like you'd find in a car.

She sits there gazing at me, so I add, "Where would I find a book of sales slips?"

Rising from her chair with grace and elegance, all size two of her, she leads me and my plus-sized cowboy shirt to a room that houses the office supplies. She hands me a package of sales slips and I follow her back to her desk. While she writes out a receipt, I set the package down, reach into my shirt pocket for a $20 bill, and hand it to her, along with a vintage gob of pocket lint. Holding the lint as if it's the tail of a dead mouse, she carefully drops the wad into a garbage can under her desk and hands over my change. I thank her, making my exit as gracefully as possible. Glancing back at her to smile one last time, I open the door to leave and walk into a small room the size of the chicken coop, except this one contains cleaning supplies, a broom, and a dust mop that's real and not a spider. When I retreat from the closet, find the correct exit, and get back to the shop, I realize I've left the package of sales slips on her desk and must retrace my steps to get them.

Finally, back at the shop with the sales slips, Angie tells me, "You need to cut me some strops for dese bogs. You need to order more hats. Did you call the bank?" Later, glancing over at me sewing at my machine, located exactly three feet from hers, she says, "Is your bobbin running out of tread?" and "We don't put green sliders with navy sippers." and, "You gotta sew it on the oggly side," meaning the wrong side of the canvas.

One time during a training session Jim tells me he hypnotizes a bag while he sews it, which reminds me of the horse whisperers in Montana. With so much to keep track of, I decide not to learn the art of bag whispering. Instead I'll subdue them with cussing mantras from my days of heavy-weather sailing with The Viking.

When we bought the business, only a limited number of canvas bags sported embroidered tropical motifs, the same designs that grace the caps we sell. One image is a petroglyph, the logo for St. John, taken from a series of carvings in a rock face near the Reef Bay Trail. Archeologists believe that the Taino Indians made the carvings over 1,000 years ago. We also sell embroidered hats with the saying *I Only Cuss When I'm Sailing*—the working title of my book about our sailboat experiences. The publisher changed the title to *If* The Shoe *Fits, The Shoe* being the name of our boat. These hats about cussing while sailing are especially popular with women. Another embroidery motif is that of a lizard in several different colors, always sporting red sunglasses. I like to think of this new lizard species as Art Gecko. Sales skyrocket on our new line of hats, and customers now also prefer canvas bags with embroidered pockets.

Still without a business license, credit card receipts continue to pile up without being deposited into our bank account. "Maybe tomorrow," the licensing office says, every time I call. Always tomorrow. The financial problems caused by this delay drag on. Sure, we deposit the cash we take in, but we're still running credit cards by the manual clunker method. This carries the risk that a card is no longer valid or the customer long ago exceeded their limit.

One day at the post office I receive not one, not two, but three business licenses, all with different numbers. After selecting the license to show Thelma at the bank and post on the wall above the sales counter, I wait 20 minutes in line at the post office to return the two extras via certified return receipt. This way I won't have to pay to renew all three business licenses next year.

As soon as the business license fiasco is behind me, the air conditioner quits. It might seem counter-intuitive that we have an air conditioner running in the back of the shop when the front doors are wide open, but by doing this we can maintain a temperature of about 78 degrees. WAPA—the initials for the energy company that I've heard stands for Worst Available Power Anywhere—is expensive. We can't afford to keep the shop any cooler. Now, as summer arrives, the loss of air-conditioning coincides with a rise in temperature toward 90 degrees. To communicate with the repairman responsible for our unit, I must call and leave a message for him at Connections, an office in Cruz Bay that handles many media tasks for people, including phone calls. A couple weeks later, when I mention to a fellow business owner that this repairman never returns my calls, I learn that the guy operates on island time. The rest of the time he's drunk.

The overhead fans cool the air, but not much. The other day I was sewing a duffel the size of Rhode Island when I felt an insect crawling on my skin between my unrestrained breasts. I threw the duffel on the floor and leaped up, screaming, but it turned out to be nothing more than a large bead of sweat.

I have to hand it to the former owners. They didn't have air-conditioning for the first 17 years in business. And now they won't have to suffer the lack of air-conditioning because they have left on the same boat they sailed in on twenty-some years ago, a boat that was wrecked by Hurricane Marilyn and rebuilt by Jim using new parts and hypnosis.

Almost every day someone enters the shop soliciting a donation for a good cause, including The Safety Zone (to help abused women), The Animal Care Center (St. John's answer to The Humane Society), public schools, private schools, Mr. Emancipation (for the carnival activities related to the emancipation of slaves on the island, coinciding with the Fourth of July), The Pan Dragons (for the kids who play steel drums), for individuals who need surgery but have no health insurance, for kids to go on field trips to Washington, D.C., and so on. Since we don't want to seem *chip,* as Angie calls it, we always make a modest donation. One woman my age tells me that last year she

collected enough money and sponsors to hike in Nepal for breast cancer research. I'd be happy to take a hike for a good cause, or no cause
at all. And if it would get me to Switzerland, I'd even do a fun run for
my pet affliction—one I've always felt should receive more attention,
more funding for education, more awareness—hemorrhoids.

Luna, a local street person, sidles into the shop now and then asking for lunch money. She never once suggests she wants to hike in a
foreign country or travel to Washington, D.C. to advise the president
not to drill for oil in the Arctic National Wildlife Refuge. Tall, angular
and dressed in layers of surprisingly elegant clothing, she skewers me
with penetrating dark eyes when she asks for money. She's my age but
thin, possibly hungry, and is prone to wild-eyed outbursts and verbal
assaults, so I'm usually generous with her. But if I'm overly quick to
hand her money, she'll come in every day. To entice me, she says she
has some seeds of the flamboyant tree to sell. This tree, shaped like a
giant oak tree, blooms flaming red blossoms every summer.

"Okay," I say, thinking I'll plant them on our lot in Fish Bay. "I'll
buy some seeds from you."

As I hand her a five dollar bill, she says, "Ma'am, you're puttin' on
weight. Your underarms got quite a jiggle to 'em."

When I tell Tom on the phone about the exchange, he says, "She
really knows how to close a deal."

We also get celebrities in and out of the shop, and as I sew I think
how nice it would be to match up the solicitors who need money with
the celebrities who have it. But if celebrities will just buy some hats
and canvas bags from us, that'll do it.

One day I'm certain one of my favorite actors is in the shop. I do
know, of course, not to hound him. So I get up from my sewing machine and lean forward on my elbows at the sales counter, smug that I
haven't been in the sun enough that my cleavage has crow's feet. I ask,
"Are you Tom Hanks?"

He flashes a smile I know from *Sleepless in Seattle*, *Apollo 13*, and
You've Got Mail. "Hah!" he says. "I wish."

One day when I'm working alone at the shop, I help a beautiful young blond woman find a perfect hat to wear sailing. With her looks, she could qualify to work in that office where I bought the sales slips. And she's nice, too. I promote our new bucket hat, because the hat won't blow away in the wind and if there's no wind you can tie the strings up over the top of the hat and look downright stylish. I don the hat to demonstrate to this babe the art of looking stylish.

Meanwhile, the man she's with is trying on a turquoise bucket hat. I tell him, "Those are kid's hats." When he removes the hat I think, Lord that guy has a big head, and it's shaped like a watermelon. But wait. I know this man from somewhere.

I say, "You look really familiar."

He looks directly at me, smiles, and says one word, "Television."

I have just hit the celebrity jackpot. "Kelsey Grammer?!"

He comes right over to me and shakes my hand, and his hand is warm and generous, not sweaty. Finally, an actor with enough starch to admit his identity.

As they purchase the bucket hat with strings, the three of us make small talk related to sailing, with me holding back my true sentiments about the activity. All the while I strain to think of one specific and witty thing to say to Kelsey Grammer, to show him I'm a knowledgeable fan, but the best I can come up with is, "I love your shows." I'm so flustered at the moment, not one brain cell is acting young and nimble.

ST. TRAUMAS DAY

*T*o reach St. John, you must fly into the Cyril King Airport on St. Thomas. That is, unless you arrive on a small cruise ship or a private yacht. From the airport, it's easy to take a taxi van to either Charlotte Amalie or Red Hook to catch a ferry to St. John. St. Thomas is almost twice as big as St. John and, as of the 2010 census, has a population of 51,634 vs. St. John's 4,170. St. Thomas also has a shopping mall, discount stores, and hundreds of duty-free jewelry and perfume shops to serve the cruise ship visitors. St. Johnians go there to stock up on supplies. On foot, you can take a ferry from Cruz Bay and arrive 15 minutes later on the east end of St. Thomas, at Red Hook. There you can walk from the dock to the street and wait for a safari taxi, which will set you back a dollar and take you to the Tu Tu Mall where K-Mart and Office Max are located.

If you want to go to St. Thomas in your car, you must take a barge. One day my roommate, Colleen, invites me on a shopping trip to St. Thomas. We get in line early for the barge, since one barge is still out of commission due to that collision with a ferry. When the barge arrives the crew drops the metal ramp onto the edge of the parking area. To back up onto the barge, as instructed, Colleen has to crank her neck around in an unnatural position. If you're a passenger and feel the need to be involved, your neck will also feel the strain. Once parked on the barge, other vehicles are guided into place just inches from us—nice cars, island cars, a dump truck, a stinky garbage truck, and a truck hauling blue porta-potties with the slogan on its door, WE'RE # 1 IN A # 2 BUSINESS. Colleen and I are able to open our doors far enough to squeeze out of the car. Others exit their vehicles through open windows—first their heads, then elbows, butt, knees, and feet. On the three-mile barge ride, Colleen visits with people. I stand at the railing and ponder words to describe the water—glacier melt water, azure, jade, sapphire, in addition to words like lyrical, mystical, occult. Then there's the sky. I'll say it's the color of a robin's egg. And there are usually fluffy cumulus clouds adorning the horizon. After the previous two months of toil, I'm deliriously happy. Everyone on the barge seems enlivened. It's a party atmosphere. My roommate says, "Let's face it, if you don't get off the island once in a while, you start to feel confined."

Once on St. Thomas, Colleen follows a regular route. First we stop at a thrift store, where I buy several skirts and tops with sufficient flowers and patterns to hide the mildew spots. At K-Mart I walk around, eyes darting from item to item. I buy a little boom-box to play CDs at the shop, and bottles of B-1 and garlic pills, to help keep mosquitoes off me. At a big discount store I buy six cans of insect repellent with a high concentration of DEET. While I'm at it, I buy an extra fan for the shop, since mosquitoes can't fly in winds over nine miles an hour. I grab a bug-eating device to attract mosquitoes and drown them. By mid-afternoon, I have a headache. I'm ready to collapse on the floor. Maybe this is why people from St. John refer to an outing to this island of shops and discount stores, St. Traumas Day.

Or maybe the trauma comes when you catch a barge back to St. John. Since the barge leaves at 5:00 p.m., Colleen gets us to the waiting area by four. From a distance the place resembles a junk yard, in which vehicles have been towed and abandoned in no particular order. The dirt parking lot has potholes, some of them ten feet across, all filled with rain water. No telling how deep. When Colleen creeps forward into the sea of vehicles and drives through the puddles, water flows in around our feet. She is undismayed. Finally, she parks. We wait. Again, she visits with others. She returns and leans into the car to tell me that some people have been waiting over an hour, because there wasn't room on the earlier barge. Soon she gets back into the car to do the impossible, to turn the car around so we're ready to back onto the barge. With everyone parked in a haphazard manner, doing this requires that she pull forward a few inches, crank the wheel, and back up, over and over. But Colleen's car is tiny and it's already dented, and she's nonchalant about her paint job. Finally, we're in a position to negotiate for a spot on the barge.

The *Captain Vic* arrives. The second the crew drops the ramp, everyone immediately backs up, honking their horns. Colleen has us expertly positioned, ass-end to the ramp of the barge. She backs up a foot or so at a time, honking, playing chicken, touching bumpers, not giving an inch. I witness two side mirrors get smashed and I hear fenders buckle. Many of these people are friends, yet the drivers are yelling and cussing at each other. The most dented cars and aggressive drivers get on the barge, including A.J., St. John's ice and water guy, in his Toyota pickup loaded ten feet high with empty gallon water jugs. And we get on too, but just barely.

One of the crew members yells, "We got too many cars on, too much weight."

But no one budges, and certainly not Colleen. She says, "I know him fairly well. He'd better not kick us off."

Another crew member yells, "Nah, it's okay, mon."

And off we go, overloaded and listing, back to St. John.

SUNNY AND WARM,
WITH A GOOD CHANCE OF MOSQUITOES

Even if clouds in the sky appear to be way out there over the Bermuda Triangle and you're only walking to the post office, be sure to take your umbrella.

Hurricane season began June 1, and lately I've been hearing talk about storms building in the Atlantic, where hurricanes get started. Now that summer has arrived, business has slowed, and shopkeepers wander around visiting while waiting for customers. Unlike The Canvas Factory, most business owners don't first *make* the items they sell. They order things in, mark up the price, and wait for customers to stroll into their shops to buy stuff. This is called *retail*. What we do is called *manufacturing and retail*. And to be honest, I like their way better. Since they have more free time than I do, I leave the concern over hurricanes to everyone else. Mongoose Junction, with its thick concrete and stone walls, is hurricane-resistant. On the other hand, during Hurricane Marilyn, the roof blew off Colleen's apartment.

Every long-time resident has a hurricane story. At my first chiropractic treatment, Bern tells me that in 1995 during Hurricane Marilyn, he and his wife and their daughter, who was six at the time, rode a couch down a steep hill about a hundred feet. Most of the house came along for the ride. While he takes my neck through a series of range-of-motion exercises he says, "It was only a ten-second ride."

He turns my neck to the right, *ouch*, and then the left, *ouch*.

"If you'd been in a rodeo, you would have won a big prize," I say. "A rodeo bronc rider once told me an eight-second ride can last almost forever."

"Actually, it happened fast and we weren't hurt," he says in his high-speed way of talking. "We were lucky, since the house was made of wood, not concrete with rebar the way they're built now. Before the hurricane hit we could have gone to a safe place. But the weather report said the hurricane was on its way somewhere else, so we stayed in the house. Then Marilyn swerved and came right over us."

Tom tells me he'll be my Informed Source. On the sailboat in Bellingham, he'll sit on his chair, an overturned five-gallon bucket, and watch storm patterns on the laptop computer using a hurricane tracking program. When he calls to warn me that Tropical Storm Dean is moving our way, the sky is already raining waterfalls. Rain splashes up onto our bags displayed on the doors, so Angie and I dash to remove them. Soon the gut, the drainage swale that runs through the parking lot, overflows and water runs across the floor of Hurricane Alley, the shop next door, and onto our floor. Angie and I had already moved everything up off the floor onto the cutting table. She says this has happened before. When the flood waters recede, I borrow a mop. It's a good way to get the floor clean, and all the drama pumps my adrenaline level up a notch.

Occasionally, the active volcano on Montserrat, an island south of us in the Lesser Antilles, erupts and spews ash. This event is often accompanied by a deluge of rain, which is good because it clears the air. Meteorologists announce that rains this time of year are welcome, since they cool the ocean and that can keep hurricanes from forming. But local wisdom may provide the best forecast of all: when the island's goat herds hang out on the roads, we in for a major weather event.

Then, too, the sky can be hazy from Sahara dust. While sewing in the cave-like back room of The Canvas Factory, I worry that there is camel dung in the dust, which can't possibly be healthy. One night last week I dreamed I spoke Sanskrit, and rode a camel in a caravan with gypsies or maybe Bedouins. These tough people treated me as one of their tribe. We wandered, taking detours, gathering real artifacts and not souvenirs. I wore rough, filthy boots of animal hides on my feet as we continued our migration. There were no mosquitoes.

But, here I am, legs covered with DEET, sitting in front of my sewing machine, head bent forward. If Montserrat erupts I could be buried in dust, caught permanently in the act of ripping out an errant seam, totally ossified. Shaking that image out of my head, I take a deep breath of Sahara dust, apply more DEET, and keep on sewing.

MOPS OF THE WORLD

Without the air conditioner working, the shop is downright steamy. One day while I sit at my sewing machine ripping out a seam, I feel a drop of sweat bead up on my mustache. If Tom were around, this would never happen. Before my mustache could grow into this walrus state of affairs, he'd tilt his head back, study me through his reading glasses, and announce, "It's time to do your mustache."

The air conditioner guy finally blows in. He removes a fan that resembles a squirrel cage and says he'll find a replacement as soon as possible.

"That would be lovely," I say. I won't hold my breath.

"Oh, hi, Hermon," Angie says to a tall, thin West Indian man who materializes out of the shadows.

"Meet my boss, new owner of the shop," she says, gesturing to me. "Rae Ellen, dis is Hermon Smith."

When I shake his hand, I see that Hermon's eyes are the color of cinnamon. He's wearing a brown felt fedora, one that looks like it's been around since Jimmy Stewart wore it. Dreadlocks whisp around his ears and neck. A tie-died T-shirt hangs over his slender frame, and his baggy pants are held up with a piece of rope frayed at both ends.

"Hermon works with wood," she says to me. "Tell her what kind is dat wood you work with, okay?"

"Lignum vitae," he says, pulling a piece out of his battered Canvas Factory knapsack in the color we call forest green. "Another name is ironwood. It's so dense it doesn't float. I'm working on this pendant." He holds up a piece of wood an inch wide, two inches high, and a quarter inch thick, with a tiny eye bolt screwed into the top. He hands it to me. The primitive face carved into it reminds me of those mysterious Easter Island stones. The facial features follow the fine grain and slight color variations in the wood. The piece is elegant, timeless, and original.

"I love this," I say. "How much is it?"

"Fifteen dollars, but this one's free today, for you," he says, looking at me with his warm dark eyes.

"Hermon, I can't believe it. Thank you."

He reaches into his pack and pulls out a black cord, loops it through the top of the pendant, ties the ends and hands it back to me. I wear it the rest of the day. The wood feels light and warm, almost alive.

While Angie is at lunch, a woman breezes into the shop, looks around and makes light conversation as she clutches one bag after another and looks in the full-length mirror. She's wearing a short, colorful dress. "I'm a snow bird," she announces. "I come here for the winters from Exeter, New Hampshire, a very stodgy place. But I loosen up when I'm down here. Look at this." She lifts her dress way up to expose her upper thigh and shows me a tattoo of a big green lizard. "I'm fifty-seven."

"And you're obviously a wild woman," I say.

She smiles and drops that side of her dress, only to pull up the other side—much, much higher up—exposing her torso nearly to her waist to show me a tattoo of a flower and a hummingbird.

"You made my day," I say. "Thank you."

As soon as the wild woman leaves, Luna darts into the shop, glowering and angry, clearly frightened, yelling, "The jumbies! They're trying to find me." Before I can reassure her, she runs back out proclaiming, "You got one in your shop! The devil took him over!" But I'm the only one in the shop at the moment, and I'm neither a ghost nor an evil spirit of the dead. At least not today.

Customers often ask me to do weird things for them, and I have trouble saying *no can do*. Sometimes people—well, it's always men— will enter the shop carrying an unidentifiable brownish lump, and lay it with care on the sales counter. Today it's a World War II Army canvas bag that had belonged to a young man's grandfather. This veteran has seen combat. The bag is now being used as a briefcase, except that the owner's pens, pencils, lunch, wallet, and iPod keep falling out through holes worn in the rotting fabric. Using my emergency room skills, I assess the bag as if it's incoming wounded, then work for an hour patching up the holes. When the owner returns to the shop he's thrilled, and I hug him for honoring his grandfather in this way. It's a soulful moment.

Another man asks me to sew a horseshoe stake bag. I tell him we have a full plate already, just sewing our regular designs. And we do. There's always too much to do. Everything is always rush-rush-rush. I'm not in the mood for a special project, but the man sketches out a design. He pleads. My father had enjoyed playing horseshoes and I've tossed a few myself. I cave in. Mostly I agree to sew the horseshoe stake bag because, as he talks, I realize how much the man looks like a former boyfriend, one who was particularly good in bed.

When the next brownish lump appears on the counter, I say, "Oh, you brought us a present?"

"This is my attaché and I'd like you to repair it," the man says. And I think, *Please don't ask me to touch that thing.* This attractive, well-dressed guy continues. "I bought it here a long time ago."

"We have some handsome new attachés in several colors," I say. "Don't you think you deserve a new bag?" Clearly the man has self-esteem issues, but on the other hand, he *can* make a commitment.

"This bag has gone everywhere with me for twenty years, but my pens keep falling out. Last week I lost a calculator. It's a perfectly good bag, except for those holes."

"I might not be able to fix it. My sewing machine balks at tight corners, which is where the holes are located, as you know. But I'll do the best I can." I study the bag some more, thinking, this will be like doing plastic surgery using clothesline rope. I say, "It'll cost twenty dollars."

I work and cuss for over three hours repairing that frazzled, moldy, filthy road kill. I cringe the entire time, and I'm not that squeamish. If I were to charge accurately for my time, it would add up to more than the cost of a new attaché. Then weeks go by and the man doesn't show up to claim his beloved bag. Should we bury the thing out in the national park? After some discussion, Angie and I double-bag the varmint in plastic and store it underneath the sales counter behind the garbage can. Now maybe birds of prey won't come swooping in the front doors in search of the smell. After a couple weeks the man stomps in the shop, madder than hell. "Why didn't you call me to say my attache was done? I've been lost without this bag. You need to work on your service attitude." The customer is always right. I apologize. He does appear stressed, like he's been suffering separation anxiety. This experience teaches me two lessons: 1) always write down the customer's phone number, and, 2) if someone wants me to repair a bag, it has to be clean.

We get a lot of smart customers in our shop who use credit cards that build air miles. So I apply for a Master Card affiliated with American Airlines and start using it to pay for raw materials. Soon I discover that many St. John residents build air miles as a hobby. One local tells me, "If you eat five boxes of a particular bran cereal, you can earn 500 miles on the credit card with American Airlines. I keep up my internal transit time while collecting air miles."

Another day a woman walks into the shop and says, "A rat just ran past me on its way out of your shop. At first I thought he was your pet."

"Are you serious?" I ask. "I've never seen a rat in the shop."

"No. I'm not kidding. I looked for a collar, but I didn't see one. He was this long, not including his tail." She holds up her hands to indicate six to eight inches. But St. John has woods rats, alias *furry night mons*, and their bodies are four to five inches long plus their tails. Maybe it was a jumbie spirit in disguise.

One of my many jobs is to cut out all the batches of bags for sewing. While doing this, I am excruciatingly careful. My goal is to cut all of the canvas pieces illustrated on the pattern, as well as sufficient zipper chain segments cut to the correct length, and all the webbing pieces needed for straps. As hard as I try, Angie often yells from her sewing machine, "Where are the sippers for dese bogs?"

"This is an evil game you're playing with me, Angie. You're hiding them, I know you are, and I'm going to find them all one day and dock your pay."

"Dot's eet!" she says, laughing.

This is both funny and frustrating, and it makes me feel stupid. I mean, I've worked all my life. For years I worked as a secretary, first in the Foreign Service at embassies in Switzerland and Yugoslavia, and for a short time in the White House, never mind that Nixon was then president. After returning to college I earned a degree in landscape architecture and worked for the U.S. Forest Service in Idaho and Montana. I can build bird houses, footstools, and twig shutters. I helped renovate that brothel I lived in for three years. I even, unfortunately, refinished teak on boats for a while. And now I'm having trouble preparing all the ingredients for a batch of canvas bags. If I weren't the owner, I'd sing the country and western song, *Take this job and shove it ... I ain't workin' here no more.*

One day when Angie and I are both sewing I tell her, "I can't wait to sew as fast as Cynthia did."

"Don't worry," she says. "In twenty years you'll sew real fast, too."

"But Angie, in twenty years I'll probably be in a rest home."

We laugh. And then we sit sewing, clipping, lifting our zipper feet, and turning the bags. I feel threadbare and exhausted, but grateful beyond measure that I have such a wonderful employee.

Angie begins to work a few hours a week at another shop in Mongoose Junction, Mapes de Monde, which I'm told is French for Maps of the World. Angie calls it Mops. She works at that shop a few hours on Fridays, and works with me on Saturdays to bring her total time up to 40 hours a week. I want her to be happy, so I accommodate her wishes. After all, she's the boss.

My goal over the summer months is to learn how to sew all 34 bags and cultivate Angie's "technique of faster." When we sew together, I ask her lots of sewing questions, of course, but we often blab about more fun things, too.

One day she tells me she's had other factory jobs—one at a Timex plant in Manila, another at a Barbie Doll factory, also in the Philippines.

"What job did you do with the Barbie Dolls?"

"I poot da butts on de dolls."

"How'd you do that?"

"I feeted de parts togedder, da butt on top of de boddom, and dey got glued togedder wit sonics."

I laugh hysterically at the description of how the dolls are made, and she laughs with me.

"Dere was a lot of passing the bucket in dat factory."

"Excuse me?"

"You know, nobody took de responsibility."

In summer there aren't many customers, and sometimes the ones who walk into the shop turn around and leave so fast it's as if they smelled something dead. One evening while removing my comfortable sandals—the ones that look like rubber-tired skidders held together with lots of Velcro, the shoes I've worn all summer—I realize they might be the culprit. Now I wonder if my shoes have been attracting mosquitoes, too, or maybe even that mystery cretin the woman saw fleeing the shop. Maybe all this time it wasn't the road kill bag that smelled rotten. Lord, I could hire these shoes out as guard dogs. It's funny how things get away from a person: first my mustache, now my shoes.

The very next day the air conditioner gets fixed. To celebrate the occasion, I trek through the Junction over to the adventure outfitters store, Big Planet, wearing my rubber-tired skidders. I buy a new pair of sandals, featuring light brown leather and no petroleum products. To celebrate, after closing the shop Angie, Dennis, and I walk across the courtyard and up the steps to an outdoor café. Tonight they're serving a special treat: sushi for beginners. While I understand that sushi can consist of rice with octopus, eel, and squid, tonight's sushi is vegetarian. Dennis asks the waitress, "What's vegetarian sushi, if it isn't raw fish?"

"It's white rice and raw veggies wrapped in seaweed."

And I notice on the little menu that it isn't cheap, either. But Angie says, "I gotta feed my pork chop somewhere."

I agree with a smile and a shrug, although I don't understand why she refers to her stomach as her pork chop.

"Well, we're here and we're hungry," Dennis says, "Might's well try it."

We sit down at a tiny, black wrought iron table with matching chairs, and place our order. We wait. We wait some more, which gives me time to think about the closest thing to sushi I've eaten to date. It has to be perch eggs. In the 1950s and early 60s in northern Idaho, my father fished through the ice in March to catch perch. This may have been illegal, and hopefully the statute of limitations on this crime has passed. In any event, some of the perch, when eviscerated, contained a sack of tiny eggs the size of your thumb. My mother rolled the egg sacks in seasoned flour and fried them in Crisco. This delicacy became my favorite treat in a childhood of good meals: venison and fish my father brought home, rabbits and chickens we raised, homemade bread, and fruits and vegetables, fresh-from-the-garden or home-canned.

Finally, our small plates arrive, each with six pieces of sushi and a green marble of condiment. We each take a small bite. The seaweed tastes like fish skin, or maybe it *is* fish skin. Not one of us can chew it into submission. Angie chews in earnest. Dennis chews and makes a face. To me sushi tastes like scrapings from the ferry dock pilings. This has to be an acquired taste, like green tripe. We inspect the sushi pieces left on the plate. Maybe they're served with a piece of protective black plastic we're supposed to remove before eating.

Angie gives one of the little sushi roll-ups to the café owner's black lab. He's overweight and looks like a blowup dog, like he'd eat anything, like he already has. He sniffs the sushi and looks away in a disgusted manner, reminiscent of the postal clerk who doesn't like me.

But I paid good money for the six little sushi deals, so I surreptitiously remove the piece I've been trying to chew and put it on the edge of my plate. It's not a pretty sight. I pick up another one and attempt to unwrap the seaweed or plastic from the rice and veggie portion, which finally requires that I *chew* it off. This doesn't go well, since the cook has apparently glued the wrapping to the rice and veggie ball. After a busy day at the shop, I'm hungry, so I pop the thing into my mouth and chew with great determination. In frustration, I also take a big bite of the green stuff on the plate that I think must be avocado. This turns out to be very hot horseradish. I choke and spit rice all over the table, and grab for Angie's iced tea to put out the fire. We all laugh as we mop bits of food off ourselves and each other.

Still hungry, we give up and pay our bill. As we walk past the cook shack, Dennis stops by to tell the cook, whose car he fixed once, "The next time you make vegetarian sushi, you should just use peanut butter for the centers and dip them in some nice melted chocolate."

With that we head to the parking lot, climb into the shark mobile, honk the horn, and drive, fan belt squealing, off to Starfish Market for some real food.

EMBRACE YOUR INNER BITCH

Business is slow. We're still catching up on back orders, but I always make time to visit when Captain Phil of the charter boat, *The Way-ward Sailor*, stops by. He usually has a story, and this time he tells me that on a recent sunset sail he had a guest who sells Depend® brand adult diapers.

"The guy told everyone on the boat that the diapers are sold by how many ounces they can hold," Phil says. "Did you know that?"

"No, and I always wondered."

"Well, I didn't know that either, so this morning while I'm hav-ing coffee with my geezer buddies at The Dockside Pub, telling them about the diaper salesman and how he plans to send me and my crew some Depends for Christmas, I see a West Indian man on the shore throw his sandal at a brown booby flying overhead. His sandal lands way out from shore in the water. The man grabs my dinghy, unties it, and rows out to retrieve it. His sandal isn't far out there, but when the guy reaches into the water to get it he falls overboard. So I wade out to help him. The man tells me, 'That damn bird followed me all the way from St. Lucia. He's stalking me. I can't get rid of him. What should I do?' and I tell him, 'I think you should get to know the bird. Maybe he's following you for a reason. Learn about the bird. Become his friend.'"

"I love that story," I say. "But what does getting to know the bird have to do with wearing Depend diapers?"

"Not a darn thing," he says.

And then he's gone. I smile off and on all day. On St. John, you never know what you'll see or hear next.

The word *carnival* is in the air for months before the actual event in early July. The word finds its way into all sorts of conversations. After work one evening, while riding with Angie and Dennis to the grocery store, Angie says, "I need some meat to cook for dinner. You know I like meat, dat I'm a carnival."

"Yes, Angie," Dennis says. "You're a carnival."

"Why are you guys laughing?" she asks.

"Because you probably meant to say carnivore," I say from the back seat.

"Dat's what I said. You gotta listen to me."

And Angie, being a good sport, laughs too, and for just a few minutes life is wonderful.

Finally the week-long event arrives. On the last day of Carnival—this annual celebration of emancipation for slaves on the sugar plantations—people are up early in the morning for the *juve sunrise* activities. The actual parade will start just before noon. After placing a hat order for a friend's fortieth birthday party, six hats embroidered with *Embrace Your Inner Bitch,* I lock up the shop and join the jostling mass of happy people. I circulate and take pictures. At noon, when it's 87 degrees, the parade finally takes flight with color, chaos, sweat and feathers. The music features one live band after another, the Pan Dragons playing steel pan drums, and also some recorded music amplified well beyond the threshold of pain. For me, the most exciting characters in the parade are the mocko jumbies, colorful figures on stilts that make these characters 15 feet tall. An ancient African art form, their height allowed them to see the evil jumbie spirits approaching, and they could warn the villagers. Today the mocko jumbies, dressed in elaborate pants and jackets of silks and satins, hover and sway above everyone. Now across the road from Mongoose Junction, they're eye level with a gri-gri tree, also known as black olive. I've read that during the plantation era, slave women gathered under this tree to tell stories, some of which included the evil jumbie spirits of the dead. Today these spirit-creatures on stilts are celebrating freedom.

Here comes Chester "The Mighty Groover" Brady, seen most often at the post office, movin' and groovin' to the radio music in the background. He has CDs for sale on which he croons songs with cultural lyrics, backed by music with a Latin flavor. Following him in the parade are dancers, exposing bare skin, their boobs and butts bouncing, tummies jiggling. Next a group of women carrying batons—The Middle-Aged Majorettes—and some of them are actually twirling.

The joyful music and singing continues, along with other expressions of animal vitality and long-standing tradition. According to the coconut telegraph, during Carnival numerous women have heard the invitation from an open vehicle window, *Go in da bush?* Sometimes, when vacation brain takes over or prudence falls away, the invitation is taken up. *And den dere's some big honkin' fockie, yeah, ha ha.* Sometimes dere's also a surprise nine months later. The same *ting* can happen after a long, frigid Montana winter. That first warm, sunny spring day can cause a Montanan to feel 15 feet tall and embrace her inner bitch. New trucks are bought before old ones are paid for, and babies are conceived by unlikely couples in curious positions and locations, like in the front seat of a brand-new truck.

YOU CAN DO ANYTHING YOU WANT, AS LONG AS THE REST OF US KNOW ABOUT IT

On this sweltering September morning with no trade winds blowing, the dump is odiferous. I feel broken down and ready for the trash heap myself, and as I walk past the workers sitting under a tree, I do not say good morning. Half way up what I now call Heart Attack Hill, I stop to catch my breath and mop sweat off my face. Finally, I reach Tony's and point toward Cruz Bay. I'm in luck. A gray-haired West Indian man in a dented up full-sized tan pickup truck screeches to a stop, motions toward the back end, and hollers, "Go ahead. Jump in."

"Thanks," I say.

"Goin' 'at way anyhow," the man says, smiling, missing a couple important teeth.

So I pull my skirt up almost to my waist to climb over the tailgate, and sit on a spare tire among mysterious items that appear to be destined for the dump. The truck lurches forward. It rained earlier, and now I'm worried about the island ice, that slick-as-snot road condition after a rain shower. Suddenly it feels as if we're flying around the bends, like I'm in a tilt-a-whirl. Certain we'll veer off the road into a tree, I grip the tailgate as we take another curve, and another, and when the driver hits a sizable bump, tools and debris on the bed of the truck leap up all around me and crash back down. My breasts levitate. Did we run down a small pig or a hitchhiker? As we skid around an elbow turn, the two inside tires lift off the pavement as if we're on a racetrack, and when I close my eyes, my life flashes before my eyes. But when I open them, all I see is blue smoke. So far, this trip to town wins the trophy as the wildest ride.

Another morning while waiting for a ride up at Tony's, an elderly red jeep stops. I climb in and sit on the passenger seat, which is wet where rain blew in. The driver tells me his name is Boiler Al.

"So, how'd you get the name Boiler Al?"

He slowly turns his head to look at me, closes and opens his eyes, and just as leisurely turns his gaze back to the road. He shrugs. "Beats me."

When my roommate leaves for two months in Maine, she entrusts me with her car, graciously telling me I can drive it once a week. Right away I reinforce the duct tape and cardboard on her torn vinyl back window. I shoo out the chickens and wash the interior, using a vinegar rinse to diffuse the odors of mold and barnyard. And when I drive it to work the first day, I'm a nervous wreck. Almost every turn is a blind corner, and while I'm somewhat familiar with the curves between Tony's and Cruz Bay, I'm usually hitchhiking, sometimes hanging on for dear life. Now I concentrate on keeping left, remembering the obstacles I've seen on the road—herds of goats, cows, chickens, donkeys, pigs, pedestrians carrying snorkel gear, and cars blocking traffic while the drivers chat. I creep along, watching for hitchhikers to pick up.

After a few trips to town, I become more comfortable. I take the roommate's car more often than "only once a week," usually Sundays and one more day a week, for instance if it's raining. What can I say? I'm an over-achiever. One day I pick up a young West Indian woman, and when I drop her off in town she says, "Thanks, ma'am. Dat was the slowest ride I ever had."

Another time I pick up a man who tells me his name is St. Croix Tom. We make the usual small talk, and then he tells me a line he heard in the 1980s on a radio show out of Puerto Rico: *It's good to live on St. John, where you can do anything you want, as long as the rest of us know about it.*

"Good one," I say. "I've heard a different motto, *We're all here cuz we're not all there.*"

"There's some truth to that line," he says. "I moved to the island in '89, just before Hurricane Hugo. Then, in '95, I went and bought a sailboat. But Hurricane Marilyn sank it before I even had a chance to go sailing. The boat's still on the bottom out there, and now my friend, Capt. Phil, uses it as ground tackle."

I hear great stories, while hitchhiking. At the shop I tell Angie, "It would sure be more convenient if I had a car. And I could get to the beach more often. But then if I don't hitchhike, I wouldn't meet so many interesting people."

"Oh," she says, sewing a hundred miles an hour. "Don't stop hitchhiking. Just use your own car for going to the bitch."

It's important to escape paradise once in a while, to visit the place you came from. That way you can be reminded why you left in the first place. I'm scheduled to fly up to the old country on September 17 for three weeks to see friends and family members, do some book readings, and help Tom deal with his mountain of junk in a fisherman's storage locker four times bigger than The Canvas Factory.

On the morning of September 11, I'm working alone when Jim from Wicker, Wood and Shells walks into the shop. Always lighthearted and cheerful, today his face is pained, like he's been in a car accident out front and has wandered into the shop for help. I study his face and arms for signs of blood.

"Two airplanes just flew into the World Trade Center in New York City," he says. "They think it was terrorists. And another plane just hit the Pentagon." He tells me people are stranded all over the world and relates other details he's heard, and then he wanders off in slow motion. Everything is suddenly unreal, as I sit alone in the little shop that has, until now, so completely taken over my life. None of it is important now, when I think of the innocent people inside the twin towers and their families. Staring out the open front door to the palm trees, seeking respite, I sit, eyes hollow, face sagging, feeling isolated and hopeless.

The phone lines are tied up, so there's no contact with the outside world. For days the sad and terrifying events of September 11 are the topic of discussion in the shop, at the post office and the bank, and on the streets. Not having a television is a good thing, because seeing and hearing the news of the events would not be therapeutic for me. Images can stay with me for years, and pop into my head at odd times. My negative image file is already full. After a couple days, Tom gets through on the phone to commiserate. A nephew of his works in Manhattan, but he's all right.

Air travel is suspended internationally but expected to resume shortly, with increased security. Should I fly? Will my reservations still be valid when the time comes? Book readings are scheduled. Tom and I have business to attend to. And I'm desperate to visit friends and family—now more than ever. After talking through the pros and cons with several people, I finally agree with Tom's assessment that it's probably safer to fly now than before, that if we allow terrorists to keep us from living our lives we've allowed them to win.

Angie and Dennis deliver me to the airport on St. Thomas in the shark mobile. As you might imagine, we're directed aside and thoroughly searched before being allowed anywhere near the terminal. Due to heightened security, there are flight delays, connections almost missed, and passengers erupting in cheers each time a plane lands safely.

While I'm in Bellingham, Tom and I succeed in dispensing with layers of detritus in the storage locker, items including odd sailboat gear, downhill and cross country skis, and lots of mystery crap. The recent terrorist attacks have dampened everyone's spirit, as we all try to figure out what it means. The only thing for certain is that life will be different, but it's impossible to predict how. Our own lives go on. We find that the contents of our locker are easier to dispose of now, and many items are donated to a thrift store with rather low standards. Other junk simply ends up in a Dumpster.

And then, after a side-trip to Idaho and Montana, where the air was so dry that my skin appeared to be two sizes too big for my face and body, I say goodbye to Tom until November. I cross my fingers and board a red-eye flight out of Seattle—final destination St. John.

The next afternoon when I open the door of the apartment on Gifft Hill, I trip over a dead cockroach, which, oddly, makes me smile.

After a sound sleep under the mosquito netting, I awake to the inertia caused by jet lag. A friend of the roommate's has picked up her car to do some repairs on it before she returns. So now, revived by strong coffee, I drag my butt past the dump and up Heart Attack Hill to Tony's, where a veteran jeep with no doors stops to give me a ride. There are already three people in the front seat–a blond woman driving plus two young West Indian men. It's starting to rain and I'm running late, so I attempt to climb in. But there's only room for half of me, so that one cheek and a major portion of my body hangs off the seat. The seatbelt doesn't work, and there's not much to hold onto.

"Just drape the seatbelt over your shoulder," the driver yells, lurching onto the road, into the flow of traffic headed toward Cruz Bay.

The seatbelt ruse is to fool the police, and I do as requested. Then I link my left arm around the arm nearest me, and grip the edge of the roof so tightly the knuckles on my right hand lock up. But I'm smiling as we careen around corners on our way into town. It's a good ride, and half of me gets rained on, but this trip into town makes me feel right at home—where I should have been all along.

VILLA DEBRIS

The ad in *Tradewinds* for the studio apartment on a hill in Cruz Bay did say "small." And now, when I stand in the doorway with the land-lady, I look and I look some more. This isn't small; this is a nice-sized walk-in closet. But at 125 sq. ft. it's roomier than either the chicken coop or the sailboat, and it has running water, even indoor plumbing. Views through a wall of jalousie windows include the vast Caribbean Sea. There's even a chest of drawers, a table almost big enough for two, and a kitchen area consisting of three shelves, a counter space with a hotplate for cooking, and space beside it for a spoon or two. Tom and I will be able to walk to and from the shop up a very steep hill—good training for a future hiking trip to Switzerland. Tom and Twodot will be arriving soon and this place just might work.

On the down side, the walls are yellow with pepto-*dismal*-colored trim, but I can wield a paint brush. And the place is dirty. But I see no cockroach corpses or termite tunnels. I'll draw a careful floor plan down to the square inch. I'll buy a futon so the room won't look like a bedroom all the time. The best part is that it rents for less than $1000 a month. You get what you pay for. A decent sized apt, especially one with views and breezes, starts at $1200 to $1500 a month. If you can find one. I sign a lease for a year.

With Colleen's help and a trip or two in the shark mobile, I get moved into the tiny apartment on the last day of October. After a bout of intense cleaning, I sit on the little balcony as the sun sets, pleased with my new digs. Then I inflate a new air mattress with my hair dry-er, putting hot air into my bed in the 80-plus degree heat, while burn-ing my fingers. I settle onto my bed of hot air and listen to the frogs sing their catchy serenade. Soon chickens begin to cackle and crow. Dogs bark. Cars start up, tires screech, horns honk. If it's happening anywhere in Cruz Bay, I'm hearing it. Well, of course. It's Halloween. No wonder it's so noisy. With earplugs muffling the noises, I drift in and out of sleep, hearing party sounds, hollering, and excruciatingly loud rock music of an amateur bent, until 2:45 in the morning. Why aren't they playing steel pan music—that happy sound made by banging a rubber-headed stick on a drum made out of an oil barrel? Or that quelbe music, traditional scratch tunes made by playing gourds, washboards, ukuleles, a saxophone, and an instrument called an *ass pipe*, made out of an old car exhaust tube. Right now I'd like to get my hands on an ass pipe. I'd march right down town and bang a few heads.

At 6:00 a.m., after only a few hours of sleep, my eyes jerk open. A diesel engine is starting up right in my room. I leap out of bed. It takes a minute or two of stumbling around before I get oriented and realize that the noise is the first ferry of the day starting up. Thanks to the way sound carries near the ocean, you don't need the ears of a bat to hear the din around here.

Only good, strong coffee gets me going. As I leave the apartment to walk to the shop, I see my neighbor, and ask, "Did you think it was especially noisy here last night?"

"We've lived here seven years," she says. "We run a big loud fan every night to muffle the noise."

"Oh," I groan. These are tolerant people.

When I signed the lease, I immediately applied for a phone to be installed. Phone installation or repairs can take months, people say, but through some miracle or scheduling error I get my phone the third day after moving in. I call Tom. He and Twodot left Bellingham a couple days ago to drive across the U.S. in our tiny 1986 Suzuki Samurai, purchased for use on the island. Not much bigger than a riding lawnmower, with sides and a convertible top, the car is an embryonic version of most cars. As a method of cross-country transport, the car is noisy and probably unsafe. Tonight he's visiting his kids in northwest Montana. My son and his wife drove up from Helena to see them all, and now I visit with everybody on the phone.

During my third night of little sleep, I hear screeching brakes, crunching metal, and the smashing of glass. And … there it goes again. I leap up to look out the window. A white safari taxi screams around the block again, crashing into cars parked along the streets. This time the truck bounces off my neighbor's car. Someone calls the police. When the driver hears sirens, he abandons his pickup and runs off into the woods. I hear voices, but roosters are crowing and I can't hear actual words. At least I'm not lonely. It's 2:45 a.m. Might's well try to sleep. At 5:50 a.m. a garbage truck arrives to empty the two nearby Dumpsters. Then the first ferry growls to life, right next to my bed.

Bedraggled and listing, I stagger down the steep hill to work. When I enter the shop Angie looks up, stops sewing, and says, "What hoppen to you? You have beeg bogs under your eyes."

Since the lease I signed states clearly that I'm entitled to "peaceful and quiet enjoyment of the apartment," and because the landlady is a reasonable person, I'm able to annul my lease. I'll move out by December 1, a time when every available place on the island is already rented. The next day, the landlady finds a new tenant, one who will pay $50 more a month.

Jim from Wicker, Wood and Shells is always looking out for me. He knows of a cottage on Mamey Peak near Bordeaux Mountain, available December 1. "The cottage is rustic," Jim says, "but it has two bedrooms. You can use one bedroom for an office, which makes it a business expense."

The big problem is that the rent is $1250 a month. The place will rent immediately, so I arrange to see it and Jim drives me out there. The cottage is one of four in a row, marching up the hill, and trees screen one from the other. The view from the decks and glass walls on two sides encompasses nearly all the British Virgin Islands. According to a glossy magazine, this view (the same as Chateau Bordeaux, the restaurant just up the road) is one of the ten best in all the Caribbean. And even better, you can enjoy this sights while getting clean, since the shower is outside on a small deck on the side of the cottage. The kitchen, dining room and living room are all in one room, well-lit by the south- and east-facing glass walls. After my adventures in housing, this place is not what I'd call rustic.

So what if I must immediately produce the first and last month's rent plus a month's rent as security deposit, and then buy groceries with a credit card?

When Tom calls again from his slow migration across the U.S., he's in Miles City, Montana. I describe the cottage and he agrees that we deserve a decent place to live, that we'll work out the cost. On a sad note, his mother is gravely ill and is staying with his brother near Minneapolis, Tom's next stop. Otherwise, he's enjoying the drive and the drive through the Big Sky Country of Montana. But he's also looking forward to finally crossing into some other state, even if it is North Dakota, where Tom, his first wife and their six children had lived on a farm near Fargo.

The next time I hear from Tom, he's in Alexandria, Minnesota, only a few hours from his brother's house. He has other news. Wes, our friend and sailboat broker, has sold *The Shoe*. And while this relieves us of a boat payment, it turns out we're selling the boat for exactly what we paid for it. The $20,000 we invested to make a silk purse out of that sow's ear must be chalked up to *experience*. Buy high, sell low; that's us.

The sleepless nights in the tiny apartment continue. Tonight a train roars closer, chasing me, hot air from the noise-pounding engine scorching me as I run faster and faster. I'm breathless as I glance over my shoulder, hoping not to trip on a giant, dead cockroach as big as a wild pig lying ahead on the trail. The monster train is gaining on me. The screeching of the wheels on the track reverberates all around me as the monster train grows closer. Seconds before the train flattens me, I awake from my bad dream to the ear-splitting, pounding base of a hard-rock band, playing in one of Cruz Bay's night spots.

The phone rings at 7:00 a.m. It's Tom calling from Tuscola, Illinois. He'd driven 500 miles after visiting his brother and mother. His mother is back in the hospital because her kidneys are shutting down. Tom is sad, but also glad he could be with her for a week. Part of him wants to go back to see her again in the hospital, but he decides to continue on. He's anxious to get to St. John, and all the arrangements have been made for his travel from Florida and for shipping the car.

His next call is from Jacksonville, Florida. He made it. Tomorrow he'll deliver the car to Crowley Shipping and then he and Twodot will fly to St. Thomas. We're both amazed that he made this odyssey across the country in the lawnmower car with his cat.

On my last morning alone, I am apprehensive. I write an affirmation: *Life with Tom is pleasant and enjoyable. We treat each other with kindness and respect and work together efficiently. We have adequate time to rest, hike, and go to the beach.*

And when Jim takes me to the ferry dock and we pick up Tom and Twodot, I'm happy to see him. It's time to get started on the next chapter of this big adventure we bought for ourselves.

Twodot sleeps stretched out along Tom's back in the spoon position. He's mostly white with a tiny black beret, black tail and two black spots the size of silver dollars on his starboard side. With the moon shining in on us, he's easy to see. Later when I wake up, Tom is sleeping on his back and Twoey is reclining on his chest like a lion. When the ferry starts its diesel engine, he jerks his head up and looks around the room for the big dog that made *that* growl.

The day before our move to Mamey Peak, Tom and I catch the foot ferry to Charlotte Amalie on St. Thomas to claim the car, and after an hour at the customs office we drive away. Tom is at the wheel. My job is to remind him to keep left, while I refer to a phone book map to find the discount stores. We can't buy many supplies, since the back of the Samurai holds trunks full of Tom's treasures. With all barges now operating, we have no trouble getting onto one, but as soon as we head east toward St. John, the barge begins to dip and sway like a teeter totter in the ocean swells, lurching and pitching from the right front of the barge to the left rear, deeper and deeper each time. I'm reminded of our sailing days and the precarious nature of all watercraft, and at the exact moment I'm certain our life together in paradise is over before it starts, the barge pulls into the safety and calm of Cruz Bay harbor and prepares to drop its ramp.

After saying goodbye to the tiny apartment in the sky, we drive the seven miles to the cottage. Together we unload Tom's trunks and bounce them down a flight of wood stairs, to be stored next to the cistern.

"What do you have in these things, anyway?" I ask. "I thought we got rid of all our extraneous items."

"Machining tools, hardware, and some sailing gear, just in case."

"Oh, blue stuff," I say, which is what we jokingly call his favorite macho junk. "Let's call this place Villa Debris."

The owner of the four cottages is a retired actor who, in the land of 1950s television advertising, served honorably as the Tidybowl Man. Gerry has a booming voice and can spout the lines of Shakespearean characters he's played on stage. You do not want to engage him in a discussion of politics.

Christine, his lovely Austrian-born wife, met him through mutual friends in Amsterdam. When the Tidybowl Man invited her to visit him on St. John, she did, and when she returned to Vienna, she lost her job. At the same time, Hurricane Marilyn struck St. John and two of the four cottages, including ours, ended up down the hill. Gerry invited Christine back to St. John to help him rebuild, and she came.

Our cottage hovers on a steep hill above the Centerline Road, directly on the route of the trade winds. Some evenings the trades blow so hard it sounds like a howling gale in Bellingham Bay. Based on my sailing experiences, I'd have to guess 40 knots, although it's hard to tell without the ropes and metal gewgaws clanging against all the masts in the harbor. At least up here on dry land, the railing of the deck is not in the water.

Our neck of the woods also catches more moisture than many areas of the island. The saturated air seeps into fabrics and cushions, resulting in a prevailing odor of mildew. If you were to put clothes inside a dresser drawer at Villa Debris, they'd turn moldy within hours.

I order four open wicker storage boxes on the Internet. When they arrive, I place them on a shelving unit in the upstairs bedroom, and Twodot immediately claims one as his bed.

Showering together conserves water. And we begin our shower with cold water, because we cannot afford to waste water by letting it run down the drain until it's warm. Tom and I take turns operating the flexible shower hose, and today Tom has the honor of bestowing the stingy ration of water. He sprays my head and body as I turn around, and then he sprays himself before turning off the water. We lather up, soap down, and apply a minimum amount of shampoo while looking at the nearby termite nest in a leafy tree, or out to the sky and ocean. Cars on the highway down below us drive toward our nakedness. We joke that someone will look up at exactly the right moment and catch us nude. But, no worries. Drivers must watch the twisty road, not feed our fantasies.

Wet, soaped up, and waiting, I stand shivering in the cool breezes. Lizards dart around on the walls of the shower. A garbage truck empties the Dumpster down by the highway. Dogs bark in the distance. A rooster crows. When Tom grabs the shower hose and turns the cold water back on, I surrender, turning again to receive the cool spits and trickles that rinse my head and body. Then he sprinkles himself. Every morning, at exactly the moment Tom reaches to turn off the water, he says, "It was just starting to get warm."

Refreshed and clean, we towel off. We're on a tight schedule. With no extra time and no loose change, we dress quickly in the minimal clothing required. We can't ignore the tyranny of responsibility, or we'll be scratching and rooting for food alongside the chickens and pigs.

CHRISTMAS IN THE TROPICS

On the day before Thanksgiving, in 85-degree heat, we decorate the shop with strings of lights, big red bows, and fake Christmas tree greenery. We don't normally engage in Christmas activities, but now with additional lodging costs, we're motivated to promote sales so we can pay down the credit card and meet next month's expenses.

As high season kicks in, the biggest selling bag colors are black and purple. We believe this is a response to the lingering shock and sadness over the events of September 11. Fewer people are visiting the island this year than last, yet with three of us now working, we're still too busy. My goal is to shave seconds off of each task. One day Tom and I are working at the shop alone, and I'm cutting crop, knowing that I *should* also be sewing. Tom sits sewing mini bags, carefully trimming the zipper ends with several slow, careful cuts, as if he's machining another door handle for Bill Gates. I tell him, "We don't have that kind of time to waste. One quick snip is all you need."

He defends his way. "It's important to do quality work."

"Of course, but we both have to work fast or we'll never have time to go to the beach."

He lays down the scissors, sits back, folds his arms, and says, "You have all the time you think you have."

"Right," I say. "I'm going to the post office."

I walk slowly, an exhausted zombie, as if I have all the time in the world. There's no mail in our mailbox, but as I leave the post office a West Indian man whistles at me as he drives past. I'm wearing a simple sleeveless dress and sandals, and since I know they like white women with big butts I don't feel particularly flattered. But still, it's *something*, and then I ponder that mystery of West Indian manhood—you know, the *big bamboo* question. And for a few precious moments, my mind enjoys a respite from the shop.

At the little park across from the ferry dock I collapse onto a park bench under a tree and stare, feeling homesick for the *me* I was while Tom was gone. And I'm exhausted. If I can't have two days off a week at my age, after working or going to school full time all my life, something is seriously wrong. A pitiful sight, I sit slumped on the bench, thighs spread out like Christmas hams. I'm staring past the ferry that just arrived from St. Thomas, when a bird, sitting on a tree branch overhead, drops a comment about my sorry life right on my lap. My eyes focus on this new addition to my attire, yet I feel no surprise at all. I simply get up and plod along back to the shop. As I walk, the bird shit solidifies enough to drop off onto the bare toes of my right foot. Back at the shop I take a tissue and clean off my toes, then resume cutting crop.

In mid-December, Tom's brother calls to say their mother has died. This is sad, indeed, and Tom takes time off to be alone. Cremation will be followed with a memorial service in early summer, when the weather is nice in the upper Midwest and the birds are singing. Tom and I reminisce about Alta's many fine qualities, and how she was involved in our St. John adventure from the beginning. Back in 1995 when she was in the hospital for a new heart valve, we tried to visit her but could not find her. As we searched the hospital, we made up a story about how she'd hooked up with a geezer she met in the hospital and they ran off together to the Caribbean. We found her, of course, but later started a novel using our goofy story line about two senior citizens escaping to St. John. There was no choice after that. We had to make a trip to see if our location would work, and … here we are!

Alta's birthday was April 1, and we also recall the early evening when we took her to dinner for her eightieth birthday. We drove on a back road from Bigfork to Kalispell, Montana, and when we saw llamas standing on the other side of a fence, she asked us to stop. She walked up to the fence, and this woman who loved her three sons with so much abandon, leaned forward and kissed one of the llamas.

In the days leading up to Christmas, we get a string of customers who value beautiful and durable handmade gifts for the special people in their lives. A local woman buys mini bags with our label for members of her bridge club.

"So," I say, ringing up the sale, "do you actually play bridge?"

"Oh, no," she laughs. "We never play cards. And the bridge thing? We just build 'em, cross 'em and burn 'em. Then we go on a cruise together. And we're all members of The Middle-Aged Majorettes. We march in the Carnival parade every year."

"I saw you there," I say. I want to close the shop and follow her around like a puppy, become her friend, join her club, take up a baton, and then go on a cruise with these people. And I'm suddenly giddy at the idea of burning a few bridges.

A few of the women who visit St. John sport diamonds so big they should, by law, come with dimmer switches. One of these women, from France, wants the handles replaced on an old canvas bag. In the interest of world peace I perform this task for her. Another woman, visiting from Mazatlan, brings greetings from Bellingham friend, Jon Lawler, who sailed his boat solo down to Mexico, where they ended up in the same marina. When I think of Jon, I remember what he told us about sailing in heavy weather: *A knockdown lasts only thirty seconds, but wet Triscuits are forever.*

At home in the evenings I describe the customers to cheer up Tom. But he's doing all right and before long, he's back at work.

In desperate need of some fun, we close the shop on Christmas Day and drive out to the East End, a curved tail of land. We find the trailhead for Brown Bay and hike through stands of century plants and organ pipe cactus to a ridge 200 feet above sea level, then down the other side to a deserted beach facing north over the Atlantic Ocean. Not many island visitors find their way to Brown Bay, but *someone* comes here. Abandoned clothes and shoes are scattered in the vegetation at the shoreline and all along the trail. We see enough apparel to outfit the entire population of a small town in Montana. Near one pile of clothing, we spot a used douche bag.

Illegal immigrants from China, Haiti, the Dominican Republic, and Cuba come ashore in the night at various places on the island, and this appears to be one of them. By the time we sit on the beach to rest, clouds cover the sky. A nearby ghost crab scoots sideways, stops suddenly and buries itself in the sand, with only its black eyestalks visible. Tom swims and I rest, then we explore the plantation ruins in the area. Near the remains of an estate house we find a crumbling concrete plaque inscribed with the date 1872, bearing the initials G-N. The stone and brick work is beautifully crafted. The ruins include a sugar factory with its boiling room, cisterns once used for rum distillation, and an ancient copper boiling pot. We find two horse mills, where horses or mules harnessed to long poles once plodded around in a circle, producing the power to crush sugar cane into juice.

At the end of the afternoon we walk back to the car and drive the roller-coaster road home. Christine hears our car grind up Mamey Peak road, and as soon as we step inside our cottage she calls us to join them on the roof of their cistern for a drink and to watch the sunset. As we sit on top of the cistern with the Tidybowl Man and his Austrian bride, the sky, now mostly clear, offers up the usual robin's egg blue with big fluffy clouds above the horizon. As the sun sets, the clouds turn every shade of pastel.

The day after Christmas it's back to business. We arrive in town early, refreshed and ready to work hard. When we stop at the post office at 8:15 to mail a package, the following note is posted on the door: *Until further notice. Closed until a later, sometime today.*

A NAKED MAN FOUND WALKING

Dear *Tradewinds* editor:

I am writing to you about your police log for New Year's Eve that indicated there were no arrests or disturbances—except for a naked man police found walking on the Centerline Road. The folks back home in Idaho enjoy hearing what's going on down here on St. John, so I send them reports, sometimes with quotes from your newspaper. My poet friend, Kathryn Hamshar, elected three times as poet of the year by the Idaho Writers' League, penned the following poem about the naked man:

> The road was empty, so I heard folks talking
> Except there was a naked man police found walking
> And I wondered, were there nudists camping near?
> Or was it just a case of too much beer?
> I am wondering just what happened to his clothes
> And if he had some more, or only those.
> Was he kicked out by his lady friend, who kept
> His gear because his spear was quite inept?
> Just barely there, he's not here to defend
> His honor, he's just naked to the end.

My letter and Kathryn's poem appeared in the January 19-25, 2004, issue of *Tradewinds* with the bold headlines, IDAHO POET IMMORTALIZES ST. JOHN POLICE REPORT.

DRIVE IT LIKE YA STOLE IT

I swore I'd never live in a gated community. But Villa Debris has a rickety, moldy gate at the entrance to our driveway to keep feral goats and donkeys from eating the ornamentals.

Every morning our perilous drive to Cruz Bay begins when I open a rickety, moldy wood gate. This gate is the closest we've ever come to living in a gated community, although it exists only to prevent feral donkeys and goats from eating the ornamentals surrounding our cottage, Villa Debris. These plants include hibiscus, frangipani, and a grapefruit tree.

After Tom drives through this gate, I close it and climb into our little Samurai. We crawl down the Mamey Peak road, rough as a Montana stream bed, in four-wheel drive low until we reach the Centerline Road. While Tom shifts back into two-wheel drive, I peer through the frangipani leaves that block our view of oncoming traffic. When it looks all clear, I yell, "Tromp on it!"

We lurch over the lip of concrete at the edge of the highway and navigate as quickly as possible into the left lane, where we will remember to stay as we drive the 7 miles and 114 curves between Mamey Peak and Cruz Bay. We roar uphill as fast as we can, maybe 15 miles per hour. In spite of a blind corner just ahead, a black low-rider is suddenly behind us honking, and then passing, with his stereo booming rap music.

Shift down, turn left. Shift up, turn right. Apply brakes. Accelerate. The drive is more comfortable if you're the one gripping the steering wheel. Riding shotgun as I am, in the passenger seat, I sit only inches away from the oncoming traffic. Our toy car rides rough, too, so my tummy vibrates like a bowl full of jello.

Sometimes when we're driving along, a gecko will be gripping the hood of the car, peering at us through the windshield, as if pleading a rescue. And while couples on their way to work on the mainland might stop for a latte, we stop to clear lizards off the windshield. They're my friends. They eat mosquitoes.

Back on the road, we approach the highest point on the Centerline Road. Over the roar of our engine I now hear a truck horn off in the distance, between us and our destination. This horn could be attached to a water truck or a cement truck. But this horn is more or less continuous, which means it's a truck pulling a flatbed trailer carrying a colossal piece of construction equipment. And this monstrosity is coming toward us. It will take up most of the road. We will meet it on a hairpin curve, and our microscopic version of a car will end up like a lizard on the giant's windshield.

"Do you hear that horn?" I ask.

"What did you say?"

During Tom's odyssey across the U.S. in this noisy Suzuki Samurai with its new ragtop, he did not wear earplugs, and now he often says, "What did you say?"

"I said, there's something big coming toward us, and it's blowing its horn!"

He looks out his window to the ocean. "Will you look at the size of that sailboat."

This odd comment reminds me of our swashbuckling days of sailing in gales with every sail up. I was the designated worrier while Tom might be meditating on the aerodynamics of a sail and how similar it is to the cup of a bra.

Behind us a car is following too closely. They can't help it. We don't drive very fast. As we do nearly every morning, Tom pulls off the highway into a parking lot to let the faster drivers pass. A rental car follows us into the parking lot, but soon realizes where they are and pulls back onto the road. We wave at them and smile.

From here it's all downhill to the Reef Bay trailhead. Tom coasts. The car backfires.

The monster truck coming toward us is a lot like life. When you need to make an exit from a bad situation, there isn't always a safe place to go. But so far, when we've met a truck barreling toward us in the middle of the road, we've been lucky enough to drive into a ditch instead of a tree or off a cliff.

The bellowing horn echoes all around, thanks to the way noise is magnified by water vapors in the air. What will happen if we meet this horn-blowing monster at the Reef Bay trailhead, with cars parked on both sides of the road and hikers opening their doors to put on their packs? If we need to get out of the way will we really, as claimed, be able to put the Samurai in four-wheel-drive low and climb to safety up a tree? We shoot down the road toward the trailhead, and thundering toward us and taking up most of the road is a truck, and it's pulling a flatbed trailer carrying a gigantic Caterpillar tractor. At the exact location of the trailhead, we meet the enemy in an explosive whoosh and blaring of horns, with only inches to spare. I needn't have worried. Even with a dozen vehicles at the trailhead, no one was getting in or out of their car at the precise moment the truck stormed through. In the rearview mirror, I see that all hikers are still standing. Every jaw is dropped, but only a few hikers are missing their hats.

Tom double-clutches and shifts into second gear for the grind back up a hill and around several switchbacks cut into the rock cliffs. Soon we'll stop at another pull-off, coming up on our side of the road, where we'll let the new crop of faster drivers pass by. But today the pull-off is filled with police cars. In lieu of an orange traffic cone, an office chair with wheels is held in place by yellow crime scene tape. Across the road, plowed into a concrete drainage abutment, is a public works dump truck. We drive by slowly, gawking, but can't figure out what happened. There are always so many island mysteries, and here is yet another one.

Our toy car farts proudly onward, with several faster drivers still on our tail. Now we're on a straight stretch of a couple hundred yards where even *we* exceed the speed limit. We fly past the Cinnamon Bay trailhead going 25 miles per hour in third gear, neck and neck with a tricked out Isuzu Passport attempting to get ahead of us. Tom tromps the accelerator to the floor, but we notice danger up ahead and he steps on the brake. The Isuzu swerves back into our lane, seconds before meeting a water truck head on.

Shift down, turn left. Shift up, turn right. Apply brakes. Accelerate. Now we round the curve where we always try to straddle the brown and crumpled leaves as big as throw rugs. Soon we arrive at the biggest curve, where once a stolen red Samurai ended up in the limbs of a tree below the road. Next we enter a couple miles of open range, with no sign announcing this as a wildlife viewing area. The longest straight stretch on the entire road–an eighth of a mile, straight as a string–brings us to The Pig Dumpster on the left, where bags of garbage and cardboard boxes spill over the sides, pigs snort through torn bags on the ground, bed springs lean against the trees, and feral cats sit nearby in a tree on a feeding perch. This morning an enormous toy gorilla sits on top of the debris in the dumpster. Next we slow down for a herd of goats, walking along the road in sufficient numbers to qualify as a migration.

A half-mile further three donkeys graze politely near the road, not far from several cows that are mostly white with brown spots. Some cows are hidden by large trees that are growing in the right-of-way. Other cows stand, dumb as a box of rocks, in the middle of the road. One cow seems to have bonded with an abandoned car. In Montana, deer leap out in front of you or sometimes smash into the side of your vehicle. Here the animals amble, and the 100 or so deer on the north side of the island tend to stay off the road.

We pass my old hitchhiking spot, Tony's Concession Stand, and find ourselves driving behind another Suzuki Samurai, one even older than ours. One of many bumper stickers on its rear end says, *DRIVE IT LIKE YOU STOLE IT.* Soon we meet a car with a windshield decal that says, *LET DEM TALK.* Here comes one that says, *YO MAN IS IN HERE,* followed by a vintage open-air Samurai with a small fiberglass dinghy strapped to the roof. The driver told us one day that the dinghy serves as a perfectly fine car roof and if she goes off the road and lands upside down in the ocean, her car will float. Stranger things have happened. One acquaintance had parked her little Suzuki, proudly wearing the bumper sticker *EVE WAS FRAMED*, at Red Hook on St. Thomas. She caught the foot ferry to St. John for the evening, and when she returned to Red Hook, her car was gone. Stolen. On St. John, a bright red Jeep Grand Cherokee disappeared from a nice neighborhood. These islands aren't that big. Where do thieves go with these cars when they don't end up in the treetops?

As we approach town, houses line both sides of the road, many of them unfinished, the homes that look like bunkers with pieces of re-bar sticking up in the air. Now we see an enormous filthy pig walking on the road with a tiny mutt of a dog, a coconut retriever, running along beside it. Tom brakes suddenly for a huge tarantula making its way to the other side of the road. With so many people heading toward Cruz Bay to work or to catch a ferry, the tarantula is at risk. I think of Thelma, the friendly arachnid who lived in the door back at the shackteau.

Twenty minutes after leaving Villa Debris, we dock safely in the parking lot at Mongoose Junction. We're parked next to another old Suzuki with an epiphyte growing out of the grill, and a bumper sticker that says, *DOG IS MY CO-PIRATE!* Sitting a moment, we both sigh. We have survived another trip to town. Thank *Dog!*

BIG DOROTHY AND *LITTLE* RITA

Long after the thrill of holiday visitors is gone, the island is so quiet it's like a nuclear bomb went gone off. And yet the Christmas rains continue. The trees around Villa Debris plump out in luminous green radiance. We peer out through our walls of glass as if from inside a salad bowl. Mosquitoes bloom in profusion. Mold sprouts on books.

During this dank, gray time we discover the wonders of Wash, Dry, Fold. We drop bags of moldy, sour-smelling laundry off at the dry-cleaning establishment, say those three little words, and pay a dollar a pound. You can't buy potatoes for that price.

Another antidote to the weather and our general feeling of exhaustion is called Drink More Scotch, which began with Tom's arrival. And why not drink more rum, too, since it's cheaper than water? If I weren't so weak of character, I'd stop participating in this debauchery. I'm reminded of the slogan on a customer's T-shirt: *My Drinking Team Has a Fishing Problem.*

Is all this scotch killing our brain cells? Maybe Tom is concerned, too, because he recently listened to an audio book, *Mozart's Brain and the Fighter Pilot,* and learned various techniques to enhance his brain-power. But all I've heard is talk, in between sips of scotch. And he's acting weird, even for him. For instance, the computer is in the downstairs guest room/office next to the cistern. One evening I'm down there checking my email when Tom tromps down the stairs, opens the sliding glass door, and says, "Are you communicating with someone by email that you don't want me to know about?"

I don't believe it. I say, "Here. Read my emails. I don't have time to read them all. You can check them any time you want." I remind him of my email address and password, and then I stomp up the stairs.

After this, every time I go downstairs to check my email, I say, "Guess I'll go see if I have an email from one of my boyfriends." When I come back upstairs I tell him things like, "I heard from that guy competing in the Olympics. He's a speed skater and he's worried that his timing is off. The other guy is French, and his command of English isn't real great, but *I* know *exactly* what he's saying in his emails. *Oh may oui,* those French men are soooo sexy. They're simply *on-kray-dee-bull.*"

When we lived on the sailboat, a pilot berth served as the computer desk, and an overturned five-gallon bucket was the desk chair. Above the computer, Tom used clothespins to attach important papers to a clothesline—inbox on the left, outbox on the right, unpaid bills in the middle. And now Tom is our business manager. He's better than I am with Quickbooks, not to mention spreadshits, and he's skilled at shooting the breeze with other merchants. Plus, he's handy with technical workings and enjoys comparing the qualities of one piece of equipment over another.

Since buying the business, I've lusted after an electric scissors or cutter that can slice through several layers of canvas at once. So I ask Tom to do the research and present options for our discussion. Before you know it, an electric rotary device called an Eastman Chickadee Fabric Cutter is on its way. This long-awaited addition to the shop looks like a pizza cutter with an electric motor. While this newest employee doesn't talk back or get hungry, it is noisy. In fact, it sounds like the mother of all cicadas, or maybe an entire swarm of cicadas emerging and finding their communal voice. But, I'm not complaining. The thing cuts through up to four layers of heavy canvas easily and quickly. It's important to pay attention, though, because quite suddenly the edge of four layers of canvas can end up as crooked as the Centerline Road. With a little practice, this purchase just might save my life. If three of us work, two at a time, I'm hopeful that we can operate in a normal pattern of work and fun. In other words, maybe someday Tom and I will be able to take a trip together. They say married people do that.

The notion is fleeting. In January Angie gives notice that she's quitting. This is a catastrophe. She'd been complaining that working with the heavy canvas was hurting her hands and even a shoulder. However, for more pay she'll continue to work one day a week. She deserves the wage and we need her help, but Tom declines her offer. He's convinced we can do all the work ourselves and save a lot of money. He says, "Sure, we might sew fewer items and sell less, but we'll just do it."

When Angie leaves, I feel lost and sad. I love her big personality, and admire her exceptional skills at sewing and relating to the customers. How will we manage?

One day after Angie leaves, a customer makes a face and holds up one of our small zip totes—a popular bag, with its embroidered outside pocket, three inside pockets, and a zipper across the top. "The sewing is crooked on the top of this bag," the woman says, staring at me as I sit today at the sewing machine closest to the counter. Most people are intelligent enough to notice that we aren't robots, that we hand-make each bag. This isn't some sweat shop in a third world country sewing canvas bags. No, it's a sweat shop on the island of St. John.

I smile and say, "Straight sewing costs extra."

Instead of finding me amusing, she drops the offending bag onto the display table, turns on her leather sandals, and leaves. While it's painful when someone is rude, especially when we work so hard day after day, the worst thing that comes out of this event is that it fuels Tom's longing for a brand-new walking-foot sewing machine. I, on the other hand, would prefer to use the money to hire a new employee, one who is young and quick, sews real fast, and flirts with the customers—someone just like Angie—not someone like us, so often wondering who put the flashlight in the refrigerator.

But, since I harbor residual guilt because Tom no longer has the sailboat, I give in. After the new machine arrives, some assembly is required. Tom spends two days putting it together, and then this sewing machine doesn't sew any straighter than the old one. Worse, this new piece of equipment is stiff and inexperienced. Tom spends additional hours talking with Elias, the technical person at the company in Florida that shipped the offending contraption. Elias' first language is not English, but Tom is thorough in his discussion of the problems with the new machine. Elias promises to ship some extra parts to solve the problem.

At one point I overhear Tom saying to him, "I'd sure like to know more about that than I don't already know."

And in spite of that statement, Elias seems to think Tom is the owner of a huge factory down here in the islands, because he tells Tom, "Make sure you tell your girls not to turn the wheel backwards."

Tom says, in a remark that will rise up and bite us in the future, "Well, Elias, this shop isn't what you think. You're *talking* to the girls."

We name her *Big Dorothy*, after a prominent prostitute who worked along Last Chance Gulch in Helena, Montana, in the 1800s. My machine in the corner is smaller, more soulful and seasoned. So what if she jumps a stitch now and then. Her name is Little Rita, a prostitute who worked for Big Dorothy. As the former owner of an old mining camp brothel myself, I should know some of their trade secrets. But while the madam who haunted my brothel appeared in a dream or two, and later in a novel I wrote, she never enlightened me. Come to think of it, I wish I still owned that old bordello back in Montana. I'd hire a couple girls, set them up in business, and earn passive income as an absentee madam.

Ah, yes. The brothel project. For three years I lived in the building while it was being remodeled. I had electricity but no indoor plumbing, which meant hauling water from a spring on the Continental Divide. I used an outhouse, even in winter, on a shoveled path lined with snow banks so high I couldn't see over them. After Tom and I married in 1993, he continued to live and work in the Kalispell area, 200 miles north of Helena. On weekends he commuted to my brothel up in the mountains, where he hoped to find some conjugal bliss and sometimes did. But since many weekends started at the office of a marriage counselor, it could be said that both our new marriage and the old brothel were undergoing renovation.

One thing I know for sure, though, is that our new sewing machine is unlovable. At least this interloper in our lives will be a good-sized tax deduction.

With just the two of us working during high season, it's even more difficult to take time off. The shop is like a blender on high speed, and soon the place is a shambles. Display shelves are empty, the cutting table looks like the landfill near Tony's, and we're dangerously low on our most popular items. It would be ruinous to take even one day off. I must cut and sew special orders, request more canvas, order more hats, and find a new source for white number five zipper chain. One day I take a purse down to show a customer and on top of the bag is a dead fly resting on a bed of Sahara dust. And now I must clean the bags and purses.

Our inventory boxes stored in shelves overhead are now empty, and we're working at an emergency-room pace to replace items as soon as they sell. At least now I can cut crop in multiples with the little chickadee, and Tom is getting better and faster at sewing on Big Dorothy. One day he flies into a rage and throws a small bag he's sewing against the rock wall. Lizards leap and drop some scat. Little Rita jumps a stitch.

I am calm, matter-of-fact, when I say, "If you do that again I'll walk out and you can do the shop all by yourself from now on."

He says nothing. We both know he can't do the shop by himself. We can't even do the shop together, except, of course, that's what we're doing.

"There isn't enough Geritol in the whole world to keep me going at this pace. Let's try to find another full-time employee, or at least two part-time employees."

"No," Tom replies. "We can't afford an employee."

"But we would have kept Angie. We would have found money to pay her."

No reply.

After a few days, Tom finally agrees that we'll try to find an employee. But first we'll somehow get through this coming summer, when it isn't usually as busy. We'll hire someone in the fall so we can train her before high season.

Some of our customers are so appealing and fun they make the long hours and hard work almost worth it. I've wanted to go home with many of them, or at least become their next door neighbor. I've even dropped hints that I'm up for adoption, but so far no takers.

A nice couple from Paris buys an XXL duffel and several other bags. The man says our bags are o*n-kray-dee-bull,* and that's what Tom and I say over and over at the end of the day, as we tally our sales. In the morning the man calls from their boat to order another XXL duffel and more bags. I rather like the French. After hiking all over Switzerland someday, I think I'll go hiking in France.

Another man comes into the shop, wearing a T-shirt about a landscape business. As I ring up his purchase, I say, "I was once a landscape architect; now I'm the queen of canvas."

"No kidding?" he says. "I once dated the queen of Kansas."

Today a small cruise ship, the good ship *Norway,* is anchored off St. John. The last time this ship anchored here, it had engine trouble and we joked that the ship had lost its forward momentum. This time a customer from the ship tells us, "While we were cruising away from the Bahamas, a crew member fell overboard."

"Oh," I say. "In the Bermuda Triangle?"

"Maybe," the woman says. "Anyway, the captain turned the ship around and retraced his route to search for the woman. Ten hours later she was found and taken aboard."

"That's an amazing story," I say, imagining myself being the woman rescued. Sharks circle and nip at my legs as I'm pulled, dripping and shivering, out of the water. Everyone cuddles me to bring my core temperature up to normal, and they treat me with concern and chocolates.

The Canvas Factory sells plus-sized baseball caps, embroidered with our unique tropical motifs. You'd be surprised how many big heads there are, heads larger than size eight, heads the size of basketballs. When a customer says, "I'll bet you don't carry a cap big enough for *my* head," I grab this opportunity to say, "Well, let me show you our gifted-sized caps for the Mensa crowd." Depending on the situation and the kind of energy I sense, I might continue. "You must be real smart, but don't let it go to your head." One guy gets out his wallet and proudly shows me his Mensa membership card. Now and then I tease an actual CEO of a Fortune 500 company, or at least that's what they claim to be.

One mostly bald man says, "Gimme two of those. With my reverse Mohawk, I need to wear a hat at all times."

Almost every day, I fall in love with a customer, knowing I may never see him again. It's a wonderful, pure kind of love.

At the end of March, weary and exhausted, we celebrate our one-year anniversary of being owned by The Canvas Factory. At 4:00 p.m. we put a sign on the door that says GONE TO THE BEACH. In Angie's honor, we toy with the idea of writing GONE TO THE BITCH. But we chicken out. Since we now live near the junction of the two main roads on the island, Centerline and North Shore, we have travel options and today we take the North Shore Road so we can stop at Big Maho Bay.

The surf is low, and the honey-colored sand is warm on our tender, bare feet. We splash and swim and recreate the scene from *Jaws*, taking turns pretending to be the shark, circling and nipping, but in slow motion. Back on the beach propped up on our elbows, we stare at the ocean in a state of torpor. In the late afternoon light, the water is the color of opals on fire. Tom's vocal chords are so relaxed his voice is barely audible when he says, "It's an effulgent scene."

"Excuse me?" He so enjoys using polysyllabic words when small words will do the job.

"It means radiating bright, beaming rays of light."

"Huh. All the time I've known you, you've never once used that word. Makes me wonder what else you're hiding from me."

He smiles, applies more sunscreen, and lies on his back.

Our state of bliss ends when the sun sinks toward the horizon. Island time has a way of flying by, when you're having sun. We drive home to Villa Debris, where we watch the sunset paint the clouds. Tom grills steaks and I saute some vegetables, scorching only a few.

"There you go, burning your vegetables behind you," Tom says.

Just taking two hours off together goes a long way toward restoring the notion that we're a team rowing in the same direction—upstream as it might be.

The next evening Jim and his wife, Barb, take us out to dinner at Polli's, a Mexican restaurant. The seafood burrito is terrific, the house margaritas are fabulous, and it feels great to be celebrating life on the island with friends. Jim and Barb often fly to other islands in the Caribbean for some R&R. I can't imagine why, since they live in a villa right out of the TV show, "Lifestyles of the Rich and Famous." I want to be like them, when I grow up.

In the morning, while I'm helping a young woman buy a small zip tote, Tom rises from Big Dorothy, leaps onto the cutting table, and rummages around behind the curtain for a roll of webbing. The young woman stops and stares at him. She's shocked, I suppose, that someone 6' 4" with a silver crew-cut can actually *leap,* and that he chose exactly that moment to do so. But I'm accustomed to his inconsistent, quirky behavior. Sometimes, like now, I find his antics endearing.

"We hire monkeys," I say. "They're cheaper."

Tom says, "I store my bananas up here."

"I like you guys," she says, smiling as she hands me her credit card.

"Thank you," I say. "I like us sometimes, too."

ONE GOOD CAT DESERVES ANOTHER

Given the way Twodot came into our lives, it's odd that he won't let me touch him.

After that bout of heavy-weather sailing in the Strait of Juan de Fuca, we didn't sail much. But Tom held onto his dream of sailing to the Caribbean. Since I was sailing-impaired, he'd try to find a crew or make the trip solo. But because he was still paying child support, he needed to work, and it takes five months to sail between Bellingham and St. John. The sailboat continued to be our home. I wanted to sell it. Tom did not.

So I walked the docks, talking to myself in ranting outbursts as if suffering from Tourette Syndrome. He stayed true to his Viking heritage, with his need to raid, pillage and conquer in lieu of compromise. When I first called him The Viking, he doffed his horned helmet and, with a smile, took off with our credit card to pillage a chandlery for more new boat parts. My feelings toward him alternated wildly. Sometimes my monkey mind thought, *It's as if Tom is some kind of essential dietary requirement*, while my Tourette's voice would yell, *Yeah! Like roughage.*

My good friend, Jennifer, suggested a different affliction—the Stockholm Syndrome—in which a person is caught and held emotionally in an unhealthy bond, and stays even when given chances to escape. Another friend talked to me about boundaries and used that blatantly yucky term *co-dependent*.

In the spring of 2000, I ran away from Tom and the boat, and hid for two months in a friend's cabin in northern Idaho. I prepared do-it-yourself divorce papers and returned to Bellingham, determined to get Tom's signature on them. He agreed to meet me at one of those white-bread eateries. When I arrived at the restaurant, his car was already in the parking lot. As I got out of my own car holding the manila folder, he got out of his. It was damp and chilly, and he was wearing his bulky parka. He looked forlorn.

"You ready to go in?" I asked, trying to stay focused and businesslike.

He didn't move. "I love you," he said. "I don't want a divorce."

"Well," I said. "I don't know what else to do."

"I brought you something," he said, smiling now as he reached into his parka, to an inside pocket.

Afraid of what it might be, I closed my eyes. Was it a gun? When I opened my eyes he was offering me a tiny white kitten, hardly bigger than a ball of cotton fluff.

"No, no, no," I said, backing away, making guttural, sobbing cries.

He knew I adored cats. And I knew he was allergic to them. To add to my immediate torment, I thought about how I'd had to find a home for my beloved 14-year-old cat, Fatty, in order to move to the sailboat. I set him up with a sister in the country, but he disappeared, probably the victim of a mountain lion. Before that, before we moved to the boat in 1997, Fatty couldn't come in the house because of Tom's allergies. It broke my heart to see him begging to come indoors.

And there Tom was, offering me a little white kitten.

I stood slobbering and shaking my head. Right then and there I should have gone into the restaurant and asked them to call an ambulance. Except I couldn't move.

"I brought a little box," he said, calmly. "I'll just put him in the car so we can go inside and talk."

When he returned to where I was standing, he wiped the tears off my face with a handkerchief and led me into the restaurant.

We waited dutifully by the *Please wait to be seated* sign.

The waitress looked at Tom, then me, then back at Tom. She probably thought he was taking me on a nice little outing from the mental hospital. She took us to a corner booth, where we each slid into place and sat facing each other. He said, "I apologize for my behavior that caused so much harm and drove you away. I want to make things right. I love you."

"You're impossible," I said, shaking my head in total resignation.

"I know. I totally agree." He almost seemed proud of it.

"I'm not hanging all our problems on you," I said. "I know I can be overly sensitive."

"Well, all I can say is that I really am sorry. I love you like crazy. I haven't been sleeping; I'm barely functional. And I've decided that I'm not going to sign any divorce papers. It's all too abrupt. I need more time to try. I want to do some counseling, first alone and then as a couple. I want us to have a life together."

And so I fell for what I would come to think of as *the little white kitten trick.* Twodot is the name we gave the kitten, with his two black spots that resemble the cattle brand of a large ranch near Twodot, Montana. Tom was no longer allergic to cats.

After we'd been together again a couple weeks and the idea of counseling came up, Tom said, in his most charming Minnesota accent, "Counseling, yeah, sure. But we'll still enable each other."

"Absolutely," I said. "We won't let 'em take *that* away from us."

Except, we got busy and never went to counseling, although we did, slowly, begin to make plans to return to St. John, without the sailboat.

Now here we are, finally—boat free and in recovery. And the cat who doesn't love me has been attacked by a feral island cat. We're at the vet's office with him. After Twodot gets his wound cleaned and we're back in the waiting room, Tom pokes his finger into a cage where a little black kitten is standing up on his hind legs like a grizzly bear. And just like that, we acquire a second cat.

Because the kitten's nose looks as if it touched an ink pad, we call him Inkspot, or Inkie. Mostly black, his white chest makes him look like he's wearing a French maid's apron. Adding to the ensemble are white hussy boots on his front feet, and the last inch of his black tail is white like a paintbrush. Wild and playful, Inkie is a little wild *mon.* He sleeps with us and wants to play during the night. He's all tooth and claw. When we lock him out of the bedroom so we can get some sleep, he meows and doesn't quit. We joke that both Tom and Inkie should be sent to reform school.

Every morning and evening I sit with Inkie, petting him, trying to calm him down, but it's a lot like socializing a tackle box. Occasionally, I socialize Tom, too. It calms him down.

The Animal Care Center (ACC), in cooperation with the vet's office, offers a spay and neuter program for feral cats. Once a month citizens capture wild cats in cages borrowed from the ACC. Then you take the cats to the vet's office, where they're tested for diseases. If the cats are healthy enough, they are spayed or neutered. Cats with pet potential go to the ACC to be adopted out. The too-feral cats are delivered to one of a dozen feeding stations scattered around the island, where volunteers feed them every day. One of these stations is in a tree near The Pig Dumpster. The first cat Tom captures, the monster that attacked Twodot, tests positive for feline AIDS and is euthanized. We worry, of course, that Twodot got infected during the attack. The next stray we capture has a liver tumor and is put down.

We keep a box of cat litter in the bathroom next to the toilet. Our goal is that when Inkie is bigger, both cats will go potty outdoors. There's usually cat litter spilled on the floor, and walking in the bathroom can be like a trip across the Sands of the Namib. The throw rug in front of the bathroom sink serves as the cats' sacrificial altar, where we often find the remains of creatures the cats have caught, tormented and chewed up. Among the detritus are pieces of those huge flying cockroaches called mahogany birds.

This morning I forget to inspect the rug before entering the bathroom after my shower, and the bottom of my foot touches something round and soft, yet firm. My foot knows instantly that it should not continue to step down. My foot remembers, from growing up with free-range chickens, how something strange and gooey can get into every crack and crevice and be difficult to remove. With a jerky little dance step, I avoid disaster, but my face frowns up into a horror movie scream. Tom grabs the millipede, big around as a pencil and three inches long and throws it outdoors into the jungle. There's something to be said for being married to someone bigger, smarter, stronger and braver.

Now what to do with my face? With this expression, you would not want to meet me in a dark alley. Tom glances at me and immediately looks away. Even I don't risk a look in the mirror. Sitting on the toilet to recover, I massage my face so it will relax into its more normally haggard morning appearance.

Always a little demon, Inkie begins to run up the walls and walk overhead on the rafters. It's eerie living with a mostly black cat slinking around overhead. He leaps like a flying squirrel onto Twodot, padding around in his slippers like a *Gentlemen's Quarterly* cat.

One morning Tom decides to empty out his tote bag, the one that's been serving as his attaché, lunch box, pending file, and mini-storage facility. In the bottom, among the crumbs and pieces of thread, he finds several giant mahogany birds milling around. When he empties the bag onto the deck, the creatures flap off into the sky.

He comes back indoors and says, "I wondered what was making my bag so heavy."

I feel smug. At last, a chance to set the record straight once and for all. As I open the cupboard to get a cereal bowl, I say, "You're a pack-rat. You collect junk, and now you're paying the price." When I reach for the bowl, a mahogany bird flies into my face. I scream and slap the giant bug to the floor. The bowl shatters around my bare feet. The creature scuttles along the floor. Inkie pounces, and when he bites down, I hear the crunch. My face screws up again and my hands reach up in an attempt to civilize it, while Inkie bats the creature this way and that like a hockey puck.

Sometimes the cats sit side by side looking out the glass walls. They study lizards on the deck, and watch the trade wind breezes move the leaves. Or they get a bead on a sailboat out on the ocean and give it the same attention they give the cursor on the computer screen. Tom keeps sugar water in a pop bottle that hangs near the entry porch. Both hummingbirds and bananaquits take turns at this feeder, and the cats watch the birds for hours, their whiskers twitching.

At the shop, we routinely sew Twodot's fine white hairs into the bindings of our bags. After all, he sleeps on our folded clothes, on the bed, and on the couch. And while we don't notice his hairs on our clothing, they're easy to spot on dark-colored canvas. So, while Twoey stays right here on St. John, his hairs go everywhere. Some of the bags and places his hairs are off to include: a large zip tote to New Zealand; a large knapsack, this one bottle green with a black petroglyph embroidery, off to Tuscany and then to Shanghai; and now in a large cargo bag on its way to Tierra del Fuego, a place I know not where, but I'm in love with the name. The singer, Carole King, has Twodot hairs sewn into her new large knapsack. And we just sent off that collection of bags to the south of France. A local birdwatcher is carrying a small tote on a bird-watching safari to Costa Rica. But while Twoey hairs can be found in bags en route to exotic places, you can also find them in English-speaking locales such as Cleveland, Omaha, New York, and even The Hamptons, which I understand is an English-speaking country near the mainland. We call this our Cats Without Borders program.

Inkie sails through being neutered. In the middle of the night of his surgery, I awake to find him lying on my chest. I'd been dreaming that I was sewing two cargo bags, and had stopped sewing to pet Inkie. When I wake up, I realize I'm not sewing and that my two foam earplugs are missing. Inkie must have fished them out of my ears while I was dreaming.

One day when I am at the shop, Glen and Radha invite me to join them on their patio to honor of one of their cats. They had discovered Chester, a lovely one-year-old black cat, lying on his side as if he'd died mid-stride. This is a mystery, but then there are all kinds of dangerous, toxic leaves and creatures a cat might ingest. I had become fond of Chester on those occasions when I fed him.

"It's sad," Glen says.

We drink sparkling soda in wine glasses as we discuss Chester's qualities. He was black, sleek, Egyptian-looking and elegant, yet down-to-earth. He was adaptable, curious, lovable, and playful. He got along well with all the other cats, even those with bad temperaments. We clink our wine glasses together in a toast, and Glen says, "May more people be like Chester."

While some islanders try to adopt every cat they see, we've decided to stop at two and capture all the feral cats we can for spay and neuter day. We've spotted a mother cat and two tiny kittens down near Big Maho Bay. It's my turn to pick up a trap at the ACC, and this morning the waiting room is crawling with adoptable cats. Some are sleeping piled on top of each other like a stack of cat rugs. Others surround me, sniffing my feet, smelling Inkie and Twodot. I have to watch out so I don't step on one of them.

While I sit at a desk filling out the form to borrow the trap, a slinky young gray and black striped cat with enormous ears, one of them clipped (to show she's been neutered) leaps onto my lap. I absent-mindedly pet this cat, whose fur is amazingly silky. While I complete the form, this cat stretches way up and nuzzles my neck, and then somehow slithers her way up onto my shoulders and begins to purr and rub her face on my head. It's like I'm catnip. I feel chosen. I don't want to leave this cat, but I must. Holding the cage now, I take one more glance at the cat, who watches me leave. Back at the shop, all I can think about is the cat who loves me. Twodot is unfriendly to me, and Inkie won't hold still to be petted. I'm cat deprived. Tom is home, and when he calls me, I mention the cat.

He says, "If it has short hair, bring it home."

So I call the woman at the ACC and place a "hold" on this cat, and when I do this I learn she's the poster cat for the Center and appears on all the flyers announcing the upcoming fund-raising gala. Even better, she was born in Rupert's Junkyard on the edge of Coral Bay, near where the largest herd of goats on the island hangs out.

Now I'll have an emotional-support animal, one that's affectionate, one that lets me love her back. I name her Lucky, because that's the way I feel.

We now have three cats leaving dead offerings on the sacrificial altar. On a trip to the bathroom, Tom discovers most of a dead walking-stick insect, so large it's more like a walking branch. Its torso is 3/8" in diameter, and it's at least six inches long. Another morning he nearly steps on a dead snake.

Lucky turns into a wonderful pal. One afternoon while sitting on the couch together watching the national dog show on TV, we agree that someday we'll have a dog in our lives, and then we'll really be lucky.

In the morning I hate to leave the cats and drive away from the happy domestic scene. During the day I picture Inkie asleep in the wicker basket full of my panties; Lucky will be sitting on the deck watching leaves move, birds fly, and boats on the water; Twoey will be draped on top of the refrigerator—the three of them languorously enjoying Villa Debris in our absence.

When I take Lucky to the vet for her booster shots I meet a couple, carrying a trap in each hand. They're bringing in captured feral cats. The wife says, "We caught seventeen cats this time. It all started out so innocent. I subbed at a feeding station and now I have thirty-six cats. Kept the first one I ever caught. She turned out to be a circus cat. Performs dozens of tricks."

APRIL FOOL

We are now officially crazier and even more likely to kill each other. We have agreed to produce 75 deluxe, small open totes for a long-time corporate customer. But these totes aren't difficult to sew, and the additional income will give our bank account a needed jolt. Finally we'll pay off some moving expenses. And maybe I'll get a massage or two for my ailing body parts.

On April fool's day Jim saunters in wearing a colorful, painted T-shirt he tells us he bought at The Fabric Mill, a nearby shop that sells clothing. He tells us this line of cotton clothing is painted by an artist out on the east end, named Sloop Jones. And even though I should wait until we get paid for the corporate order, I make a quick dash into that shop to try on a sleeveless, above-the-knee dress. The simple knit dress in orange, pale yellow, and peach, flows over my body in a way that smoothes out my bulges but isn't loose like, say, a muumuu. Even I'm surprised how good I look. "That pattern is called Peach Bamboo," Bonnie, the sales lady, says. "These dresses put new life in the men. Wearing one can be a life-changing experience. Leave it on," she says. "Go show Tom."

When I step through our open shop door, Tom begins to glow or sweat or both, and immediately hands me the cash to buy the dress. After paying for this fashion version of Viagra, I return to the shop. Tom's eyes follow my every move. He's transfixed and finally speaks his mind, "Let's lock the doors. I'll clear off the cutting table." But while the hanky-panky has to wait, other things cannot be put off. For instance, buying this dress turns out to be like buying a horse. Next thing you know you need accessories: a barn, hay and feed, then a saddle and a halter. First I notice that both pairs of sandals in my shoe wardrobe are hideously incompatible with my new dress. Not only that, my toenail polish is jarringly discordant and my cheap little toe ring looks like a pop top. It really should be gold to go with my peach bamboo dress. Next I discover that my cotton granny panties and my new dress sort of hang up on each other. I place an order with Land's End for a pair of beige sandals, a package of nylon panties, and a new black swimsuit. I buy toenail polish the color of the inside of a conch shell, and a gold toe ring. I get a haircut. I go hog wild.

Since I've made this additional investment just to wear a Sloop Jones dress, Tom encourages me to return to check out their other patterns. After all, my birthday is coming up.

"Absolutely not," I say. "These dresses are frivolous and expensive. My birthday is months away."

The design and color of my second Sloop Jones dress is Red Guadeloupe, and this dress has the same effect on Tom as the first one.

What I want more than clothing, however, is to get rid of my neck headache and the growing numbness in my arms and hands. So I go to see my chiropractor. Bern is bright and cheerful, and I can count on him to say something meaningful or entertaining, sometimes both. Today he tells me that years ago he and his wife danced profession-ally in Las Vegas. After an appointment with Bern, I always feel better mentally and physically. When you don't have much of a social life, the moments you spend with your chiropractor, massage therapist, or the person who cuts your hair can be meaningful beyond measure. Who says you can't buy love?

My friend, Jennifer, arrives in January and stays with us three weeks before landing a seasonal job at Maho Bay Camp doing house-keeping. Her job includes lodging but no choice of roommates, and she ends up living with an angry, misogynistic chain smoker. On the other hand she, too, has a knockout view of the ocean.

One day I need to go to St. Thomas on an errand for the shop, and Jennifer is on her way to Red Hook to visit a new friend for a couple days. Since it's her birthday, I hurry to ride the ferry with her so I can take her to lunch at Molly Malone's, an Irish open-air pub near the fer-ry dock at Red Hook. While we eat lunch in a courtyard, a small herd of iguanas hangs around begging like dogs. I know they sometimes attack people's feet, mistaking their polished toenails for berries. Since I'm wearing my peach bamboo dress, I'm also wearing my new toenail polish, which I call *Booze Hound Blush*, a pale color that should not invite attention. However, with my history of attracting trouble, I keep my feet safely up on a chair while Jennifer feeds the iguanas pieces of onion and pickle from her sandwich.

We chat and listen with care to each other, offering thoughtful, honest yet kindly comments, as lifelong friends do. I reveal the depth of my disenchantment with the business and the lack of time for fun or rest. "Maybe I'm just a malcontent, because living in the brothel didn't suit me, and then living on the boat and sailing didn't pan out as a lifestyle, and now ... here I am in paradise. Same thing. Sure, paradise is a lovely place to suffer, but wasn't it Jimmy Buffet who sang about laughing at life so you won't go crazy?

"First of all," Jennifer says, handing a pickle to a begging iguana. "I visited you in the brothel. I couldn't have lived up there in the mountains with no running water and an outhouse for three years with those winters. I don't know how you did that. And your neighbor... the one who shot up the Capitol building a few years ago." Jennifer has big green eyes that study me now, as if she's seeing into my soul. "Next you sell everything and move to a sailboat? Why you thought you could live on a boat, I'll never understand. You're just too willing to try new things. And all of that on top of a troubled marriage. Now, take me. I'm too much the other way. I've lived alone in Moscow in that same apartment since 1985."

I listen to my good friend, and suddenly stop chewing. "Jennifer, I just realized something. I think I'm addicted to novelty."

"That would explain a lot," she says. "But you need to take it easy on yourself. Let me come to the shop and work for you on my day off. I can at least cut straps and zippers to help you with that big order."

And finally, with a little help from Jennifer, Tom and I finish and ship the last of the corporate order of tote bags. By the time we fax the invoice, we're both exhausted zombies, and Tom's back has been out of whack. We leave the shop a couple hours early and stop at Big Maho for a swim. As I float in the water, a big green turtle pokes its head up a few feet from me. Tom takes a long swim out to the anchored boats to check for nude women, which makes his back feel better, and then we drive home in time to sit on the deck and catch the coloring-book clouds over the British Virgin Islands. As dusk descends and the quadraphonic frogs begin to sing, the full moon rises above the ocean among glowing pink and lavender clouds. Watching this scene, Tom says, "I just love living here on St. John. And I love doing life with you."

THE BLACK MAW OF DEATH

I've always known the universe isn't that into me. And now I think I'm going to die. We're way behind at the shop, as usual, still working 60 to 70 hours a week. I don't have time to be sick, but during my first pelvic exam in three years, as the nurse practitioner feels around *down there,* she says, "There's something here and it isn't normal."

I want to be big and mature about my probable demise. At least now I won't have to get that root canal. Then I remember that I don't have health insurance. I'll probably have to wander from shop to shop soliciting money for treatments. A sonogram is prescribed. I'll go to St. Traumas to the radiology clinic, then come back to St. John and wait for the results. Otherwise, I'll act like nothing is happening to me. But when I see Bern for a tune-up, I blurt it all out.

"Stick your neck out as far forward as you can," he says, taking my neck through the range-of-motion exercises.

A model patient, I do as I'm told while saying, "I think I'm ..."

"Now pull your neck back as far as you can."

"... going to die." I start to blubber as I explain myself. So much for being big.

"It's probably something benign," he says, gesturing for me to lie on my back. "If you hear hoof beats look for horses, not zebras."

"Excuse me?" Bern talks real fast. I don't always catch what he says.

"Okay," he says, behind me now, his hands on my neck. "If you're on a ranch and you hear hoof beats, you don't look around for zebras. You look for horses ... right?"

He holds my neck in both hands, feeling for errant vertebrae. I know that any second he'll say something to distract me, like "think about your left big toe," but this time he doesn't. And, anyway, I'm busy considering his absurd analogy. As if reading my mind, he gives my neck a quick yank and says, "Okay, think of zebras as cancer."

"Does this advice cost extra?"

Laughing, he helps me to my feet and leads me into an adjacent room where I lie on my stomach on a table. He hooks me up to some wires and adds ice and hot packs to my neck and back, before leaving to greet his next patient. While lying on my face in the dark, I reach for what he said like the drowning person from the cruise ship *Norway*, as if it's a life preserver. Maybe he's right.

Tonight I feel unlocked, as if some nerves in my neck are no longer pinched and that my brain is, once again, receiving a nice little flow of blood and oxygen. I say a little prayer. *Dear God. If I get to live, if you will allow that, I promise not to complain so much, and I'll stop cussing. This time I mean it.*

The sonogram costs $250 at the radiology clinic on St. Thomas. I pay with our credit card to build air miles. Maybe I'll run up enough miles by the time this thing is over to finally get to Switzerland.

On the ferry ride back to St. John, after the sonogram, I sit near an open window. The ferry bashes into a big wave, and when salt water sprays onto several passengers, everyone but me utters a surprised outcry and scoots away to a dryer seat. I sit, staring, sopping wet. What's a little salt water? I really do enjoy living. I'd like another twenty years, anyway, although I'll take ten if that's all I can get. Yes, ten good years with a full-time employee just like Angie. That's all I ask.

While waiting for the sonogram results, I alternate between making funeral arrangements and researching travel to Switzerland. I find a site on which a young man catalogs his moonlight hikes in the Alps. This inspires me to start walking in the mornings before work. The first morning I start out with great purpose, determined to get my heart rate up as I walk the steep, rutted Mamey Peak road. When I swing my arms they bump against the sides of my hips just below my waistline, that now bulge out like shoulders, and well-developed ones at that. I call these prominent growths my *lower shoulders*.

The road continues uphill and I follow it one-half mile to the top, to an enormous villa that looks both south to the Caribbean and north to the Atlantic. The windows are covered with shutters. I've met the owner, a woman my age named Jan who came into the shop to introduce herself a few weeks ago. The road continues and forks a little farther on. This road was the original route between Coral Bay and Cruz Bay, back when people rode donkeys. Where the road forks, I turn around.

On other mornings I walk down the edge of the road to Colombo's, a concession stand like Tony's that sells smoothies, trinkets, and beer. This one is wisely located at the junction of the Centerline and North Shore Roads. A dirt jeep track also dives off to the south. Deep ruts keep most vehicles off this route, but it does go all the way to Coral Bay.

On my walks I make bargains with God. Sometimes I pray. Other times I cuss. When I return to Villa Debris I lie on the floor with my feet up on the couch and a rolled-up hand towel under my neck. I listen to meditation music. And I summon a healing energy in my neck as I breathe in, picturing plump, healthy, pink disks between perfect neck vertebrae. I see myself hiking near the Matterhorn. The weather is perfect. I am strong and slender. Tom is with me.

A solo hiking adventure on the island is in order; to heck with the business. After all, once I'm gone who's going to applaud me for working myself to death? I arrange with Tom to drop me off at the Reef Bay trailhead on his way to work. As we drive on the Centerline Road toward the drop-off point, we joke about all the things that could go wrong on my big adventure.

"There'll probably be a big rainstorm," I say, "followed by clouds of giant killer mosquitoes."

"And then you'll walk right into a yellow orb spider," Tom says. "It'll fall in your hair and you won't be able to find it."

"I'll get exhausted and have to be carried out on a stretcher," I say. "Actually, I'm already that tired."

When Tom pulls off the road at the trailhead, I grab my knapsack.

We both look across the road at the opening in the dark rock wall—
the start of the trail. Tom says, "There it is, the black maw of death."

As I walk alone in the humming stillness, a mangrove cuckoo hollers from the trees to my right, and another bird answers to my left.
They're welcoming me. The trail passes thickets of sansevieria, with
its sword-like leaves as tall as humans. I walk under guava, mango,
and bayberry trees. The shiny, leathery leaves of the bayberry tree
holds an aromatic oil once used in the production of bay rum cologne. I stop to crush a leaf. The warm fragrance of citrus and cinnamon makes me feel downright euphoric. I continue past a turpentine
tree, with its reddish, flaking bark and breast-like knobs. On our 1996
hike down this trail, the park service ranger, Denise, who led the trip,
told us that its nickname is "tourist nose tree." On this tree is an enormous termite nest, with termite tunnels running up and down the tree
trunk and across the trail.

When you're not with a ranger to tell you what you're seeing, you
can read interpretive signs: about sugar plantation ruins, the names
and lore of the trees, and the petroglyph site. I read the signs, redis-
covering all the facts I learned last time and forgot. A favorite is the
giant kapok tree, soaring about 150 ft. up. Looks like another jumbie
hangout. The massive trunk near the ground has strange fin-like but-
tresses that help support the tree's height. Its white, fluffy seed covering has been used for pillows and mattress ticking, as well as floatation
devices. Another strange tree is called "monkey-no-climb," because of
large thorns that cover the trunk.

When I reach the short side trail to the petroglyph site, I follow it.
The island has been in a drought for weeks so there's no fresh water
spilling into the pool. But I sit near the pond and watch the light re-
flecting off the shiny mica wings of dragon flies, and picture the Taino
Indians carving their symbols into the nearby rock face.

If I get to live, I will enjoy more outings like this one. Otherwise,
why be on the island? Why be anywhere?

Two weeks after my sonogram, I finally get the call. "You have two fibroid tumors in your uterus, and one of them is two and one-half inches in diameter. I'm not concerned, really," the nurse practitioner says. "I'll just check them again at your next annual exam."

"Thanks," I say. "That's a relief. And it explains my fluffy tummy."

To celebrate I leave the shop and drive to Cinnamon Bay, park the car, and hike up the steep trail to sit on a big flat rock. Every small tree trunk has at least one gecko scurrying up and down it. A striped yellow butterfly flutters near me, mountain doves coo in the distance, and birds tweet in the trees. The sun shines down on me while I sit, smiling at my good fortune. After a few minutes I walk back down the steep trail and drive to Big Maho, where I sit on the beach in the late afternoon sun, listening to the quiet splash of waves.

That night in bed I try self-hypnosis. First I imagine my uterus, but picture my stomach organ instead. Wait, doesn't the uterus look like a turnip? Next I imagine a shiny pink lining with bulging growths the size of baby gorillas. As soon as I get this image fixed in my head, the fibroids begin speaking to me, reprimanding me for not taking care of myself. They tell me they represent my entire body, including my soul, and they've been neglected. They're trying to get my attention. Yes, I know this is weird, but I feel sorry for my uterus. "I'll take better care of myself," I promise, as I imagine petting the fibroids back into the lining of my uterus. Over and over, I reassure them. I attempt to socialize them, calm them down, as if they're tiny, frightened kittens.

When I tell Lucy about my fibroid tumors and my attempts at self-hypnosis, she tells me she suffered endometriosis when she was younger. She chose to have a hysterectomy, and before the surgery they showed her pictures of the tumors. "They were so ugly," she says. "They could have mugged you on a dark night."

My fibroids, I decide, are not ugly. And for weeks I use my imagination to pet the growths back into the lining of my uterus, while promising them a brighter future. What happens as a result of this experiment changes my outlook on many things forever. The odd pains in the side of my stomach disappear, my fluffy tummy flattens, and my bladder control returns to normal. I risk everything, however, by returning to my former level of whining, complaining and cussing. But I am committed to keeping the promise I made to my tumors. I will take better care of myself. How to accomplish that under the circumstances is a mystery, but somehow I will succeed.

WHEN YOU *SEE*
A HERD OF *GOATS* ON *THE* ROAD

If it's springtime in Montana and you run into an elderly person you haven't seen all winter, you might ask, "How're you doing?" He's likely to laugh and say, "Well, I made it to green grass." This means he has survived another Rocky Mountain winter. And now that Tom and I have survived our first winter of high season on the island, working six and seven days a week for months, we feel like we, too, have made it to green grass. Or at least to hurricane season.

Our landlady, Christine, tells me that after she'd lived on the island for a couple years, she developed an odd marble-sized growth on the back of one hand. The local doctors couldn't tell her what it was, so she made an appointment with Jim, the former owner of The Canvas Factory, for a hypnotherapy session. During that visit she came to realize her terror of being in a hurricane. At that moment she vowed never again to be on the island between June and November, and within weeks the growth on her hand disappeared. Her experience stretches my belief that my fibroid tumors had something to do with my emotional turmoil, and that my self-hypnosis and promise to take better care of myself caused their remission. But what to do next?

The climate on the island is consistently warm and comforting year round. You'll never suffer frostbite. There are no poisonous snakes, grizzly bears, or terrorists that I know of. Even the giant spiders are quite harmless. Sure, the mosquitoes are a major annoyance; yet while a mosquito bite can cause an occasional case of dengue fever, which can be deadly but usually feels like a bout of flu, at least you won't get malaria. And you might find yourself in a batch of sand fleas on the beach or stinging jellyfish in the ocean. But all in all, St. John is a safe place. Then, too, the human scale of the island is just right, except for all those times when living on an island this small feels isolating. It's just like life: everything is fine, except for all those things that aren't.

Tom, being technical in nature, downloads the newest hurricane tracking program and does research on tropical weather systems. Every morning and evening he interrupts his hobby of downloading updates and messing with spreadshits to check for storms. He's leaving soon for Minnesota to be with his brothers for his mother's memorial service and wherever he is, he reassures me, he'll sniff out a computer to check for storms in the Atlantic.

During Tom's absence for most of June, I close the shop on Sundays. I go to bed early every night and get up in time to watch the sunrise. Today, the longest day of the year, the equinox clouds are catching and holding the pastel joy of sunrise almost within touching distance. The colors remind me of the alpenglow I've seen on snow-covered mountaintops.

It's another beautiful day in paradise, and this time of day in the quiet, I breathe in the warm, moist ocean air. Later, as often happens, it will rain, after which the colors return in the shape of a rainbow. If there is balance to be found in the movement of the sun and the patterns of climate here, I pray that I'll find it. With all this time alone, I read and think about life. Much about life on the island is quirky and entertaining, and Tom and I joke a lot. But he doesn't seem happy, either. He often sits and stares at absolutely nothing for long periods of time, with a sad, hollow look in his eyes. He did this when we lived on the boat, too. I called it his thousand-yard stare.

In a book I'm reading on mindfulness, *Wherever You Go, There You Are,* by Jon Kabat-Zinn, I read this: "Neurotic suffering is untransforming because it feeds on self pity. It is self-inflicted death. It destroys the victim to no purpose."

Ouch! That strikes close to home. It's true; my life is like a can of worms! But then, to look at the bright side, think of all the fish you can catch with a can of worms.

I continue reading. "The funny thing about stopping is that things get simpler. In some ways it's as if you died and the world continued on, as if all your responsibilities and obligations would immediately evaporate."

Does this guy realize how complicated life can get? By now, it would take a hydraulic tool like the Jaws of Life to pry me out of this predicament.

Before Jennifer left the island and returned to Idaho, she told me what snorkeling was like for her. "Snorkeling is sort of like picking huckleberries. You go farther and farther out, reaching from one berry to the next to the next. You lose track of time. Finally, you pop your head up above the water or the huckleberry bushes, only to see that this time you've gone too far. You don't know where you are. You are hopelessly lost."

I've thought about what she said and how it could stand as a metaphor for life.

There are many good reasons to stay on St. John and make things work with the business and with Tom. His qualities are complementary to mine in many ways. For instance, while I operate on intuitive knowing that's hard to back up with facts, Tom considers ideas thoroughly, then compares and contrasts them in a broader context. He helps interpret the world for me. And to be fair, I believe I do the same for him.

Imagine my surprise.

When Tom returns from his trip, he's a new person. Something is seriously wrong with him. A woman knows these things. While most of us deal with fatigue from the change of time zones and long flights, Tom is bionic. He goes to bed late, gets up early to walk, and spends lots of time on the computer downstairs. He eats almost nothing except protein, because he's now on the Atkins Diet. On a day off, he vacuums every room of Villa Debris, changes the oil and filter in the car, helps me learn to use the digital camera, and defrags my laptop computer. He's animated, energized, lively, and happy. I'm thrilled for him, except this total change of behavior smacks of the little white kitten trick.

The break from each other was good. And now that summer is here, there aren't many customers. I have more time to rest, and we each have some time to explore the island. I feel hopeful. Later in the summer I'll leave for Montana and Idaho to visit family and friends and do a few book readings. During September and October, business drops off into the toilet. Anyway, the trade winds stop blowing. It's the height of hurricane season, and the island population declines drastically. Still, it's an opportunity to catch up at the shop and sew inventory ahead for high season. When should I go? How long should I stay? A month, I think. I'm pondering this one evening as we sit on the deck at sunset. Tom takes a sip of scotch and says, "I think you need time out. Why not stay two full months?"

This should keep me from ever complaining again. Maybe with so much time away, my right hand will stop feeling numb when I wake up. My ailing shoulder wing will heal. And when I get back, we'll advertise for a full-time employee. Maybe with life in better balance, my fibroid tumors will remain in hibernation.

The evening before my departure, Tom cooks a good Atkins meal of grilled steak and steamed vegetables. As we eat Tom talks about the way he's feeling. "It's like shedding snakeskin," he says. "This is excellent timing for you to be gone."

"What do you mean, exactly? Losing weight on the diet?"

"So I can be alone while discovering who I really am."

"Oh," I say, smothering the steamed broccoli with sour cream. "But you're almost sixty. I can point out some areas you could work on, but aren't you already who you really are?"

"It doesn't feel that way to me."

While I'm in Idaho and Montana, Tom and I talk two or three times a week on the phone. I tell him that Jan, our neighbor who lives in the villa up the hill, came to my book reading in Helena. In appearance, Jan is like me in that we don't stand out in a crowd, so I didn't notice her at first. When she came up to me before the reading, I nearly fell over. I was so happy to see her. Turns out she also has a place in

Missoula. Tom tells me about the books on tape he's listening to while sewing. He also describes the antics of the cats and the summer customers, who can be even quirkier than the high season island visitors.

Another time, when I'm staying with friends north of Priest River, Idaho, I tell him how much fun I'm having with fellow members of the Growing Brainless Together Club. And I share the misadventures of the characters in the novel I'm writing. He listens politely and then announces, "There have been some changes in my underwear collection. I now wear a thong."

"You mean a penie gourd, like the bush men wear to protect their magic parts?"

He laughs. "A little like that, I suppose, but mine is yellow. I have a green one, too. The brand is Male Power."

"A penie gourd is probably better than nothing," I say. "A woman on the island told me lots of men don't wear underwear at all. I forgot to ask her how she knows that."

"Actually, I wore the yellow one to the beach."

"Are you serious?"

"Yeah, but I was too chicken to walk from one end of the beach to the other while wearing it."

"I can't wait to see how you turn out."

"Me, neither," Tom says.

And when I hang up, I look out the window of the cabin I'm staying in and watch the river down in the valley sweep around a bend and flow toward me. Besides the feeling of being swept downstream, I have many thoughts. What *will* I find when I return to the island? That is the crux or, rather, the crotch of the matter.

A RETURN TO ABNORMAL

I'm standing on the St. John ferry dock, in a climate you can count on to be sunny and warm with a good chance of mosquitoes. And sure enough, mosquitoes, using nothing but high-tech sonar voodoo, have arranged a fly-in to greet me. I swat them away and there stands Tom, looking much the same as I left him a couple months ago: tall, tanned, a silver crew-cut, and a big goofy grin that says he's happy to see me. We hug and make our way to the car with my luggage. Soon we're bouncing over the speed bumps on our way out of town to Villa Debris.

The days are growing shorter as winter approaches, but we arrive home around 5:00 p.m. in time to sit on the deck and watch the sun set. When I look out over Coral Bay to the British Virgin Islands, I'm reminded why this view is listed in travel magazines as one of the ten best in the Caribbean. Inkie, the bad cat, sits balanced on the narrow railing. Behind him the scene includes peach-colored clouds, shimmering ocean, and lavender islands. It's Inkie in the sky with islands. Tom and I chat to the tune of ice cubes and scotch, until dusk brings on the tree frog chorus and we slide open the screen door to step inside.

At bedtime Tom assumes an *aw shucks* demeanor of guilt.

"Now what?" I say, sitting down on the bed, next to Lucky, who sits looking from Tom to me. I'm prepared for anything. Our life together has featured a lot of heavy-weather sailing, in too many ways. There isn't much he could say to shock me. He probably wants to model his yellow facsimile of a penie gourd.

"I have a confession to make," he says.

"Let's hear it."

He reaches into the miniscule closet we share and brings out my goddess dress. "I wore your dress a few times while you were gone."

I grab the dress from him. "Well, get your own dress. You're too big. I don't want you wrecking the seams."

Jennifer had helped me pick it out on a trip to St. Croix. It's really two separate sleeveless dresses designed to be worn one over the other. I love the pattern of vertical stripes of lime, teal, hibiscus red, and mango on a background of purple shadows. The scoop-neck dress is a filmy rayon fabric concoction that drapes over my curves all the way down to my ankles. The slits up both sides to mid-thigh are such a tease that even I feel sexy wearing it.

"Boy, are you lucky," I say. "The seams are still okay."

I get up and walk over to the wicker baskets where I store my underwear. Twodot, the good cat, is curled up asleep in one of them, but I find what I'm looking for. "Here," I say, handing Tom a black half-slip. "You can wear this. It's too long for me to wear with my Sloop Jones dresses, anyway."

"You sure?"

I shrug. "Yeah, I'm sure." I think this is probably just a new compulsion of his, one of many obsessions that have come and gone, never to be mentioned again. There was the winter of studying for the ham radio tests and acing them, instead of finding work; the sled dog team; acquiring goats to train as pack animals; preparing to ski the Haute Route in Europe; and grinding his own flour. Just to name a few.

Next he shows me his new panties for men, called Manties, and the infamous thong underwear. He seems delighted with his new apparel. "It's getting late," he says. "The new sex toys can wait."

I stay home the next day to recover from my travels, unpack my suitcase, and ponder Tom's new interest. Did he anticipate my question, "What's in this for me?" Is that why he ordered in the sex toys? And what kind of things could they be? I've never been into kinky stuff, which reminds me of a funny saying: kinky is using a feather; perverted is using the whole chicken. I hope the sex toys are more feathers than chicken.

In my absence, Tom had received a small inheritance from his mother's estate. He doesn't say how much, and I don't ask, but in addition to the Manties he purchased a large barbecue grill for the entry deck. He also set up a computer desk and full-sized computer in the living room for me. I appreciate this grand gesture. Now, if only I can score some time to write. I remember that Tom had agreed to advertise for an employee soon, so I smile as I putter around the place, setting up my little office in the living room, glancing every now and then at the view out the windows. They get dirty so quickly, with all the dust and bugs and mold. I should really wash them, but first I turn to my desk. When I need some staples for my tiny stapler, I descend the exterior wooden steps to the office/guest room. As soon as I slide open the glass door and enter the musty room, there they are: termite tunnels running all over the bookshelves. I grab an armload of books and flee the scene.

When I call Tom, he says, "I didn't notice any termite tunnels, and I've been down there every morning and night. I can hardly believe it."

"What have you been doing down there?"

No answer.

For me, and probably for Tom, too, our ability to find humor in most everything is the life raft that keeps us afloat in the sea of matrimony. The next morning as we clean up the termite infestation I say, "Remember the woman on the docks at Squalicum Harbor who was selling that citrus cleaning spray? You asked her to remove some spilled teak oil on the deck of a sailboat, and it didn't work."

Tom laughs. "Yeah, she said, 'Well it ain't Jesus in a bottle.'"

"We could use some Jesus in a bottle right now," I say. "Spraying the walls with ant and roach killer is not my idea of a religious experience."

After using a roll of paper towels to mop up the dead vermin and toxic spray, we vacuum dirt and spider webs, and wash the walls, floor, and bookcase with soap, water, and white vinegar. The room is still a disaster, with extra furniture piled on top of the guest bed and Tom's sailing stuff, now all moldy, spilling out of plastic containers. I'm tuckered out, and now it's time to drive to the shop to sew canvas bags.

Evenings at home are lively, as Tom entertains me with show and tell. First he introduces me to the selection of sex toys he has purchased. One of them, The Hired Man, is made of high-tech silicone. He hands it to me with both hands, as if it's on a silver platter.

"Oh, yeah!" I say. "This thing has some heft to it." It's neither a feather nor a chicken, but it *is* a sight to behold.

"You can imagine how long it took to research these things on dial-up," he tells me in earnest, as if he's sharing a shopping tip. "It can take a long time for a dildo to load, depending on its size."

We laugh like crazy people at that one. The neighbor bachelors must wonder about us. When I recover, I ask, "What else you got there?"

Tom's face is a little red as he hands me a gelatinous pink thing, about three inches long and a couple inches in diameter, give or take. When I turn it on end, I see that the center of the lewd squishy deal is open all the way through.

"It's called The Pocket Rocket," Tom says. "It's guaranteed to send a guy right into orbit."

Later, we drift off to sleep, the sex toys stored in a small duffel bag hanging from a coat hook on the bedroom wall. Maybe I should just relax about his exploration of all things sexual. In fact, I think I'm in love with The Hired Man.

One night while Tom is surfing online for sex toys or whatever, he finds an organization called Tri-Ess, or Society for the Second Self. It's an international educational, social, and support group. There are thousands of members—heterosexual cross-dressers, their partners and families. Who knew?

Tom says, "The male cross-dressers have feminine names and communicate with each other in online forums. Finding this site has helped me acknowledge my own second self."

God bless the Internet.

At work one day while we're both sewing, he says, "Tri-Ess has chapters, meetings, even national conventions."

"Why don't you go if you want. But I probably won't be going," I say, glad to state my position.

No reply. He finishes sewing a bag and tosses it onto the cutting table. From his sewing machine he can look out the open front door to palm trees across the road. He does this now. He looks thoughtful. "I need a feminine name," he says.

"Why not Tomassina?"

"No. Some kid called me that once on the playground. Hurt my feelers. Maybe Janice is a good name, or Judy," he says, sewing the handles on a large cargo bag. "No, I've got it. Rebekah, spelled with the letter 'k' for added height, since I'm tall."

"Your female name doesn't have anything to do with me," I say. "I'll never call you by that name." He's certainly getting carried away with this little hobby of his. It's starting to feel like he's having an affair with this new second self.

"None of my exploring my feminine side is so important that I'd sacrifice *us* for it. If it's a problem, I'll just stop doing it. I value our relationship more than anything."

This gives me some leverage to say, "This thing isn't terribly important to our relationship. I'm assuming it's a passing hobby. What is important is hiring and training an employee this fall, like we agreed to do. We need more rest and balance in our lives."

"Okay," he says. "I do love you."

"Well, all right then. I love you, too."

That night when he declares his intention to sleep in the black half-slip, I say, "Oh, good God, what next?" And then I mentally throw up my hands in surrender and say, "Oh, what the hell."

Tom is sewing one day while I'm ordering hats, waiting on customers, taking orders and cutting crop. His son, Doug, phones. He's a chef working at a classy French restaurant in Seattle, although he's interested in making a change. He thinks he'd like St. John. Tom tells him, "Caneel Bay Resort hires trained people to cook, and I think they'll pay for your travel back and forth. I'm pretty sure they provide housing here on island, too. You might give them a call."

I'm listening to Tom's side of the conversation, and he repeats enough of what Doug is saying that I understand what's being said. As I sew, I look over the top of my reading glasses at Tom, who is leaning back in his chair with both feet up on his sewing table. It sounds like Doug doesn't want to work as a chef any more, that he wants to come down to St. John and work for us instead. He knows we need help. But Tom tells him we'll only be hiring someone part-time and that he couldn't possibly afford to live here without full time work.

I don't believe my ears. He's been reassuring me for months that we'll hire a full-time employee in the fall. He probably said that just to shut me up.

When he hangs up the phone, I yell, "If this business can't afford a full-time employee then it isn't a viable business. I'm not working seven days a week again this winter. I want a life. And furthermore, if I have to work at this pace doing six things at once while you only sit and sew, then I'll just leave. You can buy me out of this business and that's that. You can do it all by yourself."

He sits, calmly machining a classic purse, saying nothing, as if I didn't just rant in my mean and ugly voice. So I return to doing six things at once.

Soon a woman wanders into the shop and says, "It's such a beautiful thing to see a couple working so well together."

"Oh, you just caught us on a good day," I say. We all laugh. People on vacation think everything is funny. In fact, when I was on vacation here, I thought everything was highly amusing.

But life goes on. And one daring night, we find ourselves skinny dipping at Francis Bay. The moon is almost exactly at one-half, and the stars are winking as if they're in on our little fling. We aren't completely alone, because a few early-season sailboats are anchored in the bay. Their shapes are difficult to make out in the dark, and they probably aren't even occupied. While we're swimming around naked, Tom says, "See that bright light low in the sky?"

"Yes."

"I'm pretty sure that's an incoming plane between St. Thomas and

Puerto Rico. The atmospheric conditions must be just right to allow the light to glow so brightly. It has to do with fractals and reflections."

Tom continues to keep an eye on the bright point of light, even while we swim, splash, and romp like seals. Finally, he says, "You know, I think that's an anchor light on a sailboat. Yup. Now I see it. There's a dark object on the water underneath the light."

"Oh ha ha," I say. "And you thought it was an airplane. And fractals, too."

Tom chases me in the water like an out-of-control propeller. "I'll show you an airplane."

After the splashing stops, we agree that we can't take any more fun, that we might blow a fuse or jam our electronics. Swimming naked in the ocean at night makes us feel wild and crazy. We try but fail to stifle our laughter and squeals of delight. We even discuss making whoopie on a beach towel, just like in the movies, but the thought of sand flea bites squelches that idea. "Besides," I say, "we didn't bring along The Hired Man."

And it's a good thing we didn't. When we wrap our nudity in beach towels and climb into the car to leave, it's not a moment too soon. Oncoming headlights flood the narrow rutted road, and a spotlight flashes to one side of the road and then the other. Turns out there are two different sets of headlights, one a police car, the other a national park service vehicle. Either someone reported noises on the beach or they're searching for illegal immigrants. We smile and wave at them as we drive slowly past, feeling as if we got away with something very grand indeed. As we drive the two miles uphill to Villa Debris, our talk is animated. We had so much fun. Let's do it again. But since the park service has cracked down on nudity on the beaches, we could have ended up on the front page of *Tradewinds* for skinny dipping. For us, this evening is a dramatic departure, a way to live life on the edge—the two of us together—and for just a little while, everything feels fine.

All too soon the thrill of the new sex toys is gone. Tom and I are back to making occasional appointments for sex. I have assigned the event a writing term, the *obligatory sex scene* (or OSS), although I've never told Tom. And the OSS must happen in the morning, because I'm way too tired at night.

One night I'm sitting on the bed reading. Tom comes upstairs from his office to get his small duffel bag full of sex toys to take back downstairs with him. He says he became aroused while researching those seal-a-meal devices. I'd like to say that's one of the craziest things he's ever said, but I'd be lying. I mean, this small home appliance is popular in the islands. When you seal up an item, say a shoe or a book or items of clothing, it doesn't get moldy. We'd talked about getting one, and I guess tonight's the night. Later, when he comes back upstairs and hangs the duffel on the wall, he tells me he ordered a seal-a-meal device off eBay. I don't ask him any other questions, even though I wonder if he'll want to keep his appointment for sex tomorrow.

And in the morning he's up for it, as scheduled. But, frankly, I'm not interested. Having a troubled relationship hasn't done much for my libido, but not having sex at all isn't so great for a marriage, either. So I do the best I can. Without use of any of the sex toys, we're under the sheet, all lubed up and going at it with some success. Off and on I say *Oh, yeah!* while thinking, I'd really like to wash the window walls so we can see the view better when we're in the living room. All of a sudden Inkie pounces on us from the rafters. Tom leaps up, Inkie flies into the air, and I start cussing. Talk about *coitus interruptus*. And as the particles of dust, mold and cat hair settle, my first thought is this: *Well, all right, then. I guess now I can go wash those windows.*

THE WING BONE OF A CRANE

The notes are crystalline, like the isinglass of a dragonfly's wing; thin, too, like clean air on a mountaintop. Nancy Ruffer and John Anderson, the flautist and the oboe player, are performing tonight at the St. John School of the Arts. Accustomed to performing with the London Philharmonic, here they play to be heard over the frog chorus, the crowing of roosters, and Monday Night Football on a neighborhood television. Eyes closed, I listen, transported to every magic moment of my life—driving along a mountain road surrounded by butterflies, standing in a meadow of wildflowers in the Tetons, my first snorkeling experience at Salt Pond Bay. Hearing this music is like falling in love with St. John all over again.

To improve the acoustics at this proud venue in Cruz Bay, the overhead fans are turned off. The air in the room is hot and humid, and without air-conditioning the temperature must be near 90 degrees. The side doors are open to allow in the cooler night air, and the room is alive with fluttering papers as audience members fan themselves with their programs. I see most of these people only while waiting in line at the post office or bank. It's pleasant, now, to be sitting with them enjoying this special event.

When one piece ends, the duo pauses, turns sheets of music, and begins the next. Nancy and John begin again to play above the island sounds, bravely and in good cheer, clearly pleased to share their gifts and their love of music. Nancy's mother, Elsbeth Ruffer, a pianist, accompanies them on a selection or two. Then Nancy plays an ancient flute crafted from the wing bone of a crane, bringing forth a surprising clarity of notes on such a primitive instrument. I feel blessed, as if chosen to experience this magical evening. Nothing else exists except this moment. Nowhere else in the world is there a magnificent performance exactly like this one.

Eyes open again, I watch a tiny black kitten sneak into the room and scamper across the stage. Soon the kitten races out toward the audience of bare feet in sandals, stopping to lick the toes of my friend, Lucy, the island's hypnotherapist and the captain of a snorkel charter boat. The kitten must know Lucy is also a rescuer of homeless cats. Tom and I both want to coax the kitten over to us and pick it up, but we don't move. Instead, we sit smiling at the sheer joy of being here, and at the way the island's small lunacies, incongruities, and ironies have found their way into this building in the form of a kitten, performing with these world-class musicians.

Later in the week, Nancy and John stop by the shop before leaving for London. We give them each a small canvas bag bearing The Canvas Factory label. I also give Nancy information I found online about a 9,000-year-old flute carved from the wing bone of a crane. Archaeologists in China discovered the flute that is believed to be the world's oldest, still-playable musical instrument. Sue Erickson, a Bellingham poet and lover of cranes, wrote a poem to celebrate that flute, and I give Nancy a copy of that as well. If you will google *wing bone of a crane*, you can read Sue's fine poem and listen to that ancient flute—a haunting sound from the dawn of civilization.

WHERE *THERE'S* SMOKE

Yellow CRIME SCENE tape decorates the closed doors of The Canvas Factory. The moment is singular, in a time-lapse way, when you realize, *This event could change the course of my life.* Two fire trucks are spraying the building this particular morning in early January, 2003. The beauty salon above our shop appears to be gutted. The solid, stable and timeless feel of Mongoose Junction had led us to believe the buildings were bomb proof, hurricane proof, and certainly fire proof. What will we find when we open our doors? Will all our raw materials and inventory of finished canvas bags be ruined?

We snake our way through the fire trucks and find a place to park. A volunteer with the St. John Rescue squad allows us to enter our shop. When we approach the sales counter, we can't tell how bad things are. But the smell of smoke is overpowering as we slosh through an inch or two of water. We stand in the dark, stunned. Our eyes slowly make out dirty, soot-laden water on top of Big Dorothy and Little Rita. Muddy water runs down the inside of the rock walls and the one window, and a pool has formed on the cutting table. An employee from a nearby shop offers us a roll of giant plastic bags, each one big enough to hold a body. Someone else arrives, starts shoving inventory into plastic bags, and says, "Let's get these out of here."

People on the island are familiar with disasters. Suddenly four or five of us are bagging up canvas items. Many who are helping say, "Oh, this is nothing compared to Hurricane Marilyn." They know exactly what to do, immediately and without concern for reward. Radha Speer backs her car up to the entrance and we fill it with bags, which is helpful because our own car is so small. And since we're housesitting for Barb and Jim, and their villa has an enormous covered deck, we take the bags up there and spread them out. Almost none of the bags are wet, but they carry a serious odor of smoke.

One couple in the Junction gives us a lovely card with a fifty dollar bill in it, toward a nice dinner out. Other shopkeepers and even total strangers are friendly and helpful during the fire. It's beautiful, really, but I can't help but wonder why it takes a special concert or a disaster for people to assemble and interact. One answer, I know, is that others are busy like we are, trying to make a living.

By afternoon, Glen has rigged us up with power via a utility cord. With all the merchandise and most of the materials out of the shop, we clean the place thoroughly, like it probably hasn't been cleaned in years. This is hard labor. My ailing body parts scream to take a break and go to the beach, but that doesn't happen. We keep finding more dirt. Several people help us move the two enormous wood display units, and underneath we find piles of petrified scat. No telling what made the deposits. A woods rat? An iguana? Baby chicks? A mystery critter? A jumbie? At one time or another, they've all wandered in and out of our open front doors.

While I clean, Tom bundles and tapes all the shop's loose electrical wires, and installs a small fluorescent light over the cutting table. Then he sands the cutting table and adds a couple coats of urethane. We clean some more. Three days later the odor of smoke persists so I place trays of a powerful vanilla bean potpourri around the shop to camouflage the smell. Finally, after missing four days of sewing and business, we return the aired-out, smoke-free bags to their shiny clean places, and open the shop doors for business.

The coconut telegraph offers up theories regarding the cause of the fire: someone slept overnight on one of the massage tables upstairs and a candle started the fire. Firemen had even searched for a body with no luck. Another idea is that the fire started in a computer, but in the end, as with so many strange events on the island, we never learn the cause. And while we're well-insured if someone gets strangled in the straps of a tote bag, not one of us in the building carries insurance for a fire. Glen generously waives shop rent for the next month.

WHISKEY, WOMEN AND MOLD

After ten years and still no baby, my son and his wife are thinking of adopting.

"Maybe when you guys come down here to visit, you'll get pregnant," I say. "Customers have told me it happened to them. After adopting a child because they couldn't get pregnant, they visit St. John, enjoy a lovely vacation, and bingo, the wife gets pregnant."

"That would be nice," Jeff says.

"Here's another thing," I say, determined to become a grandmother. "Remember that guy named Jack I worked with in the Forest Service?"

"Yes," my son says, trying to be patient with my meddling advice.

"One time he told me his brother and wife couldn't get pregnant, and then they found a book on the topic at a yard sale for ten cents. They did what the book said to do and got pregnant."

"Okay, Mom."

It's time to get the guest room ready for their visit. Now that I have my own computer upstairs, I no longer go downstairs. And this morning I discover that, once again, termites have been making their way, undetected, past Tom, who sits so often at his computer in his black half-slip and Manties. Termites are feeding on our books, papers, furniture, the cardboard storage boxes and their contents. None of this stuff is precious to me, but what a mess. I recruit Tom. It's mostly his debris.

We bag up papers from the bookshelf, including bills, months old, that haven't yet been entered in Quickbooks. Many of them are now unreadable, having been chewed up and spit out by the termites. The familiar, tired feeling of hopelessness, of life being out of control, sweeps over me. The smell of mold and the strange, chemical smell of termites make me want to puke. But there's work to be done, a new crisis to deal with, to mop up, to transcend. Here are books with mold so thick it looks like fur, in addition to the missing corners, chewed off by termites. The particle board bookshelf is partially eaten in the back and the shelves are sagging, so we move it out onto the porch next to the bags of loose papers. Tom is wearing his black half-slip, his apparel of choice around the house.

"You didn't smell the termites?" I ask.

"Can't say I did."

A stomach cramp grabs my intestines suddenly and I groan, "I gotta run to the bathroom." I've always thought it odd that most of my nerve endings are in my gastrointestinal tract.

When I return to Tom's office, my eyes follow various termite tunnels up the walls. A sizeable one goes under the bed, and when we pull the bed away from the wall we find termite tunnels as big as ship's hawsers. Even before we lift the mattress, we know there will be trouble. The mattress rests on a wooden box frame, without springs, and sure enough, much of the frame is now only crumbs of digested wood. In fact the supports on the frame resemble vintage lace curtains.

"Good thing Jeff and Lee won't be trying to make a baby on *this* bed," I say.

When I call Richard, son of Tidybowl Man, to report our discovery, his wife answers the phone and says, "Well, that's life in the tropics for you. I'll send Richard over to take a look."

Tom hastens upstairs to change into a pair of shorts. When Richard comes to the cottage he always yells "Hello" from a distance, as long-time residents do. In this climate, people wear little or nothing around the house. Announcing your approach gives people time to throw on some duds.

As you know by now, it takes a lot to surprise lifelong residents of the island, and Richard's response to the termite infestation is minimal. The hurricanes, the general air of lunacy, the odd wrecks and other mysterious events, even fires, have left them almost immune.

Richard muscles the remains of the bed frame out the sliding glass doors and, refusing help, he drags the crumbling piece of junk down the road to the Dumpster.

Richard has no replacement for the bed frame and we have less than a week to rig up a bed before Jeff and Lee arrive. We spot a bed frame near The Pig Dumpster, but it's the wrong size. At a different Dumpster, we find the right size frame, and even though it's rusty we tie it to the top of the car and bring it home. We lay two hurricane shutters and the mattress on it. Pleased with our creativity, we agree that once we dress the bed in clean linens, it will be a perfectly suitable place to make a baby. It's better than on the ground *in da bush.*

My son and his wife are not world travelers. So I take the ferry to Charlotte Amalie on St. Thomas, catch a taxi to the airport and meet their flight. How wonderful to see them. Jeff says, "It feels like a sauna here compared to Montana. Whew! I'm over dressed." They did just come from Montana, where it's probably zero degrees F. We grab their luggage and catch a taxi van to the ferry, and by the time we arrive on St. John, Jeff has some things figured out about the islands.

"It smells a little like sweat down here." And, "Those taxi drivers are getting rich off the white tourists."

A couple nights later, while glugging down a Heineken, Jeff announces, "You gotta drink a lot, in a climate like this."

Little does he know.

Jeff and Lee sleep like logs on their makeshift bed, but they ask for earplugs because of the tree frogs and traffic noise from the Centerline Road below the cottage. I stay home with them the first day, and after that Tom and I take turns showing them around the island, doing things like hiking and swimming. One day while snorkeling they see a big green turtle and a spotted ray. On Sunday morning, Tom takes them to a little Baptist church south of Coral Bay, where they're the only white people, and everyone is friendly and welcoming. One night we go out to dinner at Morgan's Mango. Jeff wants to pay, but when the bill comes he gulps and says, "I only have enough money for the tip."

Jeff hooks our TV up to cable, illegally, and introduces us to reality television. We watch two people eating live cockroaches that look like mahogany birds, while Jeff rubs my sore hands. When he was a child, I often rubbed his feet, and so I do that again. One morning, Tom and I give Jeff driving lessons, before turning them loose with the car. The next evening Jeff shares a ditty he came up with while driving along the North Shore Road: "Keep left young man, haven't you been told? St. John's filled with whiskey, women and mold."

Our guests change their clothes more often than we do, and when they announce an immediate need for clean clothes, I take them to Santos Laundry in Cruz Bay. While Lee and I are putting clothes in a washer, Jeff sits outside on a bench under a big tamarind tree. Next thing you know we hear him yelling. My heart sinks as we run out the open doors to find Jeff talking and laughing with other customers. An enormous iguana had slithered down the tree trunk and used Jeff's shoulder as a launching pad. He says, "I felt something on me, but I sure didn't expect to see an iguana!"

One day they go on the Reef Bay hike with a ranger from the park and have a wonderful time, as I knew they would. "Be prepared for more customers," Jeff says. "I told everyone in the group to stop by The Canvas Factory to see my mom and dad." He turns to Tom, "I didn't feel like explaining that you aren't really my father. I hope that's okay."

"You can be my kid any day," Tom says.

"What's one more, when you've already got six of 'em," Jeff says.

They joke together all the time. And Jeff asks Tom lots of questions and then listens intently, and I'm pleased that Tom always has an answer. When Jeff was growing up he asked me lots of questions, too, but I never had all the information lying around in my brain. My way of rising to the occasion was to say, "Let's look it up together." And he'd never want to. I even purchased a children's illustrated dictionary that I studied in my spare time, trying to predict what he'd ask next.

One day after school he asked, "Do you know what a seminal vesicle is?"

"I'd have to look that one up."

"It's one of two glands located behind the male bladder. It's where sperm is made and stored. We learned it in health class."

"Well, we didn't learn that when I went to school."

The fact that Tom can talk like an encyclopedia is cool. Sometimes I think Jeff likes him better than me, but I don't worry about this too much. The bigger problem is that it's difficult to consider leaving someone your kid loves.

When I ask Jeff his favorite thing about St. John he says, "Driving on the left. But then everything is my favorite. It's going to be hard to leave." And then they leave and break my heart. They still aren't pregnant, either. But maybe their doctor will prescribe fertility drugs and then I'll end up with several grandchildren at once.

RACE WALKING IN PARADISE

*T*oday is Sunday, my one day off this week. After doing some needed housework, I set off walking in the late afternoon. When I reach Colombo's concession stand, I pass the smell of beer and the sound of wind chimes to make my way down the primitive dirt road. The total distance to Coral Bay down this route might be three miles, and it will take me 45 minutes to reach my destination. The first half of the steep, rutted dirt road zigzags down the south-facing mountain side, offering views of the sailboats in Coral Bay and the villas on the surrounding hills.

The temperature is perfect, now that the sun has gone down behind Bordeaux Mountain. Once I'm off the mountain side, the last half of the road is flatter and smoother. After walking by the buildings and gardens of Josephine's Greens, I enter the low rent district of Coral Bay, and smell the aroma of *Eau de Goat.* The resident goat herd begins to trot along with me on the other side of a rusted wire fence, as if we're in a parade together. I grew up with a milk goat and still view these smelly, bleating beasties with a cordial attitude. Tom and I have considered doing many crazy things together. When we lived in Montana, we toyed with raising and training a pair of goats to carry our backpacking gear. But now Tom detests the smell of goats. When we're driving, his nose twitches into high alert, long before we see a herd of goats on the road ahead.

Now the goats are bleating as if they're begging. Based on visual and olfactory clues, I estimate a hundred goats, including the kids. What have I done to attract these goats? Is it a new kind of hero's welcome or a warning sign about my life? As I walk along, the cavalcade of udders and goat cheeks spills out an opening in the fence onto the road ahead of me, and immediately all the goats begin treating me as a threat. First the goats speed up, then slow down, each one of them nervously looking back at me, bleating in alarm. When our straggly parade passes the field of rusted car bodies in Rupert's Junkyard, I smile, because my wonderful cat Lucky was born inside or under one of these junkers. Now all the goats are ahead of me, and I keep smiling because the goats are acting like I'm their shepherd. They are unaware that everything I've ever attempted to ride herd on has ended up herding me.

By the time I reach the South Shore Road and turn right, a dozen goats have decided to trail me. "Shoo!" I yell, so they'll join the rest of the goats in a vacant field around a tiny blue cottage with teal shutters. I walk a little further on the side of the road past a small cemetery of above-ground vaults. Finally I reach Island Blues, a bar and restaurant on the shore of Coral Bay. I sit at my favorite small table overlooking the bay, order a light beer at the happy hour price of one dollar, and wait for Tom.

The light turns to dark over the sailboats in the bay, including a couple of boats half-submerged at rakish angles, ever since good old Hurricane Marilyn. As the green hills gradually grow indistinct, I recall our first visit to this bay in November 1996, on the vacation that so drastically altered the course of our lives. A couple had invited us to their sailboat for dinner, and picked us up on the dock near Skinny Legs in a chewed-up dinghy they'd pulled out of a tree. This was after the dinghy's fifth hurricane. Now six and one-half years later, that dinghy is probably still in service. Tom had originally wanted to rescue one of these half-submerged sailboats to live on, but when he researched this idea he quickly learned it wasn't possible. That's when he found us a boat on the Washington coast, the sailboat we named *The Shoe.*

Tom closes the shop an hour earlier on Sundays, at 5:00 p.m., and even though the drive from Mongoose Junction in Cruz Bay to Island Blues in Coral Bay is only 9 miles, it can take 45 minutes—exactly the time it takes me to walk here from Villa Debris. When we meet on these pre-arranged "dates," I'm always glad to see him. Sure, we've already talked on the phone today but when he gets here, we'll talk more about the antics of the customers at the shop and the cats at home.

When he arrives, I smell perfume on him. No one on the island wears perfume except a few rich widows or once in a while one of the visitors wearing a diamond ring as big as a golf ball.

"You smell like perfume? Have you been hugging on someone?"

"I'm wearing your perfume." It's a simple statement, made while he ponders what to order from the drink menu.

"The *Cashmere?* I thought that stuff was extinct," I say. "I don't *want* you to wear perfume. I'd rather you smelled like an old goat." Tom's second self has crashed our little party, and I don't like her. Smells to me like I'm being dumped for another woman.

"It's not fair," Tom says. "Women can wear whatever they want and call it a fashion statement. They can wear men's boxers as shorts, men's jeans, men's cologne. They can wear any hairstyle they choose. And you. You wear those wife-beater undershirts all the time."

"Yeah, but only around the house and to bed," I say. "And so does Meg Ryan in the movies. But, actually, I guess what you're saying is true. I just never thought about it."

On the last Saturday of February, Tom walks in the 8 Tuff Miles race between Cruz Bay and Coral Bay. He's one of 420 participants, and the only person race walking. He's also the only man wearing hot pink nylon short-shorts and *Cashmere* perfume.

He calls me at the shop after the race. "Eight miles is no big deal. In fact, after reaching Coral Bay I had a hamburger and a beer at Skinny Legs, and then I walked home."

"Congratulations," I say. Mostly I'm amazed that a man who eats bacon and eggs every morning and gets sloshed every evening can actually walk that far and not collapse. Instead, he's unusually animated.

He says, "Several women told me they liked my pink shorts. They said it was refreshing to see a man so comfortable with his masculinity that he can wear pink."

"Did you describe the rest of your wardrobe?"

"Hah!" he says. "What they don't know won't hurt 'em. And next year I'll be sixty, which puts me in a new age category, 60 to 99. I should be able to win the walking time for *that* age class easily, being such a young whippersnapper and all. You should do the race next year. It's great fun. There are music and water stations all along the route. It's one big party."

"I might do it," I say. "But right now I have a customer. I have to go."

Tom orders in a book on race walking, studies it, and orders a heart monitor device to wear around his chest. It looks like a black training bra. This technology allows him to monitor his heart rate and note the improvement from week to week. He shows me the race walking technique, which basically turns your feet into wheels. You take short, quick strides and your back toe cannot leave the ground until the heel of your front foot has touched. Angie would have called this style of walking "the technique of faster."

I've been sleeping in. This morning I feel like snail ooze, like I've traveled through a half-dozen time zones. I do the rest-home shuffle into the living room, where Tom is cooking bacon and eggs for himself, wearing my half-slip, Johnny bulging out in front. He says, "I've been up since dawn. I already walked nine miles. Wouldn't it be something if I won the walking category for all ages next year?"

I shuffle over to the table near the window, where I hope to summon enough wherewithal to make my coffee. I squint out the window at the bright sun, the shimmering ocean, the puffs of clouds, the green hills. I say, "With your long legs, you just might pull it off."

I'm happy for Tom, I really am. He's got new interests. He's enjoying life, he's sleeping well, and he's smiling a lot. He has no aches or pains and his hands aren't numb when he wakes up. He doesn't suffer an irritable bowel or hot flashes, and unlike me, he's happily married.

It's hard to be married to someone so young and vital, healthy and happy, while I'm draggin' my wagon. For instance, this morning when I woke up my right hand was so numb it was as if my hand wasn't even there. Maybe this is what it feels like after one of your hands is amputated. I want to feel young and energetic, like Tom. Maybe I should make drastic changes in *my* wardrobe. Or maybe it's all a matter of attitude. I remember an old affirmation: *I am tall and lean and physically fit. I am exceptionally healthy and I feel good.*

To improve my health, I order a Stretch-assager device, like a small foam accordion that you push in and out with both hands to relieve various hand and wrist symptoms, including carpal tunnel syndrome. It's also supposed to strengthen arm and shoulder muscles. My hopes are high enough that for a day or two I enjoy a placebo effect, and that's worth something. I also invest in a fabric wrist brace. Of course, I can't actually work at the shop while wearing the thing, and I don't really need it at home, so weeks later I donate it to the thrift store. The Stretch-assager device ends up there, too. What helps most are visits to Bern. He tells me it isn't good for my neck when I work all day with my head bent forward, that I must baby myself more. I always say, "I do what the work requires, but I'll try." He continues to entertain me and take my neck through a series of range-of-motion exercises. He makes adjustments to my vertebrae, followed by heat, ice and electrical stimulation on my upper back and neck. Sometimes I think he's a magician.

This morning I'm sitting on the toilet trapped in place by stomach cramps, while a personal furnace event sweeps over me at the exact moment a mosquito bites my butt. Adding to the festivities are sound effects from the cottage down the hill—one of the young bachelors is doing some morning-after puking. The cats, by now immune to my groaning bathroom aria, sit at the screen door staring in the direction of those *other* sounds. In between cramps I recall reading that a cat has 32 muscles in each ear, and right now the cats appear to be exercising every one of them. Cat yoga. I close my eyes and smile at this thought, then let go of a little more of the past.

Another morning before work, I'm walking down the old dirt road below Colombo's under a canopy of trees and shrubs, when a gust of wind kicks up. A shower of orchid petals rains down on me—thin cream-colored petals like the 138 wt. thread we use at the shop. A feeling comes over me, one not as familiar as that associated with a gas pain, but what is it? It takes a minute, but I decide that what I'm feeling is joy. Because at the moment I am walking in the sunshine and I'm happy to be alive, feeling blessed to be healthy enough to walk down a mountainside on St. John. I smile most of the way down the road as I walk by Josephine's, on past the goats, and all the way to the junction with the South Shore Road. I turn left and walk a short distance to Pickles Deli, where I sit alone at a small table among the Willie Nelson lookalikes drinking Heinekens, the breakfast of champions. I order a veggie omelet, which is surprisingly tasty. Even the mosquitoes leave me alone, since I remembered to spray repellent all over my legs before leaving home.

By the time I pay my bill and begin my walk up the steep dirt road, it's around 11:00 a.m. and the sun is scorching hot on the south side of the mountain. The temperature has to be over 90 degrees. My face must resemble a sugar beet. Every shady spot becomes a life raft, where I sit in the dirt or on a rock, and take a sip of water. I allow my heart rate to slow and then drag myself upright. And when diarrhea strikes, I use leaves for toilet paper, hoping they aren't poisonous. It takes me two hours to reach home. The rest of the day I rehydrate and recover while lying on the floor listening to new age music, a fan blowing on me full blast. It's going to take a miracle for me to walk next year in the 8 Tuff Miles event.

YO MAN *IS* IN HERE

Luna walks past the shop one day and glances in at us. Tom is sewing away on Big Dorothy while I'm standing at the cutting table. She stops in her tracks, leans into the shop, points at Tom, and yells to me, "I see you got rid of that homosexual you had working for you and you got *that* one now?"

And then she leaves. We don't understand what she meant by her comment, but given our many secrets, we agree it's both hilarious and strange. Does she have some kind of sixth sense? Is it that jumbie-black magic-voodoo thing operating? Tom's appearance *has* changed in the year and a half since Luna first saw him. When he first arrived he sported a crew-cut and looked like a tall, silver-haired, handsome man. Now she's probably confused, since he's wearing a longer Clint-just-in-from-a-hard-ride-Eastwood hairdo.

But no one else on the island has said a thing. Tom is active with the Mongoose Merchants' Association, too, but maybe when you see someone every day, changes in their appearance sneak up on you. Like the way my son grew up when I wasn't looking. There he was, nearly as tall as a mocko jumbie, wearing a bright red high school graduation gown. That was in 1988. Or my own aging process, and how I honestly had no idea I was old enough to be attending my for-tieth high school reunion this coming summer. The invitation placed me securely in a state of shock.

It's Tom's day off and I head to work alone. He'll use the day to ex-plore life's boundaries, investigate new frontiers, and bust free of his familiar termite tunnels. In many ways I admire him for doing this, especially when I come home in the evenings and he tells where he goes and about the people he meets. As I write in my journal, I record select pieces of his adventures. There's no way to know how much he isn't telling me, of course, but his behavior doesn't seem surreptitious.

This evening he tells me he walked to Salomon Beach, where we once happened upon those nude sun bathers, both prone and cavorting.

"I wore my yellow thong on the beach," he says.

"Oh, not that penie gourd thing." I say. This would not have been a pretty sight.

"Yeah," he says. "I thought I could get away with it since Salomon used to be a nude beach. There were lots of people there, and today I was wearing less attire than anyone. I sunbathed a while and went swimming twice. But I am so disappointed in myself. I didn't even have the balls to walk up and down the beach to dry off, like I usually do after swimming."

"There's always next time."

"Maybe," he says wistfully.

Hearing the details of his day is like remote viewing, or another way to hide and watch.

At work one day, Tom receives two new pairs of nylon panties edged with lace, in the mail from eBay.

He says, "You can tell your friends if you want to."

"No thanks. But if those panties don't fit, will you give them to me?"

"Really, I don't mind if you tell your friends."

"I think it's private," I say. "I don't discuss it with anyone." That's the way I feel, too, while treating his new interest as temporary. I also hope my positive, accepting behavior will build some equity. He'll finally *owe* me. But owe me what? Respect? Consideration? Will he finally let us get the help we need at the shop?

Next, two vintage aprons arrive in the mail. Where would we be without eBay? One apron is a red gingham check with a lacy white ruffle. The other one is pink. He holds up the red one and says, "They were practically free. We can both wear them, you know. They're unisex."

"Well," I reply. "I would have preferred an apron without ruffles."

Sometimes I wonder if he's interested in lacy articles of clothing because I act so genderless, so neutral, so *un*feminine.

By the time a housesitting gig comes along again, I'm ready. Since the house is up the hill above Mongoose Junction, I can walk back and forth to work. On the day I begin housesitting, Tom receives another soft package in the mail. I think, Oh, boy, my new sports bra. But, no, the package contains a shell pink negligee with a matching jacket. He's thrilled with his purchase. For a hobby, this thing is getting a little carried away. At the end of the day after we close the shop, Tom drives home with his new nightie on the passenger seat, where I usually sit. I refuse a ride and trudge up the steep hill to my temporary villa.

I care for two cats, feed some guppies, clean the pool filter and take measurements in a water gauge. I sleep on an air bed, and hear the ferry growl to life every morning at six, not to mention hearing all the other town noises. These annoyances are diminished when I use their swimming pool and hot tub. Their house is "wired" in many complex ways, so that I can't for the life of me figure out how to watch the TV. Instead I read their *Wired* magazines.

The lady of the house is a gourmet cook and, according to her husband, she often cooks naked. They entertain frequently, wearing clothes, at least when we've dined here. On this first evening of housesitting, when I'm hungry all I can find is a jar of Kalamata olives in the refrigerator and canned snails in the cupboards, along with 12 sets of dishes and every spice known to man. So I sit out on the deck eating the jar of olives while straining to see the lights of St. Croix, 35 miles to the southwest. Later I loll around the place nude, dipping in the hot tub, then the swimming pool, and back into the hot tub.

Tom calls me later to say good night, says he has someone in mind to hire eight hours a week, which is what he figures we can afford. But first, he says, we'll wait and see what the rest of high season brings.

A lovely woman works for us one Saturday, but she can't or won't learn to work the treadle to walk the foot on the sewing machine. So she doesn't last long. The problem with finding help is that the work and the equipment are specialized. It isn't easy to find an employee, especially when hiring only part-time help.

However, instead of discussing ways to broaden our search for a suitable employee, the topic of discussion returns again and again to Tom's second self. He says what's happening to him is called *gender dysphoria,* and that it's at least partly genetic. He's found information to support this, using the term *psycho neuro-endocrinology.* He thinks he might have had this inclination all along, but it was buried in his subconscious.

"You mean to say gender is more than just the sum of one's magic parts?" I'm turning a small zip tote I just finished.

"Yes." He sews another seam before continuing. "And now I wonder if I'm transgendered, which for me would mean living as a woman and being accepted as one. I still might just be a cross-dresser. I hope that's it."

The temperature in the shop hovers close to 80 degrees, but I feel a shiver of disbelief. Tom is clever at measuring his words, and now I think he's more aware of his true feelings than he's admitting. Discontent with one's biological sex is one thing; doing something big about it is another matter.

When Tom returns from the post office, he's happy with his loot. Today he received two books on the subject of gender dysphoria, and scored a Victoria's Secret catalog from the recycle bin. One of the books is written by a wife who thinks her cross-dressing husband is wonderful. Maybe it's all right if your marriage is stable before the husband adds that new dimension. Today, in between customers, Tom steals glances at the frilly, sexy lingerie in the Victoria's Secret catalog.

I tell him, "I don't know any women who wear that fancy, sexy lingerie. We're outdoor women. We wear cotton. We're wildlife biologists, artists, anthropologists, landscape architects. My friends don't dress like prostitutes." I say this for effect. Even I don't think wearing sexy underwear makes a woman a hussy. It just makes her different from me.

One day the island is filled with visitors from a gay cruise, as well as a cruise ship with members of Tri-Ess, that Society for the Second Self, of which Tom is a member. He arranges to meet a man and woman from this cruise for lunch.

Maybe having a good personality is a requirement for being gay. And gay guys aren't afraid of spending money, either. All the shopkeepers love them. When Tom returns from his lunch with the Tri-Ess couple, he tells me the husband was portly and dressed just like any old guy. The couple was ordinary in every way, and not at all glamorous. But he's pleased that the gay guys saved the day for him when he was walking back to the shop. He says, "One gay guy yelled across the road to one of his friends, 'Hey, you! Get down on your knees.'"

The usual conversation continues as we sew. Tom says, "I can't help it. Something must have happened to me *in utero*. How can this not be all right with God?"

"Doesn't God love everyone, even criminals?" I ask. Tom has always been so religious, so outright disdainful of gays and lesbians, and even geologists with their claim that the earth is four billion years old.

"It's different with homosexuals," Tom says. "Scientists haven't yet linked their behavior to genetics."

"Well, that doesn't make any sense."

Hermon makes an appearance and saves the day for *me* when he shows us his new lignum vitae pieces. I buy one, of course, because I can never have enough Hermon Stones. While we're standing at the sales counter he glances out the open doors and spots a group of nicely dressed African American men across the street, getting out of a safari taxi. He says, "Will ya look at dem black tourists."

BETTER LIVING THROUGH HYPNOTHERAPY

Before opening her hypnotherapy practice in Cruz Bay, Lucy invites a feng shui expert from St. Croix to assess her new space. Lucy tells me, "I want to create a calming oasis filled with positive energy for my clients." The feng shui person recommends that she cover her file cabinets and the louvers on the bathroom door. She requests that I sew purple canvas panels for her, which I do in exchange for a two-hour hypnotherapy session. Some folks say the Bible refers to things like hypnosis as witchcraft, but I know people whose lives are better, thanks to this alternative healing method.

At the beginning of our first session, Lucy does an extensive intake, inquiring about my childhood, family, current health, and any personal issues I'm dealing with. I don't mention Tom's special gender gift, because it's incidental to the bigger picture. She has me kick back in a recliner, and I lie looking up at the ceiling. According to feng shui, open rafters should never be exposed. Rafters are exposed all over the Caribbean, and Lucy has solved this problem in her office by tacking mosquito netting up there. She instructs me to close my eyes as she counts backward from ten, assuring me that I will, at all times, be conscious and in complete control. She has a soothing voice. I trust Lucy.

"Where are you?" she asks. "Describe your surroundings."

Slowly the scene is revealed to me. I am very small, a year or so old, and I'm with a band of travelers. Bedouins? No, gypsies, I think. It seems I am both participant and observer. My tribe is olive-skinned. I see their faces, dark eyes, and long, black unkempt hair. We're all around a campfire. Sparks are flying up as they discuss what to do with me, since I'm unable to make sounds. Next we travel in a slow caravan to a village in the Italian countryside, where they leave me on the doorstep of a large villa. My name is Samanta (not Samantha). The rich family takes me in and raises me. I'm a mute person, and I learn to express myself by playing the harp for appreciative audiences.

After the session, Lucy relates my past-life experiences to my present struggles, all in a positive, healing way. For instance, there are lessons to be learned about finding my voice, about making myself heard. I need to exercise my vocal chords, send up an alarm so loud, so thunderous that everyone, including Tom, will be startled. This all gives my mind quite a workout. I mean, is death the great exit ramp to rebirth? Is it an opportunity to recover or uncover what is underneath, between, behind, and on the other side of a mysterious trap door? Nothing is certain, but then I don't feel the need for guarantees.

I schedule another session with Lucy, this one for pay, because I've heard that if you don't pay your exorcist, you could get repossessed. And Lucy thinks she can help me with the pinched nerve in my neck and the numbness in my hands. Maybe she can. She was instrumental in curing a man's brain tumor and a woman's lung cancer. She also tells me about a hypnotherapist in Florida who specializes in working with cancer patients for whom conventional therapies haven't worked. After a series of hypnotherapy sessions, many of these patients enjoy a long-term remission. The day before my appointment, Lucy calls to reschedule because she'll be taking Judy Collins out snorkeling. Lots of people on the island have more than one job.

During the second past-life regression with Lucy, I begin trembling violently and exhibit symptoms of a massive heart attack. The pain in my chest is acute, an anguish greater than any I've ever suffered. Remaining calm, Lucy asks where I am and what I'm seeing. I'm unable to talk for several minutes. Slowly, in a guttural voice, I reveal that I have taken an axe and killed a lover, one who has *done me wrong* in some serious ways. My hideous criminal act is followed by time spent shivering in an unheated prison, and finally I'm set free into the sunlight. I see a small ranch, a herd of sheep, a black and white dog. During this session I expel a lot of anger. I mean, I killed the S.O.B. Lucy turns the experience on end, leading me through a series of forgiveness exercises all around, in my past-life as well as in the current one.

When I tell a neighboring shopkeeper that the hypnotherapy sessions have helped me, she goes to see Lucy, too. But during her session she's unable to relax enough for her subconscious to be tapped. Now, days later, she feels like a failure and has suffered a headache since the session. Her husband comes into the shop to see me.

First he asks, "When you were an axe murderer in that past life, did you use a double-edged axe?"

"Are you kidding?" I say. "Those things are dangerous."

We joke, but I do want his wife to feel better, so I tell him, "I probably made up those past lives. I do have an over-active imagination. I think she should try hypnotherapy again and just go with whatever pops into her head."

Maybe it's true. I can't be sure, with my ability to exaggerate, to catastrophize, that I didn't just make it all up so Lucy wouldn't feel bad. I am skilled at anticipating and then subsidizing other people's feelings to the diminishment of my own. It's one way I can contribute to world peace.

I remain open minded, however, and believe I'm being helped. Lucy suggests a hypnotherapy session that will specifically introduce me to my spirit guides. This process begins with another past-life regression in which I discover just how versatile and varied my lives have been, over the centuries. This time I'm a sub-intelligent man in his early thirties in a primitive culture. There were so few people and structures around then, but I was definitely on an island. In this past life, I'm hungry, so I steal a domestic animal to eat, after which I flee to the jungle with my dinner—only to get caught and killed for the crime.

The strong message from this past life is that I'm much stronger than I think I am. I mean, I might not have been the smartest human being, but at least I didn't die hungry. When I get home that evening, I pick up the cheap spiral notebook I'm currently using as a journal. The Scorpion King character on the cover bears a strong resemblance to the knuckle-dragger I looked like in my most recent past life.

Since my hypnotherapy sessions, Tom likes to point out that I, too, have other selves, not all of them so wonderful.

"Yes," I say. "But at least all of my other selves are dead. Your second self is a bratty teenage girl, except when she's cooking a meal dressed like a 1950s housewife. And by the way, didn't barbarians wear skirts?"

"Yes," Tom replies. "And so did the Vikings. In fact, my mother's family claimed to be distant relatives of the King of Norway. My father's kin claimed Lighthorse Harry Lee in their lineage. He was an American Revolutionary War officer and the father of Robert E. Lee. Of course, that's suspect. My father also told us a World War II story about how he captured a Japanese man named Toshi Myazockee when he threw a hand grenade and it didn't go off. Then I got older and found out that during the war he'd been in the dental corps on a training base. He couldn't have captured a guy named Toshi."

"You know, you should really do a past-life regression with Lucy," I say. "You might be surprised who'd turn up."

At the first hypnotherapy session, Lucy prescribed a book that introduced me to the law of attraction. *Excuse Me, Your Life is Waiting: The Astonishing Power of Feelings,* by Lynn Grabhorn. Apparently, *the law of attraction* has nothing to do with finding a customer attractive. I order the book online, and when it arrives I read it morning and night, and now I'm even more motivated to change my ways. Plus I read in *Time* magazine that chronically anxious or pessimistic people are 50 to 60 percent more likely to develop Parkinson's Disease. It's all about attitude. Supposedly, you get what you think about. All you have to do is ask the universe for what you want and it's yours. That is, if you believe you can have it, that you deserve it. This notion reminds me of a saying I once heard, *In an abundant universe there is always enough.*

I'm ashamed that my thoughts have been so often negative during the last ten years, or maybe forever. I'm proud of my German turnip farmer, peasant heritage, especially the good parts. We're survivors,

we're storytellers, and we've always tried to make fun of the maraud-
ers: "Hey, did you see the one that knocked me down? His hair shirt
had a bird's nest in it!" But I must stop feeling so much *weltschmerz*.
My marriage simply provides fuel for my angst, and that, apparently,
can give birth to ailments.

When I revise my list of affirmations, I combine what I want in
life with suggestions from Louise Hay's book, *Heal Your Body*. What a
lovely respite it is, to feel that I'm not responsible for every little thing,
that the universe will help me. And what can it hurt if I stop my negative flow of energy and use it instead to picture what I want? I'll focus
on all the things I'm grateful for, like Tom fixing my laptop computer
on his day off, when he ran a diagnostic while on the phone with a
technician in India. After that he vacuumed the house and cooked
dinner. I'm determined to feel joy more often, to generally feel good
and hopeful. Never again will I reach for a free rum punch and notice
that the glass is half empty.

Back in the shop it doesn't take long before I'm anxious, overwhelmed, cranky, and mad at myself because my new religion isn't
working. I'm a failure at the law of attraction. Maybe a new way of
thinking is like riding a horse. If you fall off, you have to climb right
back on.

While the hypnotherapy sessions have been helpful to my psyche,
I still have pain in my neck, arms and shoulders. My hands continue to be numb when I wake up. So I make an appointment with the
massage therapist who has an office near Pickles Deli in Coral Bay. I
walk down the mountain to my appointment. This massage therapist's
name is Cathy, and while she works me over I tell her about the law
of attraction.

"I'm interested," she says, hooking my arm in a double axel and
pulling.

I say, "You're really strong."

"I'm an ox," she says, now grabbing my shoulder blade, all 95
pounds of her leaning back until she nearly sits on the floor.

After the massage Cathy shows me exercises to do, and I get the feeling I'd better do them or I'll be in big trouble with her the next appointment. We agree that we can't make me feel like I'm 25 again, but we can help me turn my head a little easier. By the time I leave, I feel more hopeful.

On my way into town one day, I pick up Hermon on the Centerline Road. He's carrying his new cinnamon-colored Canvas Factory knapsack and a small leafy branch with tiny white petals that smell like perfume. As I drive and shift and keep left, Hermon tells me he's worried that he'll go back to jail for an incident that got blown all out of proportion, the way things sometimes do on the island. I tell him I'll picture him free, carving his lignum vitae sculptures in a nice shady spot. It's what Lucy would have said. Then Hermon shows me a large clunk of wood about six inches tall, five inches wide, and two inches thick, into which he has carved a primitive face. The wood is so lustrous from his polishing, the face is so striking, that I nearly drive in the ditch while looking at it.

"How much?" I ask.

"Thirty dollars."

"Sold."

When we arrive at Mongoose Junction, I pay him for the sculpture. He then gives me a small carved wood pendant and the branch with the aromatherapy flowers. All day long The Canvas Factory smells like a flower shop, and sales are strong.

OBJECTS IN MIRROR ARE BETTER LOOKING THAN THEY APPEAR

When people try on bags or caps and look at themselves in the mirror, some of them notice the affirmation I have taped to the top of the mirror: *Objects in mirror are better looking than they appear.* They smile. And I hope this little surprise contributes in some small way to their vacation.

Many customers are fun and smart. Some days, however, we get customers who are unfriendly, even rude, and these people are often from a low-rent cruise ship, the cruise ship equivalent of a turnip truck. While we sew, Tom and I talk about them, probably so we can feel superior to *someone*. (And right now I'm going to ask forgiveness from every farmer who reads this. We really *do* love you and all the organic foodstuffs you produce.)

After one such unfriendly group leaves the shop, I say, "Yeah, sure. You betcha. They're rural folk from one of them Northern Plains states." I strain to talk with flat vowels, the way Tom does. "Got themselves a special deal on a cruise for farmers before planting season."

"Jeez, yeah," Tom says, not straining one bit with the accent. "They're scairt to reply when we say hello to 'em. The last time they answered the door, they were so thrilled to see a new face they bought a free set of pots and pans that turned out not to be free."

"You got that right," I say, remembering this line from the film, *Fargo.*

"Ya darn tootin.'"

Other customers come in groups, like an entire family from Hilton Head, South Carolina, here celebrating their mother's birthday. One daughter flies in from Ukraine (formerly *the* Ukraine). Another daughter has a baby named Jimmy I get to hold. The 70-year-old mother is slender and attractive, and guides kayak trips. I hope I look so good and feel so feisty when I'm that age.

One day a family from South Dakota buys several bags with a credit card bearing the roman numerals III after their names. Another day a man who tells us he's an appliance repairman comes in with his family, and he looks exactly like one of the guys in the Maytag commercial.

A West Indian man walks into the shop to buy some heavy black thread for a project. "You look a little familiar," I say. It's the same line I use with celebrities, although I don't believe I've ever seen this weathered West Indian man in a movie.

"Well, I'm Fred the Dread."

"What a great name," I say, studying him. "You know, I think we were both in the back of a truck hitchhiking a couple years ago."

"That could'a been me," he says.

"Fred the Dread, what's your last name?"

"Can't tell ya cuz I'm on the ten most wanted list."

"Maybe I saw your picture at the post office, then," I say, hoping he's kidding.

He says nothing; just grins.

I hand over the thread. "There's no charge today."

Tom and I continue to work together at the shop, often laughing, discussing something we hear on public radio, and joking. It's as if we're happily married. If you came into the shop during this time, you wouldn't have noticed anything wrong, other than a longer hairdo and a few colorful wardrobe changes on Tom.

Lucky for us, Capt. Phil stops by once in a while. This time he tells us about an event that happened at one of the shoreline drinking establishments next to the ferry dock. Some tourists met a local diver who had caught a giant lobster. The lobster was still alive in an informal creel near his table. When the guy left to go to the bathroom, the tourists grabbed the lobster and, in a *Free Willy* moment, they ran with the crustacean to the ocean and tossed it back. When the diver returned to his table, he announced, "I will never again go to the bathroom without my lobster."

A mature, handsome man of Italian descent comes into the shop. Talkative and friendly, he says he buys and sells businesses. In one deal he suffered a hostile takeover by the Mafia and almost didn't get out of it alive. In fact, he lost millions. He wants to buy The Canvas Factory. He won't change a thing, he promises, although he admits to a fondness for neon. We tell him Glen would never allow neon at Mongoose Junction.

After the man leaves, Tom mentions that the guy's fingernails were manicured. Later, on my way to the post office, I stop by The Pampered Pause to pick up a gift certificate for a manicure. This seems like a culturally acceptable way for Tom to care for his hands and pamper his feminine side.

After his manicure, his nails are trimmed and buffed to a nice sheen. And he learned that if you work in sales, manicures are considered a business expense. Lots of people on the island do this, he says, so he went ahead and made another appointment.

"I'll bet you're glad that Italian guy came in."

Tom stops sewing, holds up his right hand to admire his nails and says, "Oh, yeah! You got that right."

The saying "Oh, yeah!" always makes us laugh. We've watched exactly one porno movie during our marriage. The woman in the movie kept saying "Oh, yeah!" over and over, even though she did not appear to be enjoying what she was doing. It's hard to get some images out of your head.

"I think it would be nice if he'd buy our shop right out from under us," I say. "We could play hard to get, act like it's a hostile takeover, and run up the price."

"I can see the neon sign out front already," Tom says. "TATTOOS WHILE YOU WAIT — WALK-INS WELCOME."

One day I'm cutting crop when a young man comes into the shop wearing a big cowboy hat in addition to a T-shirt, swim trunks and flip-flops. "Look, Tom," I say. "A cowboy!"

Tom looks up from sewing a small zip tote.

The cowboy says to me, "An' don't you ferGIT it, neither."

"Where are you from?" I ask.

"Florida."

"Florida?"

"You doggone right," he says, doffing his cowboy hat in a way no cowboys in Montana ever do. "Did you know there are more cows in Florida than in the entire state of Texas?"

"No," I say. "I didn't know that."

And then the cowboy asks, "Where's Woody's?"

In our continuing effort to surprise returning canvas addicts, we order in some tangerine-colored canvas. The neighboring shopkeepers even get a little excited. Jim, always good with marketing ideas, recommends we call the color *mango*. And when the roll arrives and we rip off the heavy plastic wrapping, the color turns out to be hunter vest orange, construction cone orange, MEN WORKING orange. My stomach gets queasy just looking at the color. Disgusted, I leave the roll of canvas on the cutting table and pretend it isn't there, which is impossible because it's so damn orange. Later in the day a young man walks in and looks around.

"Oh," he says, acting like he just won the lottery. "You have orange. Can you make me an attaché in that color with black straps? I go to Oregon State University. Orange and black are the school colors."

"You got it." I reach for the special order log book. "Will that be with cotton straps or nylon?"

"Nylon. I'm tough on bags."

"Okay," I say. "How about a large duffel bag, too, while we're at it?"

"Good idea."

From the day we receive that first roll of canvas, we enjoy an adulation for orange bags that's just shy of *on-kray-dee-bull*. This does wonders to quell my gag reflex while cutting and sewing the orders.

We get visitors in the shop who aren't even human. In addition to lizards on every surface and the occasional jumbie, there have been chickens and rats. One day when Tom and I sit sewing our little hearts out, a day with so few customers we don't even sell a bag that's orange, a woman appears in our open doorway and screams, "You have one of those *creatures* in your store!" And for just a moment I think she means Tom. But as she flees, she points at the showroom floor. I leap up so fast I get a head rush, and she's right. The creature is a large, frightened iguana. I escort him slowly out the door, walking behind him as if he's on a leash. We make our way past the entrance to Hurricane Alley, and when we reach the edge of the parking lot he slithers up into a tamarind tree. While I'm sorry we lost a potential customer, I'm relieved the iguana is safe and that he didn't turn and assault my toes.

One day a man comes in wearing band-aids all over his legs. "The heck's the deal there?" I ask.

"An iguana attacked me," he replies, proudly.

"You should have seen it," his wife offers. "Blood all over."

"They *do* like red toenail polish," I say, just joking.

He smiles. "That's why I took it off."

Something tells me these fine people will tell this story over and over when they get back home.

And speaking of toenail polish, one afternoon when I return to the shop from doing errands, Tom tells me, "I had an interesting customer while you were gone."

"Oh, crap," I say, tossing the mail on the counter. He knows I live for the entertainment value of the customers.

"Yeah, a big guy came in. You know the kind. Drinks beer and belches loudly, squats down to fix something and flashes you a vertical smile."

"The kind I call a white-rumped geezer?"

"That would be him," Tom says. "And that alone isn't so odd, but the man was wearing bright red toenail polish."

"Did you tell him to watch out for iguanas?"

"No, but I did say 'nice pedicure.' And the guy says, 'I always do it when I come down here.'"

During this time a very rich customer and part-time island resident comes into the shop and orders a few bags. We always get excited when we see him. He appreciates the quality of our bags and buys or orders them in a quantity sufficient to make us cheer. And because I want his shopping experience to be memorable, I always try to tell him something interesting. This time I dramatize the recent incidents featuring iguanas.

He watches and listens, then says, "Several large iguanas live near my house on the southwest shore. They like tomatoes, you know, but they're so darned expensive on the island that I started feeding them bananas instead. I read that in the book, *Iguanas for Dummies.*"

Just as the man who feeds bananas to his iguanas leaves the shop, a large woman in a print house-dress, the kind worn by 1950s housewives, appears in the open doorway. She's fanning herself with a *Little House on the Prairie* bonnet, and pants, "I cannot wait to get back to Kansas."

ISLAND ICE

These days, we're only taking "a whore's bath," which means we wash only our smelly parts. We do this to save water, thanks to an early spring drought. It hasn't rained much since Christmas. And now I picture rain falling until our cistern is full. It's another way to practice the law of attraction.

It works. The rain starts and doesn't stop. Lizards and frogs rehydrate before our eyes. Bananaquits resume their twittering. The frog chorus reaches a new decibel level. Mosquitoes hatch and flourish and swarm around my ankles. It rains so much that we have the wettest April on record. The roads become glazed and treacherous with island ice, resulting in a rash of accidents, some of them serious.

One rainy evening when I arrive home after working alone at the shop, I slap my way through the clouds of mosquitoes to find Tom lying on the couch. He's drinking scotch and watching news of the Iraq War on TV.

"I fell down the stairs," he says. "I was wearing my flip-flops. I thought the steps might be slippery, so I held onto the railing with my left hand, while gripping my drill and drill bits in the other hand. Next thing you know I'm on my butt bouncing all the way to the bottom—slide, bump, thud—holding the drill high like I'm carrying the torch at the Olympics. Groan. I landed at the bottom right next to the potted banana palm."

"Oh, no." The man has no padding on his butt. I picture broken bones, a trip to Myrah Keating Clinic, medical bills. I see myself working alone at the shop for weeks or months. My new religion, the law of attraction, has slipped on the island ice and fallen down the stairs with Tom. "Can I get you something?"

He holds out his glass. "Another scotch," he whimpers. "And don't be stingy."

This drinking for medicinal purposes I can understand. Listening to his tale of woe, I hand him a glass half-full of scotch.

"I bruised my left elbow and a few ribs on my lower right back side. Might have broken something, the way it hurts. It's like there was grease on those steps."

For three days he mostly sits or lies on the couch drinking his meds. He applies an ice pack alternating with heat and arnica salve, all the while watching the Iraq War on TV. I can't bear to watch or listen to this particular U.S. invasion. I'm no mental giant, but I can see it's morally, politically, and economically stupid.

I insist that Tom use the head phones. "I don't want to hear about the war, and don't you fergit it, neither."

By nature ambivalent, I take the occasion of Tom's Olympic performance on the stairs to explore both sides of his accident. I'm working alone at the shop, of course, and in between customers I sew and think. For one thing, I must confess it feels pretty darn good, for a change, to be the one who is more lively and healthy. On the other hand, I'm not *that* frisky. Also, the shop is emergency-room busy. After working alone for three days, I drive the 114 curves home feeling exhausted and cranky. As I cook dinner, I announce, "You'll be all right tomorrow. I'll help you to the car. I'll drive. When we get to the shop I'll strap you onto the chair in front of your sewing machine so you won't tip over."

Tom is still groaning as he moves around the house at the speed of a glacier, but he agrees to work at least part of the next day and then drive home early. I'll catch the bus or hitchhike home. And that's what we do. After a few days of this routine, Tom is able to work full time and, slowly at first, he resumes race walking.

While Tom's accident doesn't make headlines during the rains, other events do. A house under construction up the Mamey Peak road takes a nose dive off the bluff and slides on a bed of mud and rocks several feet down toward the Centerline Road. By the time this occurs, Tom is well enough to walk up the road to see it. To his amazement, a West Indian man in his underwear is jumping up and down on the ground near where the house once sat. It's one way to make sure the ground is suitable for construction, although it's a little late for that.

By the time it stops raining, the trees and shrubs have begun to sprout new leaves and blossoms, some that smell like jasmine. A flock of mangrove cuckoos flies into the nearby trees and make their jungle sounds. I look out the wall of windows to the blue sky, the ocean, the islands, and feel at once happy to be on St. John, and lucky to be alive.

WALKING WITH SPIDERS

Clutching my day pack and spider stick, I step out of the confines of the tiny Suzuki Samurai into the subtropical morning sunlight. From this location on the Centerline Road, you could look north to the Atlantic Ocean, then turn south and gaze upon the Caribbean Sea, except you can't because the vegetation is too thick. It's a jungle out there; it's perfect spider habitat. Tom revs the engine.

"Well, I guess this is it, then," I say, glancing down the grassy trace of road I'll be following on my trek to the ocean. "If I don't make it back, I've got my driver's license with me so they can identify the body."

"What should I do with your remains?" Tom asks. "We've never discussed that."

"Oh, just ship me back to the old country," I say, adjusting the straps of my pack. "Actually, do whatever you want. Surprise me."

"You know," he says, revving the engine on the Sammy again, "We really should get those burial life insurance policies through AARP."

"Now you think of it."

"Have fun," he yells, driving off to spend the day working alone at the shop. It is his turn.

I could holler at him to stop, to come back for me. But I won't. I need this day off and I intend to have an adventure, even if it's my last one. While the Virgin Islands National Park is a safe place, my outing in this little-used area is not without risk. But I'm determined to seize the moment, the day, the week. My time and opportunities are evaporating. Today's motto is *carpe diem, not carpe mañana.*

The rusty metal gate stands open, inviting me to explore this route that isn't shown on many maps. According to a ranger at the visitors' center there are some ruins from two sugar plantations a mile or so down the road. She told me, "The trail beyond the ruins comes out at Fish Bay, but be careful of the wild pigs along the way."

A journey starts with a single step, and I walk now, no faster than a graduation march, constantly waving the spider stick in front of me. Before we left home this morning, Tom presented me with the stick— a teyer palm stalk almost four feet long. First I'll deal with the spiders; then the wild pigs.

Ever since I developed a fondness for tarantulas while living in the shackteau, I've longed for the same feeling of camaraderie with golden orb spiders. I've done my homework. This spider is generally harmless, but they're such large creatures–six to eight inches overall, mostly legs–and that's just crawl-space creepy. One time I found myself up close and much too personal with one in her web. For a brief moment of terror I observed the lovely, speckled pattern of her body. My fear involves becoming hopelessly ensnarled in yet another tangled web. How easy it is to be lured into an ambush, to live a troubled story because of past choices. But that was yesterday. Today I'm prepared to avoid new booby traps.

A golden orb spider spins lines to anchor her home address. These lines can reach 15 to 20 feet across little-used trails and roads. Like this one. Their placemat-sized webs of intricate silk filigree hang at eye level. The female spider suspends herself upside down in her dining room and waits for large insects to fly into her lair and get caught. Then she dines alfresco on the catch of the day. To maintain her ambience and keep birds from flying into her space and wrecking it, she leaves insect husks on her doorstep. This way, birds are likely to see them and avoid such a mishap. In dual-purpose brilliance, she even allows her much smaller mate to loiter at the edge of the web to eat leftovers. Then if times get lean, he serves as a snack. Her decision to leave dinner scraps on her placemat helps me to spot the trap before I, too, become prey. I admire the golden orb spiders' home decorating skills.

This particular spider is the only arachnid known to spin silk strong enough to be woven together and used for fish nets. Its webbing is actually tougher than steel. In fact, scientists are attempting to duplicate their silk for use in bullet-proof vests. Now I'm on the lookout for the thin, strong, silk filaments that shine like gold in streaks of sunlight. So far I've encountered six. Each time, I wave my magic spider stick underneath the lines to make certain the way is clear. If it looks safe, I squat low and waddle duck-like to safety on the other side. But if my spider stick touches one of the lines as tough as filament, I stop, make a swift slice with my stick and carefully lift the line that's still attached to the web. So as not to wreck the spider's habitat, I carefully move the line to a tree branch at the side of the track, and continue on my way. Lucky for me, a single line of web is not as strong as steel.

The tangle of vegetation now lining both sides of the road is dense and lush. Zebra-striped butterflies zigzag in the shade, and a moth as large and dark as a bat flaps ahead of me, as if showing me the way. Mountain doves mourn and coo to each other back and forth across the track. Mangrove cuckoos chatter. Otherwise, this is one of the more silent areas of the island, giving rise to thoughts of the jumbie spirits said to live in large trees, especially around former sugar plantations. Such a spirit might reach out, grab me, and hold me prisoner until my spirit flies up. Distant voices will call to me, like mangrove cuckoos. In the humid 85-degree air, the thought makes me shiver.

I feel brave to be walking alone down an overgrown road where almost no one goes, risking encounters with Jurassic-sized spiders, uncertain of arriving at my destination. But then I remember the alternative: sitting around growing feeble, with no stories to tell. Either way I'm facing my fortieth high school reunion. And if risk can be measured by what you have to lose, I'm left with no choice but to launch out on this expedition alone. I want to prove to myself I can still live a full and exciting life. Sometimes when you take an unforeseen route, you might find it necessary to battle sharp teeth and venom. Or you could fall into a chasm. But it's also possible to feel an expansiveness of spirit not found on familiar, more comfortable terrain.

I was a wallflower in high school; I don't need to be one now. It's time to step into the future, to trust that a trail will emerge. So what if I've made past choices based on ignorance or misinformation? Or I was operating under the influence of a romantic notion based on false advertising.

Young trees now encroach onto the former road bed like high school seniors watching a parade of one–a mature woman wearing long pants, long-sleeved shirt, and a knapsack—eyes darting, sweat dripping off her nose, swinging a stick in front of her like a cane. The grassy road bed ends abruptly on a knoll overlooking Fish Bay. Only a meager trail is visible, leading southeast, away from my destination.

The terrain has become hotter, sunnier, drier, and still there are no ruins. No spiders for a while, either, but I can't be sure so I continue fishing with my stick. Now parts of the trail appear recently plowed up, a sure sign of wild pigs. They're searching for tasty roots to eat. According to Rafe Boulon at the National Park office, when domestic hogs become feral, they revert to the wild state within a couple of generations, growing course, red hair and long, sharp tusks. I remember the spring day in northern Idaho when, as a toddler, a giant sow grabbed my coat and attempted to drag me through the pole fence into its pen. My father hit the sow's nose with a stick and my mother pulled me back, and the pig stood staring at me with a piece of my coat in her mouth.

Yes, I will grope forward. It's time to foster open spaces in my thinking. Maybe when I finally find the ocean I'll flag down a boat and hitch a ride out. Yes, this is the answer. I'll escape my current situation, change my name, start a new life. This won't be a vacation; this will be a disappearance. Thanks to the camouflage of my ordinary appearance and my age, it should be easy to inhabit a brand-new milieu. I'll take on a new identity. Establish my own witless relocation program. Problems solved.

Alerting the pigs to my presence, I yell, "Honey, I'm home!" Funny how not one of my husbands ever hollered this greeting from the 1950s television show *Father Knows Best*. And my own father didn't act like the one in the show, either. One time he came home from the taverns, growling and scratching on our front door, wearing a bear skin. And now my husband wants to dress like The Little Mrs. in that TV show, and not the father.

While thinking of fathers, bear skins and husbands, I remember all the times I hiked in grizzly country back in Montana and how I always clapped my hands to announce myself. It isn't good to surprise a grizzly. And it probably isn't smart to catch a wild pig off guard, either. But I can't clap my hands now because I'm still casting for spiders. Instead, I talk out loud to the pigs. "You know, I'll be attending my fortieth high school reunion, and way before my time, too. What a surprise. I didn't realize how old I was until that invitation showed up. The thing should have come decorated with a black border."

Really, it's diabolical. I eat breakfast, push back my cuticles, and the next thing you know I'm staring down sixty.

While conversing with the invisible pigs, the trail becomes narrower, and now it's rocky and steep. What's left of a trail is held up by remnants of a rock retaining wall. And all around me, rocks and dirt are freshly churned up by the wild pigs. I yell out, "Are you big and dirty, snarling and slobbery? Do you have an overbite and tusks? Will you run at me, hoping I'll throw down my pack? If I hit you on the nose with my stick, will you leave me alone?"

Only when I stop addressing the pigs do I notice that the trail has disappeared into a wall of thick vegetation. And while I can't see the ocean, I hear waves washing on the shore below in a crescendo of soothing music. I duck down to scoot under low branches and vines that grab my shirt and pull off my hat. Flailing at the vines with my spider stick I struggle free, and when I stand up I'm on a low ridge of pebbles at the edge of a beach. But this is not Fish Bay. This must be remote Genti Beach. And look! There's not one sailboat off shore to rescue me.

The Caribbean Sea shimmers in silver and aquamarine in the hot sunshine. Puffs of cumulus clouds move indolently in a sky of robin's egg blue. I throw down my pack and my spider stick, pull off my hiking shoes, socks, shirt and pants, and wade into the ocean, wearing only my white cotton granny panties. The sandy bottom tickles my feet while the waves wash against my legs, shoving me back toward shore. I laugh at my good fortune and wade further out, and when I picture myself on a tourist brochure standing half naked while facing the horizon, I laugh hysterically at the image and slap the water like a child. I never found the ruins, I have no idea how I'll get home, and I'm not where I expected to be at this moment, this month, or this year. But I am still alive and in this perfect, gleaming moment, I am young again.

THE HIGHEST IQ ON THE SEA FLOOR

"**W**ill you be wearing your half-slip while Doug is here?" I ask Tom.

"Probably not," he says.

My theory is that Tom's wearing of my black half-slip at home has become a habit. If he doesn't wear it for the two weeks Doug is here, my dim hope is that he'll give up wearing women's clothing and become interested in some new hobby.

My feelings of wanting to leave and never return persist, but now it's May and Tom's son, Doug, is coming to visit. In June, his youngest daughter, Ruth, graduates from high school and will come to see us. And then, too, we've agreed to house sit for Jan up at Villa Woodbine, at the top of the Mamey Peak road, for four months starting July 15. There are always so many reasons not to leave.

When Doug arrives from Montana, his response to the island is normal. First he begins to sweat profusely and rip off extra clothing, and second, he falls in love with St. John and wants to live here. By now, though, he's given up being a chef and is involved in a computer business. Doug is shorter, darker and stockier than his father. He looks a lot like the actor, Matt Damon, but I'm not sure he's aware of this. Anyway, he's busy being Doug—smart, quick, easy-going and fun.

The shop is still busy, as high season winds down, and it's a little stressful to take time off. But we're philosophical about the importance of being with family members. The first day Tom shows Doug around the island, they swim and snorkel at Salt Pond Bay out past Shipwreck Landing. For Tom's sixtieth birthday, which happens every year on Cinco de Mayo, I gift him and Doug with a day of sailing on *The Wayward Sailor* with Captain Phil.

After their sail, Tom and Doug stop at the shop to see me.

"We snorkeled and even did some free diving," Tom says. "A squid wasted ink on me."

"And we saw an octopus," Doug says. "Did you know they're like chameleons? When they're angry they can turn bright red. And they can look like a starfish. These guys have the highest IQ on the sea floor. Phil told us scientists have observed them in lab settings. One was caught unscrewing a lid on a Mason jar. It took him sixteen minutes to figure it out and then do it. After he did it four or five times, he got it down to five minutes. A second octopus watched the first octopus open the Mason jar, and it took him only ten minutes to open the jar the very first time."

"Yeah," Tom adds. "In this lab, they had an octopus in one tank and a bunch of shrimp in a tank across the room. The scientists had a surveillance camera on the lab at night. The octopus climbed out of his tank, made his way across the table, cleaned out the shrimp tank and then went back to his own tank."

Doug says, "We saw a juvenile damsel fish. It was bright indigo, a very intense color, with spots so white that it set up sort of an optical buzz."

My head is spinning with all the excitement and images. I'm thrilled they had such a good time.

To celebrate Tom's birthday and Doug's visit, we eat dinner at Morgan's Mango. Captain Phil joins us, and during dinner he regales us with stories. We learn, for instance, that he taught Lloyd Bridges to dive. He tells us he was diving in the Bahamas with a friend one time, when a huge shark, 12–15 feet long, chomped his friend and disappeared with him down deep. Phil saw the trail of blood. The guy was never seen again, but no one would believe a shark got him. In an insurance scam years before, the guy had faked his own death in order to collect $1 million, but he got caught. "Of course," Phil tells us, "I've told some of the same stories so often, embellishing the details each time, you know, and now I don't know for sure what really happened. But I'd swear in a court of law I told the truth."

On the island an experience can be so magical, so unique and special, that you know it will never happen again—and this evening is one of those times.

During Doug's visit, Tom and I often drive to the shop to work together in the mornings, and Tom drives home in the afternoon to do things with Doug. He leaves in three days. This morning we're at the shop only a few minutes when Tom receives a call and takes the cordless phone outdoors. When a family member calls we often do this. Sometimes it's quieter outside, if there aren't too many trucks on the road, and sometimes it's quieter inside—even with the fans, air conditioner and a sewing machine running.

It's Saturday, the day before Mother's Day, and we anticipate high sales. While Tom is on the phone, I get us set up for the day. A neighboring shopkeeper wanders in to say hello and leaves. A customer buys a plus size cap. And then Tom walks back into the shop, fighting back tears.

I will summarize the phone call that changed everything, the way phone calls and accidents can. Tom's youngest son, Matthew, 23, was accidentally shot and killed by his best friend. I'm unable to describe the shock and disbelief, so I won't try. We immediately close the shop and put a sign on the door: CLOSED DUE TO FAMILY EMERGENCY. We drive home, tears streaming down our faces, to tell Doug.

Arrangements are made for Tom to fly with Doug to Montana the next day. Tom will be gone for a week. All the kids, their mother, and one of Tom's brothers will gather for the funeral and I will stay here to keep the shop open. Matthew, such a fine young man, had just started a new job he liked and had been learning to fly. He was creative and always kind. Tom and Matthew had recently discussed his coming down for a visit. None of us can stop crying.

At the ferry dock the next morning, Tom parks the car. The ferry is due in a few minutes, so we leave my keys in the ignition. The plan is that I'll walk Tom and Doug to the ferry boat, return to the car, and drive to Mongoose Junction to the shop. But the ferry is late and I wait with them until the boat arrives to hug them both good-bye. When I return to the car the keys are gone from the ignition. An elderly West Indian man standing nearby says, "Your keys are at the police station with a couple of presents attached to 'em. You parked in da cross-walk."

If it's a cross-walk you'd never know it. The stripes are faded. And we've often seen cars parked in this spot. So I walk to the police station to explain what happened and to ask for the keys. A woman on the other side of a window tells me she doesn't know anything about my keys. She says there's an officer in a police car at the ferry dock now. I should walk there and ask the officer. Back at the ferry dock I find the police car, with a woman police officer sitting inside. The engine is running, the windows are up, and the air conditioner is on. I knock on the window and finally she rolls it down. I explain to her what happened. She rolls up her window and gets on the radio. I wait. It's scorching hot in the sun. She rolls down the window. "Sgt. Adder has your keys. He's somewhere on da islan'."

"If my car is in the way, I'd like to move it."

"You shoulda thought of dat 'fo you park it dere."

I stand near the car, baking in the sun, waiting. Finally the officer tells me I should walk back to the police station. When I arrive I sit inside, waiting for Sgt. Adder. At least it's cooler. I can't stop crying because Tom and Doug just left and Matthew is dead, and now I can't get my car keys. I wait for 15 minutes before Sgt. Adder struts into the station, jingling my keys back and forth by the foam turquoise shark on my key chain.

"Those keys look familiar," I say.

"Oh," he says, puffing himself up to strike. "Are these yours?"

I'm in trouble. I try to explain why the car was at the ferry, that one of our sons just got killed, that we didn't know it was a cross-walk because the stripes are so faded, that the ferry was delayed or I would have come right back to the car. I don't want him to think I'm crying because I got caught and I'm trying to cry my way out of it.

"Two offenses," he says, clearly enjoying his position of authority.

"You leave your keys in da car, next ting you know it stolen and den you report it to us."

"We don't lock our house, either," I sob. Why I say this, I'll never know.

"What you do at home is your own business, and if you gonna get all hysterical on me you can jes' go outside and calm down."

"I'm not crying because you have my keys," I state calmly. "One of our sons was just killed."

He rants on. "Den you park in da cross-walk for half an hour."

I'm smart enough not to correct him on the time. "If there's a fine I'll pay it and then I can move the car. I'm a good citizen."

He hands me the keys.

"Is there a fine?"

"No," he says, hands on his hips. "It's Mother's Day."

Feeling stomped flat, I walk like a robot to the car and drive to Mongoose Junction. Inside the shop I lock the doors behind me and pour myself a drink, grateful that Tom keeps a bottle of whiskey within reach at all times. Finally I try to sew, but when I sew a gusset on bass-ackward, I leave. Driving home along the North Shore, I am especially careful in case the police farce is now out to get me. I've heard the term DWW (driving while white) and thought it was a joke. Now I think otherwise.

Taking some respite from the grief and police harassment, I focus on the beauty all around me—the sky and popcorn clouds, the hibiscus and bougainvillea blooms near Peter Bay, the postcard view of Trunk Bay, the mirror flashes of ocean in the afternoon sun. And all those trees, their rootedness and timelessness, and how they serve as edge habitat for all the animals and people who love them. When I see a red-tailed hawk flying overhead, I am undone all over again.

At home my son calls. We commiserate, for he had liked Matthew very much. Then he says, "I feel odd telling you at a time like this, but we're pregnant. The baby is due at Christmas time."

AS FINE AS THE HAIR ON A FROG'S LEG

During this dreamlike state of sadness, as I drag my basket of grief through the days, a strange thing happens. Trees and everything about them offer me comfort. As a child, I spent a good part of every summer sitting up in a huge fir tree, feeling safe and happy. Now I see trees, as if for the first time, and how their roots anchor them solidly to the earth, how their trunks reach up to touch the sky, how their branches draw strength from the weather and then hold fast in a storm.

The island is once again in the beginning stages of a drought. Because the soil is porous, minor bursts of rain that fall drains away quickly, leaving thirsty tree roots. Leaves, even epiphytes, are drying up and falling to the ground. Each tree's essential truth is exposed, now, like their elegant branches, arching and swaying, and the strong lines of their trunks. Strangler figs are revealed for what they are, vines using the host tree in order to reach the sunlight above the canopy. A strangler fig can smother the life out of the support tree and then replace it. The thought occurs to me that when Tom returns, I must be careful not to absorb his grief on top of my own feelings of loss.

Before driving to work one day I walk up the Mamey Peak road to see Jan Frey at Woodbine and tell her what happened to Matthew. Recently a widow, she's familiar with grief and the importance of getting on with the details of living. She offers sympathy and gives me lady finger bananas and limes off her trees.

While showing me her new burnished steel kitchen appliances, she says, "Yesterday I found a tarantula in a corner, the poor dusty thing. I picked it up and carried it outdoors."

"You touched it?" I ask.

"Oh, course," she says. "They don't bite."

I tell her about my old friend, Thelma, the tarantula in my door at the chicken coop, and confess my arachnophobia. We talk about large spiders, then, and the things we know and don't know about them. For instance, we wonder if Thelma is still alive. After all, they can live 20 years and travel long distances. And do tarantulas all look alike to each other, the way they do to us? Do they feel sad when a loved one dies?

I'm sewing as fast as I can to keep the shop from looking totally bare-naked, while thinking about how the law of attraction fits with the death of a beloved person. If we get what we think about and create our own realities, I'm confused. I've worked hard on my attitude, on getting my happy valve to open a little. Now I fear my valve has slammed shut so hard it will take Liquid Wrench to get it open again.

A woman strolls in humming, lifting up bags, trying on one after another, looking at herself in the mirror, her image looking back at her from under the *Objects in mirror* sign.

"How are you today?" I ask.

She turns, smiles at me, and says, "Well, I'm as fine as the hair on a frog's leg."

And for some reason that makes me want to cry, but I suppress it as she hums her way in a circle around the small display area of the shop. She selects a navy classic purse with a lizard embroidered on a bright green pocket. She is so pleasant and cheerful that by the time we're finished with the transaction I feel better. For the rest of the afternoon I think about frogs, wondering if they really do have fine hairs on their legs. Tom will know; I'll google him. He's faster than the Internet.

But when he calls, of course, there's no talk of the hair on a frog's leg. He tells me that over 300 people attended Matthew's funeral, that his flight instructor arranged a flyover complete with wing-dips. No one, least of all family members, knew how many people Matthew had touched in his quiet, kind-hearted, good-natured way. It's like we thought he'd always be around, that we'd catch up with him sometime later and get more involved in his life.

Alyce, a sassy blond island resident, stops by the shop to offer her condolences. She'd had a ladies' night at their villa, Plumeria, one night when it wasn't rented out, and I had missed the party. She jokes about a discussion that took place that night in her kitchen. Present were 1) herself, owner of Plumeria but living down the hill in a construction trailer with a Cadillac convertible parked out front with a flat tire; 2) a woman with a new villa at Peter Bay whose construction costs had gone $1.5 million over the estimate. Their current short-term renters don't want her and her husband to stay in the guest house on the property, so they're staying at the Marriott on St. Thomas; and 3) another woman who is living in a concrete storage bunker next to their cistern, while the rest of their villa is being built; and 4) a new nurse at Myrah Keating Clinic who is living somewhere on island in an eco-tent.

Alyce says, "The good news is that real estate values are booming, and someday we'll all enjoy a healthy return on our investments."

"I can only hope our lot is gaining in value," I say. "That would reverse our habit of buying high and selling low."

When Tom returns from Montana, he's wearing earrings, one in each ear. His youngest daughter, Ruth, had encouraged him to get both ears pierced, although she knows nothing of her father's interest in dressing like a woman. I don't like it that he now wears two earrings. His hair has grown to the length of my short haircut. I have a sinking feeling that both his hair and his earrings will keep getting longer and longer. Oddly, the more feminine he becomes, the more gender-neutral I feel.

Tom stays home for a few days. I wish he could take several weeks off, but this is still high season. The shop is usually open seven days a week until August, but we close this Sunday because I need a day off and we don't want to be around other people. We drive to the East End, park at the trailhead for Brown's Bay, and hike the two miles to the shore. We meet a couple walking out but when we reach the bay, no one else is there. The usual piles of cast-off clothing are strewn around from the illegal immigrants who have landed here. While Tom swims and snorkels, I splash a little and search the beach for sea glass without success, then pick up trash to carry out in a bag I brought along for that purpose.

Tom and I don't talk much, preferring instead to be alone with our thoughts. After hiking out to the car past bare trees and twenty-foot tall stalks of century plants, we drive to Shipwreck Landing for lunch, our teeth rattling as we bounce over the rough road.

After finally getting our food and eating, Tom wants to snorkel and free-dive some more, so we drive back out the East End to Haulover Bay. I spray DEET all over myself and sit in the shade on the beach, watching as Tom places a two-pound weight in his Speedos next to his magic parts. With this additional weight, he can descend below the surface of the salt water and do some free-diving, like he and Doug did with Captain Phil. I look up every now and then from the book I'm reading to watch Tom snorkeling, a wake of sadness behind him in spite of his efforts at distraction. Suddenly I find it hard to breathe. Seeking solace, I look up into the branches of the tree overhead and feel somewhat sheltered. A bananaquit flies out from the branches and soon returns, and I listen for the whisper of her wings, but hear nothing. Grief is like that. It rises and falls, but one day I know from other devastating losses that a shift will happen and when it does, I'll once again be able to hear the soft voice of bird wings.

Back on our morning schedule, we agree to leave Villa Debris at 7:00 a.m. to drive down the steep North Shore Road to one of the beaches. We'll walk and swim before driving to work. But Tom is still on my computer.

"You ready to leave?" I ask.

"In a minute," he says. "I'm posting a message on the Tri-Ess forum about the non-dominance of men over women. It's an issue for some members."

"What's the issue, exactly?"

"The need to dominate their wives."

"Oh, really?" This could turn into a discussion that would wake the neighbors, except I'd really rather go to the beach.

Finally at Big Maho Bay we park and walk across the road onto the sand. As usual the sand hugs my feet, and grains of sand squish up between my toes.

Tom says, "Look!" He points to the far end of the beach. A fiberglass dinghy is lying upside down with its engine bobbing in the salt water. Sprawled nearby on the wet sand is a large bloated man. At first we think he's dead, but then he curls onto his side in a fetal position.

"It's not good for his engine to be in the salt water like that," Tom says.

"Maybe when he comes to, he won't know where he is."

"Must have been one wild night at Fred's."

"At least he isn't trying to dominate his spouse."

"That's for sure."

While Tom does his 200-meter sprints on the road, I float on my back watching the sky, the clouds, the pelicans and the magnificent frigate birds. I'm reminded how affirming it is to be in the ocean and how perfect the water temperature is in early summer. Sometimes I'll be floating happily on the ocean and the next second I'll be crying about Matthew. It happens again this morning.

When we leave, the man at the far end of the beach is still asleep near his dinghy. As we grind back up the steep hill in low, the moist island air blows in on us, at its most perfect temperature. Once we reach Villa Debris, I hesitate for a moment before putting on my flip-flops.

"Darn!" I say. "There's still sand between my toes."

Tom, the big *galootimus maximus*, scoops me up and carries me from the car to the porch. He sets me down gently, takes each foot, one at a time in both hands, and tenderly brushes the sand off my feet, attending carefully to the spaces between my toes.

BEWARE OF *THE* SH*IT* WEASELS

*I*n the heat of July at my fortieth high school reunion in Priest River, Idaho, I'm the only one wearing mango-peach Sloop Jones rompers that could, with something akin to chic, hide a sack of potatoes. And, after reading that Preparation H reduces the bags under your eyes, I'm also wearing a smear or two of that. A former male classmate looks me up and down and announces, "You're the youngest-looking person here."

"Why, thank you," I say. "And I forgive you for pushing me off the monkey bars that time in third grade."

What a great bunch of kids I went to school with. Fifty of us graduated together, and most of us were classmates the entire 12 years. We all joke about life in high school, how the town kids differed from the country kids. I think about what a bumpkin I was, living on the periphery of a full life. I'm stunned at the realization that my life still feels like that. Sure, I'm doing life in paradise, and I co-own a business where the world beats a pathway to my door. To some members of the class of '63, I suppose my life even appears glamorous. But they don't know, for instance, that my husband likes to sleep in a negligee. Nor do I tell anyone I slept on the floor of the Seattle-Tacoma Airport near baggage claim, because I couldn't afford the only motel room available that night, and that, furthermore, I felt noble while enduring the discomfort. Some patterns are hard to break.

When I arrive back on St. John in mid-August, I'm standing at the ferry dock in a cloud of mosquitoes when Tom arrives to pick me up. His dangly earrings flash in the late afternoon sunlight. And the trade winds are messing with his new mop-length hairdo, causing him to look like Max Ernst, the surrealist painter. And his fingernails and toenails are now painted a glittery blush color. No matter. I'm happy to be back.

The hurricane shutters are already up for the season at Villa Debris, making it dark and unpleasant. So I stay at Woodbine with Tom and the cats, where Tom will be housesitting for two more months while Jan is at her place in Montana. Tom's been sleeping in a twin bed in the main house and wants to continue sleeping alone, so I sleep in a separate pod, upstairs in a king-sized bed. None of this is a problem for me. Besides, Tom, wearing his black half-slip, comes to lie with me and talk a while before going to his own bedroom. It's a friendly arrangement.

After he leaves my bed, I pet Lucky and I look out the wall of windows at the stars, thinking how my life is like a television sitcom or an *un*reality show. It's as if Tom and I are the only survivors of a natural disaster, and we stay together because of the dangers we've shared. And the humor. Besides that, during our first few years we hiked, backpacked, sketched, read books together, started writing a novel, and finished the inside of the brothel. It's sad to think that now about the only thing we have in common, besides memories, is our dislike of President George W. Bush.

Directly overhead is a gauzy white tarantula nest, right where the teak rafters come together like the spokes of a wagon wheel. Even though I'm a tarantula enthusiast of sorts, I don't want one *on* me. This tarantula could lose its footing and fall on my face. And in the night that's exactly what happens. Or I'm convinced it does. It's all the same difference, in terms of needing an adult diaper. However, the object turns out to be one of my earplugs. They're always slipping out of my ears and giving me a fright.

The shop is closed on Sundays this time of year. On this first Sunday after I return home, Tom and I drive early in the morning down to Maho Bay. Tom race-walks on the road while I swim, and this morning when he's finished he walks onto the beach, pulls down his shorts, and moons me. No one else is on the beach, and only a few sailboats are anchored in the bay. Probably no one but me caught sight of Tom's bony hinder.

Tom likes to watch reruns of the TV show *West Wing* every night. His bachelor's degree is in both political science and history, and he served those two terms as a Republican legislator in Montana. This show serves as his political fix. The acoustics in the cavernous great room require that he turn the volume up LOUD, and his ear phones do not work with this TV. Because of this, I leave every evening after dinner and walk the half-mile down the road to Villa Debris, to watch videos of my own choosing. I'm into *Lonesome Dove*, which takes several evenings. Sometimes while I'm watching a show, Inkie will show up all the way from Woodbine. What a surprise, since he's such a scaredy-cat and there's a big island mutt between here and there.

One night before walking back up the hill to Woodbine to sleep, I call to Inkie, to see if he followed me to Villa Debris. But I don't see him. I have a flashlight, but prefer to make my way in the dark. After all, there's nothing to be afraid of. So I'm walking along when, suddenly, I hear a soft snapping of brush off to the side of the road in the dense vegetation. I turn the flashlight on and shine it in the direction of the sound. What I see is utterly astonishing, a sight so beautiful, so elusive that hardly anyone ever gets to see it: a night-blooming cereus as big as a dinner plate, white like a huge chrysanthemum. I am blessed. But the voodoo question remains: what made the sound that brought my attention to this rare, extravagant flower?

Between five and six o'clock every morning I wake up and look out the front windows at the cloud pictures, the art gallery images of dark blue grays, pastel hues, and the distant islands beyond Coral Bay. Waking up to this view, from an even higher vantage point than that of Villa Debris, is almost as magical as seeing the night-blooming cereus.

When Tom isn't downloading updates on the computer, he's communicating online with fellow Tri-Ess members. Or he's ordering frilly items from eBay. But lately he's also tracking storms, which is how we learn that Hurricane Fabian will probably miss us. One day the program shows a possible collision between Hurricanes Henry and Fabian out in the Atlantic. When this happens, do they destroy each other like asteroids? In the end, the hurricanes do not collide. What happens, though, is that Hurricane Fabian changes direction and Bermuda takes it in the shorts.

Another morning Tom reports that a tropical storm named Isabel is forming 600 miles west of the Cape Verde Islands. It's headed right for us. Tracking this storm keeps him occupied every morning and night. Next he announces that Isabel is expected to hurl itself clockwise 200 miles to the north of us. This sounds like no big deal, but then he says the tracking error can be 200 miles off. In other words, we'd better hustle our buns. At Villa Debris we stack all loose items on the bed, wrap it all up in a blue tarp, and secure it with clothesline rope. And then we high-tail it up the road to Woodbine, with its massive yet easy-to-install hurricane shutters and thick concrete and stone walls. The island shuts down. Ferries and barges get tethered to docks. Shops and services close.

When Isabel arrives, she's a monster with an eye the size of Death Valley. The sky is milky, as the peripheral nebula of this giant white vulture brushes the island. Once in a while we peek out, but mostly we stay indoors, where it is eerily quiet except for the ice maker, the wind and rain, and the sound of a dead tree blowing down in the yard.

Very quickly the island returns to its laid back, off-season torpor, as if a hurricane scare is nothing. I work at the shop. Sometimes I write on my next novel at Woodbine. We eat good dinners together, prepared in the gourmet kitchen. I watch videos at Villa Debris. Tom watches TV at Woodbine and surfs the Web. And I do all of this in various states of physical discomfort, until one day I remember to go to see Bern for a tune-up. Why, I wonder, do I wait so long?

Before my appointment, I was going downhill fast. I was going to have to put myself out of my misery. From now on, I'll to go see him every two weeks, on the same schedule as I apply my mustache-remover cream. I write this decision in my journal, which prompts me to get up and apply the cream. When I do this, I look down to the deck and see Tom sitting in the morning sun with his coffee, wearing his pink, knee-length negligee. Usually when he hears me open my bedroom door upstairs in the pod, he hurries into his bedroom to change into his black half-slip. Now that I've seen him dressed like this, a light switch flips off inside my chest. For me, this moment signals the end of our relationship as a couple. And at the same odd moment, I realize I love him no less than before. But now the *kind* of love is different. But, then, neither of us has a libido to speak of anyway, and by now those sex toys are probably all moldy.

That night I dream I'm alone on a bicycle, towing some unknown items behind me in a two-wheeled cart. On a lonely road on the outskirts of a town, I have a general idea of my destination, but that's all. And now the sky is turning dark and the wind is kicking up. Soon it will start raining, and I think, *Oh, well, I can always call Tom to come and get me.* When I wake up and lie in bed pondering my dream, I realize I've always had this built-in notion of *husband as umbrella, husband as safety net.* The idea of living in the world with a bigger, stronger, smarter person's arm around my shoulder—a *man's* arm—is a desirable, if sentimental, notion. This could, I suppose, be blamed on that aforementioned 1950s TV show, *Father Knows Best.* And now I have to put my old notion in the context of seeing Tom in a negligee.

While working at the shop, Tom is listening to the Stephen King story, *Dreamcatcher,* a horror story populated with alien creatures called shit weasels. One day when I call him, he picks up the phone and says nothing. Did I get the wrong number? Finally he says "The Canvas Factory?" as if he's asking me.

"I forgot where I was," he admits.

"That's okay," I say. "I forgot why I called you."

That evening when he arrives home at Woodbine and gets out of the car, a huge brown curled leaf falls on his head. He slaps it away, horrified, convinced that he's the latest victim of the shit weasels.

Another day when I call Tom at the shop, he's in an especially good mood. He says, "Remember that customer you googled, the guy that was one of *People* magazine's most beautiful people in the world?"

"Oh, yeah!" I say.

"Well, he came in and noticed my pedicure, said he really liked it."

"Oh, so you had a good exchange."

"Well, it *was* nice to have someone notice my pedicure."

"He's probably a metro-sexual," I say. "I just read about them in *Time* magazine. They're hetero men who aren't afraid to wear earrings, get manicures and pedicures, and cry at weddings. Maybe that's what you are, a metro-sexual."

"Might be. Just think of it. For once I'm on the cutting edge of a trend."

"Keep in mind," I say. "There's no need to over-achieve."

"No possibility of that. With this thing, I'm just flying by the seat of my panties."

And I think, pay attention, Rae Ellen. He said panties and not Manties.

In early October, while the island is under a Bermuda high with an unusually clear sky, I begin a housesitting gig of my own. *My* villa is the one on the hill above Mongoose Junction, with the two cats, the guppies, the swimming pool and hot tub to take care of. There's plenty of time to read their *Wired* magazines and take dips in the pool and hot tub. This is the life.

On the days Tom drives in to work at the shop, he usually gives me a ride up the hill after work. We sit on the small deck perched in the sky and watch the sunset. It's like this is my house and he's courting me. If I ignore his two dangly earrings, he's still handsome, charming and fun. Anyone might fall for him, at least until he reveals his choice of sleepwear. Yes, housesitting separate villas is a fine way to conduct a relationship.

On one such evening, Tom tells me to stop by the next day at R & I Patton Goldsmiths in Mongoose Junction. They're holding a package with my name on it. When I retrieve the item, it's a gold starfish and chain. The manager who hands me the little box says, "You'd better hang onto that guy." Later Tom tells me he gave me the starfish and chain because he knows I like gold. He just felt like doing it. He's even cut down on his alcohol consumption. Is he trying to be especially nice to me so I'll accept his second self? And as we celebrate the miracle of our tenth anniversary, I find myself still hoping we might have a future together.

Another evening while we sit on the little deck, he says, "You are such a wonderful person. I'm so lucky. I really love you."

"Wow. Thank you." What I'm thinking is, good grief, now what's he up to? I've made progress at focusing on the positive, but I'm still wearing my hide-and-watch attitude. And because he keeps changing, I've always felt a little off-guard. Now I'm waiting for the other high-heel to drop. And he continues to be unpredictable. One week he'll be adamantly opposed to something, and the next week he'll act like it doesn't matter at all. It's like being married to the mob.

"I mean it," he says. "And I know you don't think so, but you're beautiful."

"I love you, too," I say. "I don't know what I'd do without our joking and talking."

We clink our glasses together and salute the sunset.

CATCH THE COWGIRL SPIRIT

One day the owners of both villas return to the island at the same time, and Tom and I return to Villa Debris—surrounded by our belongings in plastic bags, tote bags, cardboard boxes, and duffels—abruptly and rudely thrown together full-time again.

With the hurricane panels covering the windows, the living room is like a cave. After the neighbor guys help us remove them, the living room is so bright I have to wear sunglasses. Tom says "Vitamin D is good for you." So on Sunday morning he washes his panties, not Manties, and hangs them on a clothesline he rigs up on the deck. Then he sits on the couch while not wearing sunglasses.

"So," I say, looking up from my computer, "what do you want to do today?"

"Oh, I think I'll just sit here and watch my panties dry."

He's been out of sorts since moving back home. I think he loved being queen for a day at spacious, elegant Villa Woodbine, where he could wear his negligee to bed every night. Now I won't sleep with him wearing anything more feminine than the black half-slip. He could, of course, sleep downstairs in the office/guest room. But it's a moldy, termite-infested room, best used only for conducting gender research on the Internet and shopping on eBay. And that room is closest to the road, which now sounds like a monster truck rally thanks to the real estate boom and the increased construction traffic. Up at Woodbine, it was quiet.

Finally Tom gathers himself into a standing position and goes downstairs to install a new hard drive and modem on his computer. Doug has started his own computer shop and is now our personal tech guru. Tom finishes assembling his computer and comes back upstairs to sit on the couch and watch football, muted, since I can't tolerate the sound. If I weren't here, I know he'd turn the volume up and watch the game wearing a dress. Part of me still hopes this cross-dressing thing is a passing fancy, although it's been going on for over a year, with no signs of abating. In fact, his hair is growing longer every day and so are his earrings. Soft packages containing frilly items arrive on a weekly basis.

It's high time I bought something for myself, and I don't mean some measly item that's "practically free" from eBay. One early November day I wander around Cruz Bay looking for a used rental car, since this is the month the agencies import new cars. No bucket of bolts for me. I've heard about the dangers of rust on older vehicles. For instance, one day a woman living up the hill from us was driving down the steepest part of Mamey Peak road in an older pickup truck, on her way to meet a guest at the ferry dock. When she made a tight turn, the bench seat she was sitting on came loose and slid forward. She lost her footing on the pedals, but hung onto the steering wheel. When her foot found a pedal again, she stepped on it, but it was the accelerator. The speeding truck attempted to climb the steep bank, and crashed over onto its side. Being a hardy long-time island resident, she climbed out the only open window, walked back up the hill to her house, and took a different vehicle to town in time to meet the ferry. Later we heard that the metal and bolt assembly that holds the seat down had rusted all the way through.

To keep out the rain and chickens, my car will have windows that roll up. A four-door vehicle is convenient for picking up hitchhikers. And four-wheel drive will get me up the S curves by Trunk Bay on the North Shore Road, even on island ice. After kicking tires for a few days, I score a 1998 Suzuki Sidekick hardtop meeting all requirements. This is a navy blue unit with air-conditioning. We can't afford a second car, of course, but I blow a small savings account and round up the balance on a signature loan at my Montana credit union. Tom registers the car using his Old Fart Card (once you're 60 years old in the USVI, this card gives you a discount on ferry rides and vehicle registration fees). We're done with the paperwork by 9:30, in time for work.

When I park the car at Mongoose Junction I apply a yellow bumper sticker from the Cowgirl Museum in Fort Worth. On an island of cars decorated with bumper stickers, mine is the only one with the decal, CATCH THE COWGIRL SPIRIT. A favorite quote, by Patty Carey, a rodeo rider early in the twentieth century, is "I plan on growing old much later in life, or maybe not at all." My purple cowgirl shirt with the red boots on it is finally properly accessorized. Boy howdy!

Our new couch is not off eBay, either. It's a gift from Jan, owner of Woodbine, who recently bought all new furniture. The arm rests are wicker, but because the rest of it weighs almost as much as a car, the two young neighbor guys help us move it into our living room. In addition to the couch being long, the cushions hug you when you sit down. The couch has other unique properties. If you stand within ten feet of it, which is almost anywhere in our great room, the couch reaches out for you with a strong magnetic pull. I can often resist the pull only because Tom and the cats are already reclining on it. By 8:00 p.m. or so, they're already asleep with the TV on.

One night Tom is watching the Democratic president on *West Wing* ride herd on the affairs of the country. One of the lead actresses says, "Well, you know that one in forty men is a cross-dresser, so probably at least one of the former presidents roamed the halls of the White House wearing a prom dress." The topic is hard to escape.

I'm a slut when it comes to someone with a good sense of humor. And while I'm not normally competitive, I always try to score a good line before Tom thinks of it. Since I met him 11 years ago, he's loosened up enough so that no subject is taboo. In fact, the cruder the better. We're as bad as teenage boys. For instance, Tom is skilled at smashing mosquitoes after they've bit him. Streaks of blood end up on everything, and certainly on the bed sheets.

We're in the bedroom getting dressed one morning, and as Tom pulls on a pair of lacy panties, I notice a smear of blood on the bottom sheet of the unmade bed. I say, "Looks like you started your period."

"Good one," Tom says, catching his breath from laughing.

As high season approaches, we resume working together most days to build up our inventory. One day while I'm cutting crop and Tom is sewing on Big Dorothy, I say, "I think you should tell your children and your brothers about your real identity. It's a good opportunity to educate them about this thing you've been calling gender dysphoria. For the kids, this might help offset the fundamentalist views you raised them with."

"I'm thinking about it."

"Okay. I have a question, so get ready," I say. "You've read that this gender issue got started when you were a baby, still *in utero*. I'm not sure how to ask this without making a statement first, so here goes. Throughout history women have prettied themselves up to attract the opposite sex. So, do you have a secret desire to be seduced by a big strong man?"

"Absolutely not. That's homosexual. That's not me."

"Oh, okay. And another thing I've been wondering. On the Tri-Ess forum, do the single men discuss what happens when they date and find a new girlfriend?"

"Sometimes."

"And how does it go when they tell the new girlfriend about their cross-dressing?"

"It's usually all right, once it's explained. It all depends on how open-minded, intelligent and tolerant the girlfriend is."

"Yeah, right."

"No, really."

"And the married ones? What if the man was unhappy about suppressing his second self for years and years? Maybe his behavior hadn't been too shiny, so by the time his obsession with cross-dressing pops up, it's the final straw."

"There's something to that," Tom says, topstitching a tan and black classic purse. "The profile of those men is that they seek macho jobs, like the military, and are probably bullies or verbal bashers."

"Oh, and they dominate their spouses?" I try but fail to keep sarcasm out of my voice. Actually, I'm glad to know that when I catch the cowgirl spirit and disappear into the sunset, his next woman will be totally accepting of his second self, if only she's sufficiently intelligent and open-minded.

STICK OUT YOUR TONGUE

Our vet tells our cats that she's their Aunt Jan. She and her husband are building a house down the hill from Villa Woodbine, and they invite us to a party to celebrate the progress on their house. Their walls are now up. During construction, they're living on the property in a tiny but air-conditioned shed attached to a shipping container. Their temporary abode has everything they need, all arranged precisely, like in an RV or a boat. At the party there are dozens of people, almost all of them new to us, since we don't get out much. One woman talks about her bad neck and how she finds relief from an Oriental physician-acupuncturist who visits the island from St. Thomas a couple times a week. Then the subject of hypnotherapy comes up, as it often does on the island, and one man asks, "Why only past life regressions? Why not future life progressions, to learn what's ahead, to see who you'll become next?" This is a good question for Lucy.

When I arrive at my appointment with the acupuncturist at her office, she doesn't ask me what's wrong. She says, "Stick out your tongue."

I do as I'm told.

She shakes her head and says, "Not good."

"What?"

"Liver is bad. Hormones out of balance. Not good energy. Are you tired? You carry your stress in your back. Your muscles are very tight." She shakes her head again.

I'm ashamed of my tongue and my lack of self care.

"And you're angry. You must let go some more of past."

"Plus my right hand is numb," I say, "and my lower back hurts." She might's well know.

"I help you."

She has me lie on my stomach on an elevated table.

"No more alcohol," she says, poking a needle into my lower back.

"Ow."

"No more caffeine."

"Double ow."

"And no walking up and down hills. Bad for back. Walk on flat and walk in ocean. Ocean will heal you. You feel better with not many treatments."

When she's done totally amending my life, and I look like a human pin cushion, she leaves the room. My exposed left thigh suddenly itches. Is that a needle or a mosquito bite? I don't scratch it. She finally returns to add more needles and mild electrical stimulation to my lower back, and leaves the room again. Later she removes the needles and has me turn over. She pokes needles in my numb arm and hand and a couple in my feet.

I leave her office with a box of green tea and some Chinese herb pills. And I'm curiously relaxed while driving home. My lower back doesn't hurt and I have greater mobility in my neck. That night I sleep soundly, so I'm inclined to follow her advice. Drinking green tea instead of coffee grieves me, especially since the green tea smells like horse pee and threatens to diminish my cowgirl spirit. The "no coffee" rule lasts until a splitting headache wrecks my resolve about 10:00 a.m.

The next week, I find myself lying on her table again. I say, "I walked in the ocean with barracudas." I did, too, although they were only two feet long.

"This is good."

She pokes a needle into my forehead.

"Ow," I say. "You didn't do that last time."

"Is for clarity," she says. "Your third eye."

"Will it help me be more creative?"

"Yes," she says, poking a needle into my elbow.

On my next visit to the acupuncturist, when she pokes a needle in my third eye, I weep about Matthew. After a few minutes the sadness goes away. At the end of the session she asks to see my tongue. I'm a little worried that she'll know I ate a cookie and had coffee earlier, but she's very pleased. "Toxins have left your body. It is good to cry."

Acupuncture isn't the cure-all I had hoped it would be, and a couple mornings later my right hand and arm are so numb, it's as if I'm missing that limb. It's December and high season now, and I'm more angst-ridden than ever. But when I next visit the acupuncturist she tells me, "Much better energy. You graduate." She doesn't even look at my tongue. She wants me to return in three weeks. In the meantime, I'm to drink more green tea for my gastro-intestinal issues.

"Stop worrying," she says. "It doesn't change anything. You worry but everything still same. No good."

When I return in three weeks, I cry again. And when I leave her temporary office in town I'm so relaxed I float down the hill like fog, wondering if I'm capable of driving home. When I approach the main street near Nature's Nook, where I'll cross the busy street to reach the sidewalk, Lindy comes walking down the middle of the street. He's holding a can of beer, looking like a skeleton wearing rags. Laughing to himself, mostly toothless, he puts one stick leg in front of the other as he makes his way. I slow my pace so I won't collide with him, and at one point we're within about four feet of each other. He doesn't appear to see me, and as he passes in front of me he stops suddenly, sneezes, and sprays beer and spit all over my skirt and on my left foot. It's one of those startling time-lapse moments when even the traffic stops. I stand, as if frozen. Horns honk. Lindy recovers and jerks forward, never once noticing that I exist. I dart across the street where Angelo, who works for Glen at Mongoose Junction, is standing.

"Lindy just sneezed beer on my foot, Ange!"

"I saw that," he says. "What, so now you think your toenails will fall off?"

A downpour began in early November 2003—too early to qualify as the Christmas Rains. The sky usually spits a little rain every day, unless we're in one of our drought cycles. But this time it doesn't stop, and the sky stays gray like a Bellingham winter. At Villa Debris, torrents of water run down our window walls. On the Centerline Road, waterfalls tumble off rock cuts. Rocks the size of cars slide downhill accompanied by mud and downed trees. The electricity goes off and on, and then stays off for hours.

During one of these outages, I cook tofu stir fry on our gas stove for dinner by lamplight. We know that Jan at Woodbine cooks with electricity and might get hungry, so Tom drives up the road to fetch her for dinner at our place. He returns with Jan and her neighbor, Craig, who is wearing a wetsuit and a headlamp, looking like the creature from the black lagoon. So we all eat tofu stir fry cooked with gas. We trade stories and lies while the rain runs in sheets down the windows, and our cistern overflow pipe splashes water down the hill toward the Centerline Road.

The next night the lights stay on, the neighbors stay home, and we sit together on the couch—husband, wife, and the three fur children—watching a TV show on the string theory. Before you can say *quantum mechanics,* the couch has sucked us down, down, down by invisible means into another dimension, and we're all asleep.

The rain continues. Mold decorates every surface. The roof above the bed springs a leak on Tom's side, right over his pillow. We set a lasagna pan lined with a towel on the spot. Tom crashes on the couch and I sleep alone, hugging my heating pad on low because it's freezing, probably down to 70 degrees. A few nights later, it's still raining, although the leak mysteriously stops.

Every morning we wonder if we'll be able to get to Cruz Bay to the shop. We can take either the North Shore Road or the Centerline Road, and both routes could be blocked by slides. Even if we can get to town, will we have electricity? There aren't many customers, and the phone has been silent. At home, we can't connect to the Internet.

Island ice is rampant. And this particular morning someone is gunning their engine, trying to force their vehicle up the slippery Mamey Peak road. They make a run at it over and over, tires spinning. We smell burned rubber.

"Must have bald tires," Tom says, eating his customary bacon and eggs for breakfast.

"And no four-wheel drive, either," I say, before taking a bite of bran cereal.

We listen as the driver makes repeated attempts to make it up the first slippery slope. Suddenly the engine noise stops and we hear yelling. Tom changes out of his half-slip into a pair of shorts, and we trot down the road in the rain to see what's happening. Down by the Dumpster sits an old island pickup, engulfed in flames. The driver owns the house up the road that slid downhill during the spring rains. By now several people from the neighborhood are standing with the woman. She relates that when the cab filled with smoke, she let her truck roll back down the hill, and leaped out just as the engine caught fire. We watch the blue-gray smoke and flames as we wait for the fire truck to come from Coral Bay. One by one the truck's tires explode.

"My purse is in there," she says, groaning. "Along with all the cash to pay the carpenters. It's all gone."

Someone driving past on the Centerline Road stops and asks, "Whose truck is it?"

"It's mine," the woman answers. "Just call me Shit-For-Luck."

Besides the usual condolences, what is there to say? To make matters worse, mosquitoes swarm us. They're flourishing on schedule—two weeks after the initial deluge started. So I walk home to get the insect repellant. When I return I offer it to the woman first.

The rain continues. Cisterns overflow, mold grows behind our ears and between our toes. And the shop floor floods. No environmentally-responsible cotton canvas goods are damaged, however, thanks to the wonders of plastic storage bins. At a time when we usually receive calls for Christmas orders, the phone at the shop stays silent. We take this opportunity to raise the prices on our best-selling bags.

By the time December arrives, the island has received 21 inches of rain, with 19 of those inches falling in 7 days. Damage to the island is estimated at $6 million, mostly to the infrastructure that was failing anyway. Ailments to my own infrastructure reappear as I work harder, faster, longer as required when high season arrives. The phone remains dead, with no promises of repair from the phone company, so we run credit cards by the old clunker method. Fortunately, we learn we can use the credit card machine and the home phone to enter the receipts. This energizes our bank account in time to avoid a disaster.

And then Tom keels over with a ferocious cold, the worst he's ever had. But because we're so busy he keeps working. Two women who live on the mainland but own a villa on island stop by the shop. We're on hugging terms. When they see that Tom has a bad cold, one of the women, a retired physician, says to Tom, "Oh, you poor little boober."

Poor little boober's cold gets even worse. He stays home on the couch a couple days to sleep it off under a blanket with the cats. Hermon thoughtfully brings me leaves and twigs for black wattle tea to ease Tom's cold symptoms. This tastes all right if you put enough honey and lemon in it, but it doesn't make Tom feel any better.

I'm usually able to ward off a cold, but I take special precautions this time. We don't need a second poor little boober. I sleep in as late as I can in the mornings, take extra vitamin C, and work on my attitude. Maybe flirting with the law of attraction again will keep me from getting sick. And this time, too, I manage to skate, even though the glands in my throat swell up to the size of a pig's testicles.

My son calls from Montana. "We're all ready for the baby to arrive around Christmas," he says. "But I wish it would warm up. It's way below zero. I put in a fireplace insert to keep down the electric bill."

"It's not so hot here, either," I tell him. "Got down to seventy degrees the other night. I had to wear socks with my sandals, long pants and layers of shirts with sleeves. I hugged the heating pad."

"Real funny, Mom. I wish *we* had seventy degrees."

Jeff calls a couple days later. "I bought a chain saw and got a permit for firewood from the Forest Service," he says. "Drove up Magpie Gulch where that fire went through a few years ago. Cut down a dead tree and then I had to outrun it while it was falling.

"Jeff!"

"Don't worry, Mom. I'm careful."

On winter solstice, December 21, I take a needed day off to vacuum bug parts, wash windows, and debride the mold off another wall. The day is mostly sunny, so I arrange with Tom, who is back in the saddle at his sewing machine, to meet me after work at Skinny Legs in Coral Bay. Just after 5:00 p.m., I leave Villa Debris and walk down the dirt road, which is now mostly washed out. When I reach the flat part of the road, I practice the race walking technique Tom showed me. The goat herd race walks along with me on the other side of the fence. At Skinny Legs while I wait for Tom, I look through the baby clothes for sale with the Skinny Legs logo on the front. I decide to wait until the baby is born so I'll know what gender to buy for—will it be pink for a girl or blue for a boy? And then Tom arrives, wearing a sleeveless shirt, floral shorts with coordinating earrings and nail polish—all featuring some shade of pink.

TOUCH

On Jan. 3, 2004, my son calls from Montana to say they had a baby
girl and her name is Madison. "She's absolutely beautiful," my son
says. "She's a little doll."

I'm emotional at this news. I barely squeaked by with Jeff, and
now here's a granddaughter. How can I take on this new responsibility right now?

"Be sure to read aloud to the baby while Lee is nursing her," I tell
him. "That way she'll bond with your voice."

On the coldest day of an arctic Montana winter, at minus 30 degrees, they bring her home from the hospital. I ache to hold her. Jeff
emails photos of the new baby at the hospital, including one of him
giving Madison her first bath in a big shallow sink. In another photo
she's lying on a quilt made by her *other* grandmother, who is lucky
enough to live nearby. Madison is frowning in the cutest I've-got-an-
attitude way that makes me proud.

Tom says, "I think you should attend the Whidbey Island Writers'
Conference in March. You can also go to Montana to see the baby, too.
I'll pay your way."

What can I say? I'm confused. He receives a small National Guard
retirement check every month that he uses for manicures, pedicures,
wardrobe items off eBay, alcohol, and some deep sea diving he did for
a while, until he injured his ear on a dive. We're just getting into high
season, so that should boost sales. But we still need an employee, and
they aren't cheap. March is the busiest month of the year, a time when
it's not smart to be gone for ten days. But I want to go to this writing
conference again and I must get my mitts on Madison. So I make the
arrangements.

The shop is busier than ever as we cruise toward the end of January, but Tom and I agree that we'll each take two days off a week no matter what. He wants to train for 8 Tuff Miles and I need to rest my ailing body parts. The next day our main corporate customer calls to order 90 deluxe small open totes for a March 3 meeting.

"We have to hire a part-time employee," I say. "This is too much."

"We can do it ourselves, easy," he says.

Toward the end of the day Tom leaves for a hair styling appointment followed by a pedicure. He has the most wonderful time in the little nail salon, visiting with the women, hearing about their lives, trading banter. And then he takes the next two days off.

A book I ordered, *Coach Yourself to Success*, arrives in time for my own two days off. In the first chapter, the author says to deal with all the petty annoyances in your life. First she says to list them, which takes me over an hour. I read on. Three pages later the author says, *Okay, now do something to eliminate these annoyances once and for all.* So I clean the lamp shades and file some papers. I love this book. My life is better after only one chapter. I read how important it is to get help, be it cleaning your house or taking care of your kids. This leaves you more time for creative activities that will enrich you mentally as well as financially.

I'm on a roll with my list of annoyances. I call an attorney on St. Thomas that a customer had used for a real estate deal and recommended. I tell her that our lot has an easement issue. This problem has to be resolved before we can get a loan to pay it off, all of which needs to happen before the lot can be sold. She advises me what to do. Then I ask how a divorce is done in the USVI and she tells me that both assets and debts are a 50-50 proposition; however, retirement funds are not considered joint property. I reiterate that I'm still hoping to work things out, that I'm just gathering information.

Curiously, her reply is, "Call me when you're ready."

To get at the bottom of my physical ailments, I reread Louise Hay's book, *You Can Heal Your Life*. She's convinced our physical health is connected to or caused by our mental attitude and feelings. The word psychosomatic pops up more than once. My particular symptoms can result from not feeling cared for and safe. I add new mantras to my list, including *I am the power and authority in my life.*

By the end of my two days off, I'm ready to take charge. A lovely West Indian woman in Cruz Bay had once mentioned that she sews and would be interested in working part time for us. I invite her to work with me on Saturday, on Tom's day off when there's more room to move around. Tom seems fine with this idea, for which I'm both grateful and puzzled.

On Saturday, as agreed, the woman arrives. She wants to share some voodoo experiences she's had, and it takes every ounce of discipline I have to change the subject back to the work at hand. Slowly and carefully I take time to show her how a walking foot sewing machine works. I demonstrate several times, and then she tries and fails. Patiently, I show her again, focusing on exactly how you must rock your foot on the treadle. Over and over she tries, and fails. She insists on tromping down on the treadle as if she's driving a car. At the ripe old age of 40, she simply cannot learn this new thing. We part on friendly terms, but I am disheartened. Surely there is someone who wants to do the work and can learn to sew on these machines.

This morning at the shop Tom is wearing his pink patterned Sloop Jones T-shirt with bright blue and white chevron beads and matching earrings. His flowing hairdo is almost to his shoulders. He's sewing away on Big Dorothy when a large, gregarious man enters the shop, walks right into the work area, and booms, "Oh, Ma'am. I wonder if you could give me some information. Where's a good place to eat dinner?"

Tom seems unsurprised. He looks up at the man and answers in his male voice, "I've been hearing about Ten Tents, a small place up at the Lumberyard."

"Ten Tents?" I say from Little Rita, in the corner. "Do you mean Ten Tables?"

"Oh, ha ha ha. Yes. I mean Ten Tables."

The man doesn't miss a beat. If he notices Tom isn't really a "Ma'am" he doesn't let on.

After he leaves I say, "All that alcohol is killing your brain cells."

"That's ridiculous. You say dumb things, too."

"But it's funnier when you do it."

"That's because it's such a rare event."

"He thought you were a woman."

"I don't care what gender he thinks I am."

"Can we go eat at Ten Tents some time?"

"If I can wear your goddess dress."

"In your dreams."

Tom succeeds in getting his heart rate monitor to talk to his computer, so he can plot improvement in his race walking technique. And at one of the 8 Tuff Miles pre-race tune-ups he wins a global positioning unit to wear on his arm. It's not easy to get lost on an island this small, but he wears the unit anyway as he continues to train. On race day, the last Saturday of February, he receives numerous compliments on his shoulder-length hair, pink earrings, hot pink running shorts and off-white tank top. There are over 500 entrants. Tom wins a trophy for his age class, 60-99, besting his previous year's performance by 12 minutes.

The day after the race I leave for the mainland. The writing conference is wonderful, but meeting my granddaughter is like getting struck by lightning and going to heaven. She's such a doll, so adorable, so smart, and so fun to watch. We dance together, especially to Allison Krauss singing *I Will*. Madison smiles at me, which melts my heart, and one time she not only smiles but says, "Hi," which surprises everyone except me. She's clearly gifted and talented. By this summer she'll be 50 percent bigger—that much more baby to love. As I leave her, I ponder how to be the best grandmother I can be. I will encourage a love of books, of course. And I want to help her be creative, love the outdoors, and not be afraid of big spiders. We'll laugh a lot together. I want to be a wonderful grandma, like the one I knew and loved.

"Kinda heavy on the perfume," I say, standing on my tiptoes to hug Tom before we leave for the shop. A hug is in order. After all, he has just worked 14 straight days while I was in Montana and Washington.

"It's not perfume."

"Well, whatever it is, it's too strong."

"Do you really think I'm wearing too much? I can't tell."

"Yes, I do. What's the name of it?"

"*Touch.*"

The next morning I think I smell less perfume, or maybe like so many things, I'm simply getting used to it. The day is hectic, and after our lunch minute, during which we wolf down some leftover salad while sitting at our sewing machines, Tom walks to the post office. He returns with a box for me: a pair of Bose head phones. One evening before I left for the old country, I had mentioned how nice it would be if I had my own head phones to wear while watching movies on my laptop computer.

At home, however, Tom now refuses to wear *his* head phones when he's watching TV and I'm trying to read. Even when I say "please."

"Do we have a gun?" I yell from my chair at the table. How does he know I only mean to shoot the TV and not him?

He chuckles but says nothing.

I hate to be petty and dastardly, but in that nanosecond my hostility toward Tom returns. This lack of consideration is why I can love him and *intensely* dislike him at the same time. A familiar thought pops into my head: Where can I hide the body?

In the morning I stand on the porch in the balmy air, taking in the peaceful islands and calm sea. At such moments, paradise is stunningly perfect. The sun is shining, as usual. I listen to the sounds: mourning doves, honey bees, hummingbird wings at the hibiscus blossoms, a truck passing on the Centerline Road. Suddenly the discordant shriek of a donkey braying down by the Dumpster shatters the stillness. The other-worldly noise jars my nerves. It's like a donkey's been struck by the passing truck. Or maybe aliens have landed and are arguing over where to find Tom.

But when we leave for work, we see no injured donkey, no aliens. So many mysteries; so little time. At the shop it's a high-speed blender sort of day. Tom is precision-machining bags while listening to NPR. The tasks I'm doing are, by now second nature, leaving my monkey-mind free to ponder the jungle in which I'm lost.

I feel grateful for the moments of respite this morning on the porch, before the mysterious shrieking. And I appreciate the fact that Tom worked so hard while I blew around up north. I'm even grateful for the Bose headphones. But I'm like a cow chewing a cud, the way my mind tries to understand Tom's behavior. Finally, in yet another attempt to take charge, I tell myself: When I leave this summer I won't come back. You'll see pictures of me on *Unsolved Mysteries*. In a televised interview, Tom, Mr. Oblivious, will say, "Yeah, last time we talked on the phone she was getting ready to board a plane and come back to St. John. Everything was going so well with us here in paradise." Then I overhear these words on NPR: *chronic hostility can make you sick*. I freeze and stop breathing. I stare at a lizard on the wall. I listen as a woman on the radio discusses the importance of forgiveness in our lives. NPR is talking to me.

In the days following this splash of recognition, I take some action. Which means I make an appointment for both a massage and a chiropractic treatment. There are several excellent massage therapists on the island, and the one I'll be going to this time is in town. She's mature, wise, nurturing, and professional. I know that anything said during a massage is held in confidence, so when she tells me my shoulders are tight like a drum I reveal my marital quandary. She suggests I see a counselor. After my massage I visit Bern, who unlocks my neck and makes me laugh. Then I call the counselor. Today I feel mountains of gratitude for the health care providers on this small island.

Now that I've made an appointment with a counselor, I panic. How can she help me if I can't articulate what's wrong? I decide the basic problems are: feeling trapped by the business; wanting to reclaim and manage my own resources (time and money); wanting a friendship with Tom but not marriage; and the importance of extricating myself in a responsible and generous manner. I mean, holy hell, I don't want to be held hostage by mere hopefulness. Nor do I want to be held captive by pretty scenery when all I really wanted was warm feet in the winter.

The counselor is my age, a long-time island resident, and she's also divorced. She holds each person who seeks her help in the highest regard, she says. "You deserve the kind of life you want and my goal is to help you achieve it. You're a writer. Make a list of things that are missing in your life."

Suddenly, I'm not so alone.

Tom is acting like everything is hunky dory with us. This drives me crazy, because if he thinks everything's all right, then in some weird, co-dependent way I wonder if it's just me. Maybe I've created the situation or worse, maybe I'm imagining it.

Now and then I rescue another bananaquit from Inkie. I gently take the bird out of Inkie's mouth and release it, and most times the bird flies away. How do they survive this? Sometimes I wish I were one of those little birds, already taking flight.

WOMEN ARE SMARTER THAN MEN

Occasionally I wear my goddess dress to work, and this morning, after our nano-shower, I put on the dress, one layer over the top of the other. I'm in the bathroom holding the big red magnifying mirror, trying to tweeze away the errant hairs that pop up in odd places lately. Looking in this mirror is a horrifying experience. Every feature on my face is enlarged, exaggerated to landscape proportions, including arroyos so deep that food could get trapped in them. But I'm looking past the gullies and other landforms on my face, determined to pluck a chin hair I've been toying with for days, a hair long enough to wrap a small package. Tweezers in hand, reading glasses on, I finally see it. I'm poised to pluck, when something mouse-sized only squishier, more lewd, more slug-like, crawls on the bare skin of my back under my goddess dress. I scream and drop the tweezers and mirror and jump up and down, flapping the sides of my filmy dress like giant wings. The offending varmint falls with a thud onto the cat's sacrificial alter near a bird feather and the legs of a beetle. It's a lizard, larger than most and missing a tail, probably from a recent encounter with one of the cats. The poor creature thought it had found refuge in the folds of my dress before I put it on, and now it's scared and confused.

"Save it," I yell to Tom. "Don't let the cats get it. It's been through enough."

Tom picks up the lizard, sets it outdoors on the shower floor, and closes the door so the cats won't see it. While he does this, I try to reassure my face that it's over, the threat is gone. But my face doesn't trust me. Several minutes go by before the landforms settle down.

During Tom's day off, he calls to tell me he has a Viking intuition. We often joke about how difficult it is to know the difference between an intuition and a gas pain. But this time he believes it's the real deal. How about an evening at the new restaurant, Pastory Gardens? This bar, restaurant, and mini golf course a mile east of Cruz Bay, just off the Centerline Road, has been under construction for years. A weathered sign out front said SOON COME. And soon come has finally arrived. Tonight our favorite postal clerk, Chester (The Mighty Groover), will be singing with backup music on steel pan drum by a fine musician named Karl.

"I'll hitchhike in so we don't have two cars to drive home later," he says.

And here we are at Pastory Gardens, seated on an outdoor deck open to the sky. The night air is clear and balmy, and lights are twinkling across the water on St. Thomas, four miles to the west. Overhead, the moon is full and several planets are lined up. At the circular bar not far away, under a circular roof, we recognize a dozen or so familiar faces from Cruz Bay. The place has no walls, except for the restrooms behind the bar.

Tom has scotch on the rocks and I drink rum. Rum has many fine qualities. For one thing, it's cheaper than potable water in the Caribbean. And for a person with a history of early poverty followed by unrelenting frugality, the choice is simple—on my rare occasion out, there will be no rainwater drinks for me. Also, rum involves the senses in a highly unique way. At first whiff, rum smells like a promise, one it can keep. Next I inhale overtones of molasses, cocoa, vanilla, almost-charred wood, and holiday spices—and then I add caffeine-free diet Coke to my glass and dive in headfirst. A swallow or two later a benevolent force lays its warm, sympathetic hand on my chest, right over my heart. I hear the words, *You are good and all is well.* My entire body relaxes and I smile, certain that the incident with the lizard this morning is no longer written on my face. Even my exhaustion is replaced with anticipation, as the waitress delivers our organic stuffed tomatoes over pilaf.

Wearing my goddess dress tonight transports me happily outside my normal good behavior and restraint. This dress is like a parrot fish or island sunset in the way that it represents joyfulness and jubilance.

Come to think of it, this might be one reason for Tom's interest in wearing it. And when Chester, a rotund West Indian man wearing a tuxedo and a happy face, begins to sing songs of the Caribbean to the calypso beat of Karl's steel pan drum, it's impossible to sit still. So, Tom and I join several others on the dance floor. This is extemporaneous dancing, with no rules for right or wrong. You just move to the beat of the music. The sides of my hips, my lower shoulders, jostle from side to side in my dress, my breasts flop around unrestrained, and my Birkenstock sandals slap the concrete floor. The spokes of the wagon wheel ceiling spin as I dance around in circles. For a while I even forget that my marriage is falling apart. Chester is belting out a song about how women are smarter than men. I yell myself hoarse along with all the other women in the place. I scream and reach my arms out toward the full moon. For a few minutes I feel no pain, no angst, not even ambivalence. No more disappointment in Tom or in the ways that life on this small island has let me down. Yes! Let me live forever in this rum-soaked hilarity. And please, Chester, won't you run for president of the world.

Among the women cheering Chester on are several rich widows. A brilliant idea strikes me: if only I could transfer ownership of Tom to one of these fine women, it would solve a lot of problems. Over the course of the evening, I encourage Tom to dance with each one of them, and he does. But in the end, we drive home together, slowly and carefully, keeping left and staying out of the tree tops below the road. At home as we crawl into bed together, we agree that tonight was the most fun we've had since moving to St. John, or possibly forever. As I drift off to sleep, I decide that rum smells like dancing to an island beat in my goddess dress. Rum tastes like the truth—that maybe women really are smarter than men.

A WALK IN THE OCEAN

On my first day back on island after a summer trip to Montana, Angelo stops by the shop to use our phone.

"I see you're back," he says.

"Not really," I say. "Not yet."

"Okay, then I won't tell Tom I saw you."

But, of course, Tom has seen me. In fact, on our drive home after he picked me up at the ferry dock, we covered a lot of ground, in more ways than one.

"I need hernia surgery," he says. "I'm not in pain, but the doctor says I should get it taken care of soon. It'll be done on St. Thomas. Same day service, just like any beachside café. Should be a quick recovery."

Balmy breezes flow in through the open windows as I listen to this new turn of events. "Every time I leave and come back, you have a surprise. We talk so often on the phone and yet I didn't know about this."

"A young couple just bought Hurricane Alley," Tom says. "Tina and James. Maybe James can help lift the rolls of canvas onto the racks. He's a big, strong surfer kind of guy. They're both real nice."

I close my weary eyes as Tom drives us home along the North Shore. With my eyes closed, I know I'm missing out on the stunning views of ocean, beach, island and sky—views I haven't seen for the month I was in Montana. I think about reading to my granddaughter, walking with my little family in the green grass of early summer, and carrying Madison in a backpack when she met her first wildflower, an arrowleaf balsamroot. I think about how a baby represents goodness and innocence and hope for all mankind.

Tom says, "By the way, I'm going to a cross-dressing event in Maine the end of September."

"That should be an eye-opener," I say, my eyes still closed to this strange life I've re-entered.

"I'm nervous about it. I might not dress right. I might get beat up."

"You know, I don't really want to be here," I say. It's as if I'm under water with a snorkel tube in my mouth. "I want to leave and not come back, but I won't do it until late spring, after high season."

"I want to do some counseling with you," Tom says. "And I want to work with the counselor on self-acceptance."

"To tell you the truth, I'm too tired to talk. I'm overwhelmed and I miss Madison more than I can bear."

When we reach home, we know what to do. We'd worked out the logistics by phone. Even with Tom's hernia, he helps carry my luggage into Villa Debris. In turn, I help him move his things and Twodot up to Woodbine for a second summer of housesitting. Inkie and Lucky will stay with me.

Over the next week we eat dinner together every evening at Woodbine, and in the mornings we drive together down to Maho or Francis Bay to walk and swim. Tom doesn't mention my wanting to leave. In fact, he acts like I didn't say anything at all, which allows me to do the same. And in this strange way our life settles back to its usual state of abnormal.

In the evenings we sit on the deck at Woodbine like rich folks. As we watch the clouds turn peach, mauve, and pale yellow, the topic of discussion is usually what's happening with Tom. My own changes of life—hot flashes and becoming a grandmother— are only fascinating to persons undergoing those same transformations.

Tonight I long to ask him, "So, how does it feel, going through puberty while dressed like a 1950s housewife?" But I'm too fucking nice. Instead I ask, "So, how do you feel when you dress up in women's clothing?"

"Oh, tension sort of builds inside me as time goes on without dressing up. It gets relieved when I put on a dress. Expressing this side of me feels good and right. I'm happier, more comfortable."

Hearing this, I realize that's how I feel when I'm in Idaho and Montana. Not the part about wearing a dress, but the part about feeling good and right and happy.

After moving indoors to eat dinner, the discussion turns to his upcoming trip. We now call Maine, his destination, The Big Closet.

"Can't we talk about something else? I ask. "Your second self wasn't invited into my life. In fact, she's invading my space. And another thing, I wouldn't have married you if I'd known you'd evolve into someone else entirely. Talk about bait and switch."

"Fair enough," he says.

But the topic continues to worm its way into our discussions. Sure, I could eat dinner by myself down the hill at Villa Debris, but I am weak and Tom's a good cook. Plus I don't always want to be alone. Tonight while listening to him talk I realize I love him but not romantically, the way a woman should feel toward a husband. And Tom's second self doesn't exactly help the situation.

He says, "I'm worried that I won't dress right when I go to Maine."

I do the sisterly thing and say, "There is no right way. You can dress like a Stepford Wife or a rodeo queen. It's an opportunity to express your individuality as Rebekah." I want to say "like a girlie man," but I don't.

"I've been listening to *Lonesome Dove* on audio," Tom says. "When I go to Maine I don't want to look like the Buffalo Girl from Oglallah."

"Well, then leave your elk hides at home."

"Can you teach me some makeup techniques?"

"You know I don't wear much makeup," I say. "My mascara, hose, and lipstick days ended in 1978 when I stopped being a secretary. And I'm not going to up my hussy quotient now."

One day I hang out at Woodbine writing while Tom works at the shop. This morning we agree that at the end of the day, I'll walk down the mountain to Island Blues and he'll meet me there after work. I time my walk down the steep dirt track so we'll arrive at the same time. I arrive a few minutes early and sit at our favorite little table near the bar and an open window. Tom arrives in time to watch dusk descend over Coral Bay. A band named *The Iguanas* sets up. The waitress tells us they'll start playing at seven, and Tom suggests we stay and eat so we can hear some music.

The air is balmy, the hamburgers are good, and *The Iguanas* are playing soft rock with a calypso beat. The band is outdoors, under a fabric canopy at one end of a patio. On the patio, people are eating and drinking at closely-spaced white plastic tables. A drunk woman is dancing to the music between the tables, bumping peoples' elbows, lifting up her dress, making suggestive moves.

After we eat Tom says, "Dance with me."

"There isn't really any place to dance," I say. "And I've never danced on loose pea gravel before. Ask the drunk woman."

He descends the nearby steps leading down to the patio. The woman is happy to dance with him. They really get wild together, too, and when Tom lifts her up in the air *she isn't wearing any underwear.*

And I think, doesn't he have a hernia?

While he's dancing with the woman wearing no panties, others join them. A short blond woman named Julie asks me to dance, and she really cuts a rug. When I finally dance with Tom, he wants to kiss me. But I don't want to kiss him in front of all these people, or ever, so he kisses my nose and doesn't quit.

"Stop sucking on my nose!" I yell.

So he stops doing this and asks Julie to dance. She says, "You can dance better than you did with that French woman, right?"

"I don't know," Tom admits. "And she's French?"

"Yeah," she says. "Okay, I'll give you a try."

She's short and Tom is tall, and it's a disaster, with Julie catching an elbow in the head. A while later when he asks her to dance again she says, "No, you bounce too much."

He dances with someone else. Later, when he heads back down the steps to the patio, Julie yells out to him, "Yeah!"

Tom says, "Yeah!"

Julie grabs his buns then, the buns that aren't even there, and she doesn't let go. When she finally releases her grip on Tom's hinder, she walks past me and says, "You're a fuckin' good dancer, for a tourist."

"Thanks," I say, impersonating a tourist, in case she's in the mood for a barroom brawl.

Finally we leave, but not until Tom visits for quite a while with the French woman and gets her phone number. On the drive up the mountain to Mamey Peak he says, "She's lonely for women friends. She told me she really likes you."

"We didn't even dance together," I say.

Tom is thoughtful for a moment. "I'm thinking of arranging a dinner party at Woodbine for two or three couples. I'll invite her to join us."

"If she's lonely now," I say, "being at a party with a bunch of married people would only make it worse. I was single 14 years before I married you, remember. I know what it's like. Maybe you should dress up in one of your second self outfits and do something fun with her."

Every night I sleep down at Villa Debris while Tom sleeps up at Woodbine. And every morning now at exactly 6:00 a.m., Lucky, my lovable striped kitty with the huge ears, chews on my chin. This morning when I wake up, I remember where I am and how much I miss Madison.

Tom picks me up, as usual, to go walking and swimming. It's always lovely and quiet on the roads and beaches this time of day, this time of year. Sometimes we're the only ones around. We walk together or separately. In the ocean, I do arm exercises, walk in the water, or just float on my back and feel buoyant while watching pelicans or magnificent frigate birds fly overhead. This time of year, some bays have stinging jellyfish, but so far we haven't bumped into any.

This morning at Big Maho, Tom race walks on the road and I walk in the ocean. The water is crystal clear, right down to the individual grains of sand on my toes. I push each leg forward against the resistance of water, happy to be doing something good for my body. I lick a splash of wet from my lips, which always reminds me that the ocean is over salted for my taste.

Behind me I hear the shotgun blast of a brown pelican striking the surface like a spear thrown with exceptional force from high above. I stop walking and turn. The pelican sits on the water slugging back gulps of small fish. Beyond him the hills are silent and still, as if watching me back.

When I turn to continue my walk in the water, a little fish about three inches long begins to swim with me as I stride forward parallel to shore, pushing hard in chest-deep water. The little fish is tireless in its determination to keep up with me. It's silly, but I start to feel loved by the little fish. I'm its big friend, its new family, its reef. I'm where the little fish lives now. As I walk faster the little fish easily keeps up with me. We're together, my little fish and I, on this calm early morning before the tropical sun reaches the bay.

For three long trips back and forth, keeping parallel to shore, my body pushes against the water. The little fish swims to keep up, first in front of my chest, now under my right arm, now under my left arm. But it's time for me to wade to shore, to return to reality. With all my heart, I don't want to leave the world of the little fish that chose me. But I must get ready for work. At great risk, the little fish swims hard to keep up with me as I make my way toward the beach. When I step ashore, the little fish tumbles back out to sea in a wash of sand. Tears stream down my face. I must be losing control. Reaching for the towel I left hanging on a sea grape bush, I hear the familiar gunshot sound of a pelican striking the water behind me. I do not look back.

The next morning when I step onto the beach I pray my little fish will swim with me again. But I walk alone in the water, back and forth, this morning and the next and the next. I miss my little fish and I miss my granddaughter. I am sad for all the loved ones I have lost. And for others I've left behind so I can live on a small island surrounded by water the color of faded turquoise, with a husband who is becoming a total stranger.

MY NEXT HUSBAND WILL BE NORMAL

This summer when I was in Montana, Tom went to Jost Van Dyke, one of the British Virgin Islands, with his manicurist. She's a beautiful blond woman 15 years younger than I am, and she has bodacious ta-tas. Tom says they're just friends, and I believe him.

Even though Jost is only five miles northeast of St. John, I've never been there. Tom arranges for us to stay two nights at White Bay, and here we are, in one of four beachside cottages at The Sandcastle Resort. Only about 200 people live on the island, and most of them own beach bars. The Soggy Dollar Bar here at White Bay is one of them. Sometimes boaters anchor out past the reef and swim ashore to the bar. They buy drinks with soggy dollars, hence the name. After putting our stuff in the lovely cottage Tom had reserved, I follow him through the sea grape bushes and palm trees to the bar. It's 11:00 a.m., and he orders us each a drink with a friendly moniker—the painkiller.

"You'll love it," he assures me. "This bar invented the drink."

The beverage is cold and the temperature is hot, so I glug it right down. And I do love it. A painkiller tastes like fruit juice, only better. But before I can reach for another one, my head starts to spin and I collapse in the shade of a sea grape. It's like I suddenly have the flu. For the rest of the day I lay around in a hammock or on the bed in our cottage. As I lay dying, Tom joins in the loud talking, laughter, and shrieking at the bar, while drinking more painkillers. Everyone but me is delirious with joy and happiness. Apparently, there are several shots of alcohol in these drinks, and these days I'm only good for one rum drink. By evening I begin to recover from the painkiller, and I make a decision: no more alcohol, or at least not much. Lately every time I drink even a little, I get a headache and feel like shit. But of course I want to consume alcohol now and then, especially rum. It tastes good. It dulls the sharp edges of my world. And most everyone else can drink. No doubt some of my ancestors are disappointed in my inability to drink. So I silently reassure them that even though I'm unable to hold my liquor, I will, under the slightest duress, revert to a redneck, knuckle-dragging fit of cussing and sarcasm that'll curl the weeds on their graves and make them proud.

The day is rescued from being awful when Tom insists on buying me a short-sleeved, peach-colored pullover top that says *My Next Husband Will Be Normal* on the back. It's our little joke. My spirits lift immediately. I put the shirt on and for the next two days I only take it off to shower. This shirt is my new best friend. Who needs a little fish to swim with? The real joke is that if I can somehow manage to extricate from *this* husband, there won't ever *be* a next husband. Tom is husband number three. How many exes does a person need?

The second night the proprietors of the Sandcastle take all guests to a BBQ dinner at another beachside establishment, the world-famous Foxy's at Great Harbour. We dine on a Caribbean buffet of salads, fruits, vegetables, BBQ chicken, ribs and mahi-mahi, after which a calypso-rock band starts playing. My birthday is past by several weeks, but Tom arranges for the band to play "Happy Birthday" while a cupcake with a lighted candle is delivered to me. Everyone sings and cheers as we stroll onto the dance floor, especially the women, probably because of my shirt that says *My Next Husband Will Be Normal*. Later I dance a lively swing with a tireless West Indian man. What a great time. I love the band and the dancing at Foxy's.

The next morning I'm ready to catch the morning ferry back to St. John to open the shop. Tom has had such a wonderful time on Jost that I encourage him to stay and catch a later ferry. The later ferry, however, breaks down and he and the other stranded passengers catch a ride with a guy in a power boat. When Tom shows up at the shop, he's filled to overflowing with his extra day of fun. He tells me boat loads of people showed up and danced dirty to Soca, a style of calypso music with a cardio beat. A young hair salon owner from Puerto Rico fell in love with Tom's long platinum tresses and plans to come to St.

John to cut and style his hair so she can photograph him for her shop promotion. I wish women would stop encouraging him with this feminine appearance thing.

On the morning of Tom's hernia repair, he gets himself over to the hospital on St. Thomas via the foot ferry and a dollar taxi. In the late afternoon, I take my car on the barge to pick him up at the hospital. He sails through his surgery and generally had a pleasant experience. Over the next few days I work at the shop during the day and take over chef duties at Woodbine at night. Tom reads and finds frilly new duds on eBay for his trip to The Big Closet.

The evening after his surgery, he shows me his new MP3 player and how the names of the songs are displayed. "See," he says. "Here's *Confederate Railroad*."

"Can you plug this thing into the big speakers?"

"Sure."

Only one day after his hernia surgery, we're dancing nice together—one step one way, one step the other way. He doesn't bounce. He doesn't yank my arm out of the socket. Then one of our favorite songs plays and we dance our version of the Western swing as we shout out the familiar, goofy lyrics, *I like a woman just a little on the trashy side*. We both laugh so hard together that I almost start crying. And then we dance to Jimmy Buffet's "Margaritaville," hooting along with the line *at least we don't live in a trailer*. Our voices echo around the cavernous villa. We have a Grand Ole Opry time. While country and western music is perfect for the theme of a love triangle, tonight we're not discussing his second self, he's not wearing jewelry or perfume, and he isn't drinking because he's taking pain medication. It's just the two of us.

The next few days, however, Tom lolls around Woodbine, wilted and sagging. After a week he resumes race-walking in slow motion. And he returns to the shop to work a couple hours, but not before getting a manicure and a pedicure. Of course, after he gets a manicure he can't do much work with the canvas or anything else because he doesn't want to screw up his nail polish. He informs me, "Properly applied nail polish can take hours to dry."

While sitting on the deck at Woodbine this evening, Tom admires his manicure. He looks thoughtful. "I'm really struggling with this second self thing. It's like I need new wiring. I mean, I've been a homophobe all my life and now look what surfaces."

"We could call Chris at Angel Electric," I say.

"Speaking of the name Chris, I'd like to talk with Chris in Helena. When I was a Republican representative in the legislature, she approached me about introducing a gay and lesbian rights bill. She thought that since I'd worked so hard on an environmental bill I might consider it. But at the time, I was still so narrow minded I could look through a keyhole with both eyes."

"What would you say to her?"

"I don't know exactly, except that now I understand her point of view. I'd apologize for being so … something, so ignorant maybe. And I'd like to talk to that person in Bellingham who went from male to female, the one I refused to call by her new name. Now I better understand LGBT issues."

"L what?"

"LGBT. Lesbian, gay, bisexual, and transgender."

"Oh. That's funny. I'm a member of GBTC."

"G what?"

You know, my friends in Priest River. We started The Growing Brainless Together Club."

"Oh, that."

"Maybe while you're recuperating from your hernia surgery, you could journal about seeing those two people again and figure out what you'd like to say to them."

"Good idea."

When I was in Idaho, my fellow GBTC members were all on the South Beach Diet, and doing very well. In fact, Kathryn, the senior member of the group, recently reported by email that she's still losing weight. But she's longing for one of those giant Viagra-sized hotdogs with all the trimmings from the Costco store in Spokane.

Since my lower shoulders and I are looking a little too Rubenesque for my self-image, and Tom wants to reduce his growing tummy bulge, we decide to go on this diet together.

He says, "It's getting so I can't look down and see below my stomach to the *other* bulge."

"And you'll look better in your dresses without a paunch."

"That's why I'm doing it."

One winter while living on the sailboat in Bellingham, we owned a bread machine. We hauled it with us to our various housesitting gigs, and during those cold, bleak Pacific Northwest months we baked a loaf of bread every day. Neither of us was employed at the time, although I was writing and Tom was taking computer classes. But mostly, life revolved around our daily bread. The big question every morning was, "Hmmm, what kind of bread should we bake today?" One answer was, "I don't care. Whatever floats your bloat." Call it emotional eating or call it getting through 90 straight days of gray skies and rain. But one spring morning we woke up not just plump, but Pillsbury Dough Boy fat. We'd each gained 20 pounds. So we put on our baggiest clothing, pulled our bloated selves up the companionway stairs and stepped off the boat. We delivered the offending appliance to a thrift store. Then we joined a gym, and as we walked on the treadmill we grieved the loss of our bread machine. We drooled when we talked about how the warm bread had smelled while baking. And, oh, the taste, with butter melting all over it and running down our hands and under our sleeves. Even now, if I so much as glance at a piece of bread, I inflate.

The South Beach Diet seems sensible and healthy. We take turns cooking meals from the diet book. Tom makes a terrific tomato and onion sauté, and another night a baked salmon dish, both to die for. In fact, Tom is being so good, so nice and fun and charming again, that I'm thinking of staying married to him. So what if we no longer sleep together? I'll just go ahead and relax and be happy, which is what I want to do anyway. Is the difference in his behavior because he isn't drinking, now that we're doing the diet? Or is he just excited about his trip to Maine?

"You're so much more enjoyable to be with when you don't drink," I say. "We might even be able to stay married."

No reply. He smiles. Does he hear me? Does anything I say register?

We're both working at the shop one day when a family comes in. Their young girl watches Tom sew. She says to me, "What's she sewing?"

"Well," I say, in my nicest voice. "She is my husband and he is sewing a small knapsack. He likes to wear earrings and beads."

"Oh," she says, and doesn't seem particularly surprised.

Later a man pops his head in the door and yells in to Tom, "Oh, Ma'am? Where's the nearest restroom?"

Tom, sewing a small cargo bag at his machine, yells back in his strong male voice, "Around the corner and up the stairs. Turn left at The Clothing Studio."

The man leaves.

"We have a new threat named Hurricane Frances," Tom says, looking up from his hurricane-tracking program. "But there's only an eleven percent chance this one will hit the island." It's the end of August, approaching the height of hurricane season.

The next day the hurricane pulls up to the north of us and parks, and because hurricanes can be so unpredictable, we stay home to prepare for the worst. It's only ten days post hernia surgery, but with the help of the neighbor bachelors, Tom lifts and screws heavy 4 ft. x 8 ft. sheets of plywood over the remaining windows at Villa Debris. On the bed we stack boxes of books and suitcases filled with our clothes, throw a blue tarp over everything, and tie it all down with a mile of clothesline rope. In the great room we cover the computer desk, computer, printer, and couch with tarps and tie them in place. I capture

Lucky at tuna treat time, put her in a cat carrier and take her up to Woodbine. But Inkie's too smart to be caught, and I worry that he might get blown over to Jost Van Dyke.

Up at Woodbine, we're incarcerated for 24 hours. I sleep on the second twin bed in Tom's room, and my kitty's caterwauling echoes all around the cavernous villa, keeping me awake. The hurricane scare passes with only a bout of wind and rain, so I take my beloved, yowling junkyard cat back down to Villa Debris. The new dilemma is that we've rendered the place uninhabitable. It's dark and cave-like, and we've done such a great job of wrapping up the bed it's a chore to undo. But the pod up at Woodbine, where I slept last summer in the king bed, is under renovation, and I want to sleep at home.

Life is going along well enough during this time. I dispense useful tips for Tom's trip to Maine. "Don't shovel in your food. Don't make audible body noises. And it's going to be cool in Maine. You might wear socks. So remember, don't use them as a napkin like you used to."

"I hope the others won't want to sit around dressed like women and watch football or play poker," he says. "Some of them do that."

"You know," I say. "You might find that spending an entire weekend dressed like a woman will be a real drag."

One evening while watching the sunset up at Woodbine, Tom announces that he wants to jump out of an airplane. Where does this stuff come from? I mean, we'd been married four years before he mentioned the word *sailboat*. Next his second self falls from the sky. And now this?

"You're only 61 years old," I say. "Why don't you wait ten or fifteen years before skydiving. You don't want to rush into a thing like that."

But he doesn't think I'm funny. He's thoughtful, staring off in the direction of the clouds, now tinged with fuchsia. "And I'd also like to take a sail plane flight."

"Well, if we're still married next summer, let's do it in Switzerland. I want to go back there for my sixtieth birthday, remember?"

"I thought you were leaving me."

"I haven't made up my mind. You've been so nice lately, without the drinking, that we might be able to stay married. And when I lived in Switzerland in the late 1960s, I went up in a sail plane with a Swiss guy named Jurg Kutzli. He might still be an instructor. I could find out."

"Sure," he says.

"In any case, I intend to spend more time in Montana next year to be near Madison."

"That's okay," he says, still staring at the clouds.

When Tom calls me from Woodbine at seven, as he does every morning, his voice is raspy from some sort of respiratory virus. He sounds a little like Lauren Bacall. He says, "I'm practicing my new femme voice."

By the time we coordinate the day at the shop and discuss dinner plans, we end up talking 45 minutes. Being alone gives him the space to ponder things. He says, "I think my drinking has been a form of self-medication. It helped to soften my problems."

"Maybe you should quit drinking for good and face the music."

"I know how you feel about it."

"And you know that I'll accept your cross-dressing but only to the degree you now do it and no more. This subject can't take over our lives, in terms of what we do and what we talk about."

No reply.

I was trying to negotiate, but I guess my timing was off.

On a day in early September when we're both working at the shop, Tom announces, as if it's no big deal, that our accountant has finally completed our tax package. She's had all our info since March 1, and now the total with late penalties and fees is over $5,000. The loan we've requested from the bank to pay off the lot is $12,000. Now it will need to be more like $20,000, so we can pay all the back taxes. The boat I'm on keeps springing leaks. I can't bail fast enough. We couldn't pay our taxes, and we still can't afford an employee or health insurance. But Tom doesn't seem concerned. He has bigger struggles. He makes an appointment to meet with the same counselor I see once a month.

That evening at Woodbine, Tom models his new Jam's World shirts and floral nylon shorts, and even a dress. He's been practicing his femme way of walking, and is quite good at it. This reminds me of the time we were training for our ski trip on the Haute Route in the Alps, the trip that never happened. He read up on how to do telemark turns on his cross-country skis, and then executed these difficult, acrobatic turns easily, while I fell repeatedly at every turn.

"Have you figured out what I should tell your kids if they call you while you're gone?"

"No, maybe tell them I'm on a retreat."

"Why not?" I ask. "Men go on retreats all the time for self-improvement, bonding, and sharing makeup techniques."

"Or maybe I'm visiting a couple old friends," he says. "It's a guy thing."

"I'll just say you're on a retreat in Maine, chanting and drumming with a bunch of guys. Like with the ya ya sisterhood."

"Or the yo yos," Tom says, taking the bait.

"Then if they ask questions I'll say you'll call them when you get back."

"I was afraid of that," he groans.

"Another thing," I say. "If you come back to St. John with shaved legs, I'm out of here.

"I haven't decided whether to shave my legs or not. Anyway, hair grows back. No one would even notice."

And I know this means he'll do it. I remind myself to be nice. *I will be charitable. I will speak calmly and deliberately, or not at all.*

"It's one thing to be open-minded and liberal about the way others are," I say. "But I'm finding it's another thing to be married to someone who's different in this way. I don't like it when two or three times a week someone asks me, 'What's *she* sewing?'"

Everyone on the island seems accepting of Tom's new appearance and dress. This place enjoys a bit of a circus atmosphere anyway, with its spectrum of characters and scandals. Tom's fashion statements and appearance hardly merit comment. The island is very international in this regard. Women often say things to him like, "I love your hair." Sometimes one will say, "Where'd you get those lovely earrings."

Tom tells me he's learned some new terms: *gender bender* and *gender outlaw*. I picture Roy Rogers wearing fringed buckskin culottes.

SWEETBOTTOM

As tropical storm Jeanne blows and snorts over the island, she drops waterfalls of rain. In the middle of the night the roof at Villa Debris springs a leak again, this time on my face. I roll over to the empty side of the bed and finally go back to sleep. Tom arrives at 6:30 because there's no electricity up at Woodbine and he needs coffee. I'd been dreaming I was with Robert Duvall in a Forest Service cabin in the woods. What a rude awakening. Tom's hernia incision is somewhat infected, his cold is hanging on, his phone up at Woodbine doesn't work, and he has a big cold sore above his lip. He's grumpy but still able to be funny, which I appreciate. Tom is one of a kind. And while he isn't Robert Duvall, I do still love him, except, of course, when I hate him.

It's a fresh, post-rainfall morning as we drive in the sunshine down the North Shore Road to walk and swim. Today we're walking near Francis Bay, and when we pass the old wood sign nailed to a tree that says SWEETBOTTOM, we ponder the odd name. As we do every time we pass this way, we look beyond the sign and a rustic wood gate, at two West Indian-style cottages on the property. They're both paint- ed brown and partially hidden by an enormous genip tree. The place looks like a Southern plantation, with its sweeping lawn and enor- mous flamboyant tree. These trees sport bright red blossoms early in summer, when they appear to be on fire. Who are these people, lucky enough to live in this grand location near Francis Bay?

I'm walking as fast as I can, and Tom, who is mostly legs, is walking as slowly as he can, and these adjustments allow us to walk together. Early in our marriage, when we backpacked in Montana, he would also adjust his pace to mine. He was a wonderful hiking and back- packing companion in the Tetons, the Madison Range, the Mission

Mountains and Yellowstone. But once we moved to the sailboat in Bellingham, I never again got him up above sea level. And there we were, close to magnificent hiking trails in the North Cascades near Mt. Baker, a gleaming white tooth of a mountain.

"Maybe you enjoy the company of women so much because there's none of that male competition thing," I say. "There's no posturing to prove you're the alpha male. Maybe cross-dressing is an extension of that idea. Or, if the company of women is so comfortable, why not just become one?"

"It's possible some of that is operating."

"Don't be taking your male competitiveness with you to The Big Closet. Don't try too hard to be the alpha cross-dresser." I'm huffing and puffing, trying to keep up with Tom so I can continue to counsel him on how to act feminine.

"I just want to be myself."

Instead of telling him that's not a good idea, I say, "If someone isn't nice to you, just stuff a tube of lipstick up his nose."

"There's no need to be nasty," he says, getting into the banter. "I'll just take the tube of lipstick out and write *You stupid bitch* on the mirror."

"Before or after you stuff it up his nose?"

We laugh together and walk along for a while without talking as we make our way up the steep hill to Maho Bay Camp. I can't get enough air, and sound like a freight train, but I'm determined to keep up. Tom isn't breathing hard at all. Finally we reach the Camp's pavilion and begin the traverse down goat trail through the tangle of trees to Big Maho Bay.

"Something else has been on my mind," I say, once my breathing slows. "I'm not the most feminine woman in the world. My own hosiery and lipstick days only lasted from 1964 to 1978, and now I've become more or less androgynous. And then there's the flatulence. Maybe being a man of imagination and all, you decided to invent a wife you could have with you all the time, one you could count on and control a little more. And she'll never let you down. Maybe it's like when lonely children invent a playmate."

"Very funny."

We walk along for a while, not talking.

"How's your femme walk coming along?" I ask.

"Not very well. I could use some coaching."

By this time we're back to the paved North Shore Road, walking east. We stop so I can catch my breath again. "Well, let me show you how to walk like a model." I clomp ahead of him 20 feet, stop, and let a fart. "See. That's how you do it."

The evening of our walk past the SWEETBOTTOM sign, a surprising thing happens. We've put the word out that we're looking for a different place to rent, one that's quieter, and an acquaintance calls to say that one of the two cottages at Sweetbottom is available. The main cottage is occupied by the owner of the place, a grand dame with the nickname Diddie, and we're told she's only advertising by coconut telegraph. She's seeking a mature, quiet couple to live next door. Places like this don't last. I immediately call Diddie to introduce myself and brag about us: we're quiet, responsible business owners, mature beyond belief, hard workers, and we often walk in the area and love the location. Only the mature part is a lie. She says she already has a long list of interested people, but she'll keep us in mind.

"Oh, and we do own three cats," I admit. "I hope this won't be a problem."

"No cats," she says with vigor.

"Oh, no," I say, unable to keep the disappointment out of my voice.

A week later, in another curious turn of events, she calls to say she has selected us. Some work is being done on the cottage and it will be available October 1. I panic. Now we'll have to live up to all the things I told her. And I didn't even mention Tom's increasing penchant for dressing like a woman. Nor have we actually *seen* the inside of the cottage. These problems are resolved when Diddie stops by the shop to meet us. Tom, with his long platinum hairdo, dangly earrings and bright Jam's World top and shorts, passes her inspection without a blink. She says she'll have us over for a drink soon, at which time we can look at the cottage. This is exciting news. We'll be a short walk in our flip-flops from Francis Beach. We won't have to drive anywhere to walk and swim. We'll be right there.

THE BIG CLOSET

Vulnerable. That's how Tom looks as he waits at the ferry dock to leave. This is his first *outing* as a transgendered person. Yes, he's finally come to the conclusion that this *thing* is more than just cross-dressing. And now he's fussing in his purse to find the fare along with his senior discount card. To explain his appearance to his fellow passengers, he's carrying a copy of *The Gender Workbook* in the side pocket of his unisex black purse. He's wearing a brightly patterned Jam's World nylon shirt and dark nylon shorts. His manicure, pedicure, earrings, beads, ankle bracelet, toe ring and long flowing hair are all perfectly coordinated.

Anything could happen to him. For one thing, he might encounter fundamentalists (the "fighting fundies," Tom now calls them). He was one himself, until recently. But his second self put in an appearance at about the same time as the Republicans made some bonehead political decisions. And just like that, Tom took a sharp turn to the left and became a liberal Democrat. He was never prone to violence during his tenure as an ultra-conservative person. But he knows there are extremists out there, and some of them might believe they're doing their god a favor by ridding the world of a kook.

After hugging him goodbye, I walk toward my car, making my way around the vehicle that is illegally parked in the crosswalk. As I glance back toward Tom, he's still standing in the ticket line near his two natural-colored canvas cargo bags and one enormous black wheeled suitcase. This is a lot of luggage for only ten days in Maine, but then he did pack for two.

For the briefest moment I have the feeling that I've just said goodbye to Tom forever. This thought and the tears that go with it stay with me as I drive to Mongoose Junction, park my car, and walk to Honeymoon Beach.

Really, it's been one small loss after another. First it was the crew-cut. I'd said so often, "Why don't you let your hair down a little." Even after he retired from the National Guard, he maintained his crew-cut. But once he started growing his hair, he just let it grow and grow and grow. Then one day I noticed his Neanderthal daddy longlegs eyebrows were trimmed and elegantly arched. The feeling of loss associated with his eyebrows took me by surprise.

My walk along the path in the cool morning air is more of a plod, really, as I mull over the term The Big Closet and how apt it is for Tom's destination. Sure, he'll be *out*, but Maine is still a closet in that no one knows him. And he's not really *out* here, either. He just dresses funny.

On the beach I sit and watch the waves wash toward me and recede, over and over. The clouds decorate the mostly blue sky, and I look beyond small cays to Jost Van Dyke, home of the painkiller. At 7:00 a.m. on this September day, the beach is deserted and I feel washed ashore and all alone, like clothes left behind by illegal immigrants when they change into different attire for their hopeful new lives.

Back at the shop, I sew four small zip totes and two small duffels, and cut a crop of other bags to sew. I clean the front doors and freshen up the Caribbean pink paint. Then, to brighten the shop, I paint off-white latex over the wood on the back window panel. I don't sell one thing all day. And while shoplifting isn't much of a problem, someone manages to steal a bright red performance hat.

Two days go by without a call from Tom. I'm the only person who knows where he went, yet I don't have a phone number to reach him. In the morning I'll start calling B & B's in Maine. I've been watching one too many crime shows on TV, and I'm worried for his safety, especially with his elevated kook factor.

In the night I dream I'm in the ocean, unable to get away from sharks. I have no clue how I got myself into this mess, and to make matters worse I'm weighted down by wet tennis shoes. An idea pops into my head that just might save my bacon. I remove one of my shoes and throw it onto land, hoping it will bring help. But when a shark bites my chin, I know the end is near. The shark, of course, turns out to be Lucky. I lie in bed petting my chin-chewing kitty, happy that I escaped from my terrible dilemma, wondering if the dream carries some ominous meaning?

Tom calls at 7:00 a.m., just as he would if he were up at Woodbine.

"I'm having a wonderful time," he says.

"That's good. I was worried that some thug had his way with you."

"Yeah, well, I've been real busy. I went to a transgender makeover place and got my face made up, complete with tape to hold it in place."

"I could use some of that tape."

"I even bought a platinum wig, and went out to dinner alone, all made up as a woman. No one acted surprised or said a thing. It was no big deal."

"So how does it feel so far?"

"Well, I got lost," he tells me. "There I was, all decked out as a woman and I do a dumb-assed guy thing. I don't look at the directions, and the next thing you know I'm driving the rental car around in a construction zone with no signs. Then I finally stop at a gas station. When I get out of the car I'm careful not to snag my nylons, of course. And I walk into a gas station to ask for directions. A young couple is working in there and the guy's wearing two earrings. They don't miss a beat when they give me directions to the B & B. It was interesting how I kept wondering if I'd be safe. Now I know how a woman might feel sometimes. It's been a good education."

"It is a little different when you're six-foot-four."

"Maybe so," he says with excitement in his voice. "Anyway, tonight the rest of the cross-dressers check in. I'll call you again when I can."

I take a long lunch hour to see the counselor. I tell her how wrecked we are financially, that I want to be in charge of my own resources: my time, my money, and what I think and talk about. I confess that I'm flirting with depression. Oh, and I might be going crazy, except, of course, when Tom and I are in one of our goofy honeymoon phases. She tells me that when Tom talked with her he didn't seem to know that I wanted to leave. I try to tell her how gifted he is at denial, that when he doesn't want to hear something he simply doesn't hear it.

She's a good listener so I blab on. I telling her there should be a "lemon law" for marriages. A warranty period would make sense. But, no. Based on what a man chooses to reveal, you decide, Oh, what the hell. Then you take five minutes at the Justice of the Peace to get married. Only years later do you discover that, all along, the S.O.B was impersonating a man. But I'm not sure she believes that I've tried to communicate my feelings to Tom. How can he possibly act like a divorce is out of the blue?

At the shop after my counseling session, newlyweds from Charleston come in. Matt and Lisa are friendly and chatty, and with hardly any customers these days, I'm glad for their company.

The husband says, "We've just had two hurricanes named after us."

"Yes," the young woman says, looking adoringly at her new mate. "You know how much trouble one hurricane can be. But now these two hurricanes are happening out there at the same time."

"Do you suppose this has something to do with our future?" Matt asks me.

This young, beautiful couple is on their honeymoon. They're enjoying the irony and coincidence of having hurricanes named after them and, then, just when they get married, the hurricanes both appear in the Atlantic.

"You guys have your whole lives ahead of you. I'm envious of your happy future."

They both hug me.

At the end of Tom's trip, I'm working at the shop when he calls me to pick him up at the ferry dock. I find him at Mooie's having a beer, all fluffy-haired and perfumed. He doesn't have a single hair on his arms or legs. His demeanor is also different. It's as if he's someone else, as if I'm a taxi driver here to pick him up. I sense a new separateness, as if *we* are no longer an *us.* As I drive us to Skinny Legs in Coral Bay to eat dinner, he tells me all sorts of curious things that happened on his trip. I'm hungry for news from the outside world.

"A dominatrix did my makeup the second time."

"What's a dominatrix?"

"It's a woman who hires out to men to be the one in charge, to dominate and humiliate them. She dresses like a man but doesn't have sex with them. She was really cool, actually," Tom says. "She told me, 'Tonight I'm packing.' When I asked her what she meant she reached into a brown paper bag and pulled out a strap-on dildo."

"From a brown paper bag?" I say. "She needs a Canvas Factory duffel."

"Maybe so," Tom says. "Anyway, when she's working as a dominatrix, she wears the thing under her blue jeans so she has a meaningful bulge."

"And you trusted her with your face?" What I'm really wondering is, where am I in all of this? And I answer the question myself: Nowhere I want to be.

At Skinny Legs people stare at us now, whereas they didn't stare the week before Tom left for Maine. Something is definitely different about him, but I can't figure it out. While we eat, he talks about the other guests at the B & B, says he wishes he could have stayed longer, that he was just beginning to relax. He realized how much energy it had taken for him to make the trip, but then how comfortable he was there after all. I'm curious. I'm all ears.

But after our meal while we're on the long drive up the mountain, I find myself saying, in a hollow, flat voice that sounds like someone else's, "There are some important things I need to tell you. I'm leaving the island and I am not staying married to you."

"Oh, okay," he says, as if he's delighted.

"I can stay at Villa Debris and you can move down to Sweetbottom. I want an amicable divorce and I want us to be friends. I just can't stay married. It's getting to be a mental health issue." I hear the resignation in my voice and realize I'm talking in a monotone, and this is how I know I'll really go through with it this time. "I need your cooperation on this."

"You've got it," he says, cheerfully. "And we can both live at Sweetbottom. No need for two places."

"You can't tell me you love me or beg me to stay. If that happens, I'll leave immediately."

"Oh, I won't," he says. "It's okay."

"Well, don't act like it's the fucking most wonderful news you've ever heard," I say, glancing over at him. He's sitting demurely on the passenger side with his hair-free ankles crossed, the breeze lifting his shoulder-length platinum tresses.

He's silent for a moment and I worry that I've broken his heart beyond repair, the way mine is. Then he says, "So, do you want to go for a walk in the morning down at Big Maho?"

GIVE ME AMBIGUITY,
OR GIVE ME SOMETHING ELSE

*T*his is not dating; this is a habit. Every morning we walk and swim together, and every evening Tom wants me to eat dinner with him up at Woodbine. No one else is clamoring to do things with us. They're all preoccupied with their own lives, during this fall season of island torpor. Then, too, I want a *revised* relationship, not *no* relationship. I believe this friendly parting of the sheets is a giant leap in a healthy direction for both of us. Why *not* keep doing things together?

This evening the sky is hazy, like maybe Montserrat blew its top again. On the deck at Woodbine, Tom and I talk. As usual, the conversation gets around to his transgender experience. On and on. The subject grows more tedious by the minute. I have thoughts and feelings, too. I mean, we *are* getting a divorce, after all, which seems of no consequence to him. Finally I sneak a few words into the conversation, but he promptly informs me my offering isn't a good fit with what he's saying.

"I've got it figured out," I say, loudly enough to be heard all over Mamey Peak. "What you need is an inflatable doll, one that has a computerized talk button located in a discrete location. You can program her to say things like 'How interesting. Sounds like you've given that some thought' or 'Don't worry, darling. I love you just the way you are today, and I don't care who you are tomorrow.'"

I stomp off the deck toward my car. Tom runs after me for a hug goodbye, but I decline. As I jolt and bounce my way down the rocky dirt road, riding the brake, I make a decision. Tomorrow I'll call the attorney on St. Thomas to start the divorce proceedings. No one, not even me, is going to stop me this time.

In the morning Tom shows up at Villa Debris to walk and swim as if nothing is wrong, and we do what we've always done—we walk and swim. But this morning I stay behind him a safe distance.

During the day, when I'm at home and he's at the shop, he calls me several times, sharing news of customers and telling jokes. And I'll be damned. I catch myself thinking, I might not have to bail out after all. My indecision is like a thousand-word puzzle. Partly I believe it's possible that out of a terrible quandary, something new and shiny can emerge. But I recover my senses quickly, ashamed that I allowed myself such thoughts. And while I refuse to be fooled again, I also don't call the attorney.

The logistics of our situation is like a bad dream, one not featuring a handsome film star. We've made a commitment to move down to Sweetbottom sometime in October. Tom will continue to house sit up at Woodbine until November. And soon I start my own housesitting gig in that villa on the hill above Mongoose Junction.

Everything is compounded by the fact that I don't really want to divorce Tom. But the ambivalence—the deciding to go away alternating with a period of getting along and having fun—is making me crazy. I'm doing Tom a favor by leaving him. He doesn't need someone trying to stop him from wearing perfume and lipstick, or shaving his arms and legs. Then, too, it seems as if he's pushing me away, even if he's oblivious to doing so. Living and working with him over the next six to eight months while engineering a collaborative divorce will give new meaning to the term The Worldwide Wait. By comparison, using dial-up for Internet access, doing business with the VI government, or waiting in line at the bank and post office, will seem like amusing ways to spend time. I picture Tom being cooperative. I believe he cares about me and wants me to be happy, too. And even though we can't stay married, surely he'll want to be friends. He knows I won't simply abandon him and the business. After giving it all some thought, I develop an affirmation: *I disengage from Tom in the kindest way possible. He accepts my decision and allows an amicable, fair and drama-free separation of our finances and belongings. We remain friends.*

Jennifer is back in Moscow, Idaho, in the apartment she's lived in since 1985. On one of our phone visits I tell her, "This marriage reminds me of what my father said about the Great Depression. He said, 'I thought times'd be gettin' a little better. I never thought they'd up and get worse on me.' Jennifer, this time I'm finally ready to get the divorce."

"I've heard you say that before," she says. "Maybe it's like quitting smoking. It might take lots of times to quit, but each time you quit, you get a little closer to success."

"Jennifer, you are brilliant."

Tom looks forward to his standing four o'clock Saturday appointment with his manicurist. They have become good friends, and since he's often her last appointment of the day, they go bar-hopping afterwards. Since I'm unskilled at bar talk and alcohol now gives me a big headache, I spend my nights at home.

Tonight, on his way to Woodbine after his Saturday evening adventure, he stops at Villa Debris to see me. It's 8:00 o'clock. "Everyone asked where you were," he says. "They love you so. People's lives will be wrecked when you leave. I don't want you to go, either. Maybe you'll come back." He's slurring his words. I'm surprised he managed to get home.

"You'll find someone else," I say. "St. John has all those lovely widows."

"Oh, it's not that simple," he says. "Most women my age probably won't think being with a transgendered person is so wonderful."

"You'll have to strategize," I counsel him. "You'll want to make absolutely certain a woman is *gone* on you before telling her you like to sleep in negligees and go on cross-dressing vacations."

One day Hermon is in the shop telling me a story while I sew, when a woman my age from St. Thomas stops by. The three of us shoot the breeze a while and I mention that Tom and I are moving and have put in a request for phone service. If you live up in the old country, this might not qualify as conversation, but it can be a big deal in the islands.

The woman says, "I have a telephone story. In 1969 I came down to St. Thomas to get a divorce. Where I lived up in the states at the time you could only get a divorce if there'd been a case of infidelity or domestic violence. My husband and I simply suffered irreconcilable differences. A divorce was easier to come by down here, but you had to live here for six weeks prior to filing for the divorce. So I stayed on St. Thomas to fulfill that requirement. During this time, a friend put in a request for telephone service. After waiting a year, he bribed a telephone employee. Next thing you know the bribed employee installed phone service, but at his neighbor's house instead of his."

"Did you ever get the divorce?" I ask.

"Yes, I did. And I fell in love with island life and moved to St. Thomas."

Tonight I'm at the villa up the hill from the shop, going through one of my periods of profound sadness, loneliness, anger, and disappointment. I hate to lose the good things about our relationship, just because I can't handle the transgender thing on top of all the other problems. My neurotic suffering reaches new heights. I stop hearing the beloved tree frogs, and when I remember them I listen intently, using their peeps as both meditation and medication.

The counselor wants me to list incidents for which I think Tom owes me amends and to state why I require a response. "Don't sugarcoat it by mentioning the good things," she said. "This exercise is only about the bad times." She's a peaceful warrior. I believe she hopes that by doing this exercise and eliciting an apology from Tom, some of my angst will diminish. I blow my nose and keep trying to write out my list of grievances. I'm having trouble doing this because I don't want to hurt Tom's feelings. I'm pathetic.

The phone rings. I answer. This is not my house; it could be anyone.

"Who is this?"

"It's your soon-to-be-ex-husband."

"Oh, hi."

"You should see how Inkie runs up the genip tree, all the way to the top."

"You must be at Sweetbottom," I say. These days we are so rich with housing options that either one of us could be almost anywhere on the island.

"It's wonderful here," he says. "I just installed my new closet organizer. And I ordered sheet sets, new ones with a tropical pattern."

"Did you see the big moon up there over the Caribbean with the lunar eclipse?" I ask, not wanting to wreck his good mood by mentioning my list. "I saw it earlier while I was sitting in the hot tub. What an amazing sight."

We are intimate in our shared life topics—on the phone, at least—and this feels good. At the same time, I'm aware of the disparity, incongruity, irony, ambivalence, and downright craziness of our situation. It's a bipolar state of affairs.

"Talk to you later, Baby," Tom says.

One evening Tom brings steaks, mushrooms and squash up the hill to *my* villa to cook for dinner. He's pleasant but distant. I go on and on about how delicious the meal is, adding, "If I manage to get out of here alive, I'll probably starve to death without your cooking."

He tells me he saw the counselor, that they talked about his childhood, his kids, his second self. "Yeah," he says, "She told me I need time to process what is happening to me, to integrate my second self into my life."

"You guys ever talk about how *we're* doing?" I guess it's like a scab I have to pick.

"Oh, no. It never comes up."

"Do you mean it isn't important enough to appear on your radar screen?"

"Nope."

And when it's my turn to see the counselor I tell her that Tom doesn't seem to care that we're disintegrating. She says, "Just to set the record straight, we do talk about how you guys are doing, and he doesn't want the divorce."

"Well, this isn't the message I get from him."

She wants me to express my pain, my anger, and all the anguish at how difficult the relationship has been. I don't want to make a scene, but she's good. She knows what to say. First my shoulders ache, then my throat tightens like I'm being choked to death, and sharp pains stab me in the chest like I'm having a heart attack. This is the way I felt during the past-life regression when I realized I was an axe murderer. Now it feels like something is gripping my solar plexus. I sob and rage. She wants me to scream, too, but I hold a glimmer of self-control and manage to draw the line. As it is, I'm mortified by my lack of restraint. But the counselor is pleased, and the slutty caretaker part of my personality is thrilled that I could accommodate her.

I'd begun wearing mascara so Tom wouldn't look prettier than I do, and because I cry so much I got the waterproof kind. But this mascara smeared all over hell during my counseling session. When I get to the shop, Tom, bless his heart, reaches into his tote bag and loans me some eye makeup remover.

Tonight Tom is visiting me at my villa. We're relaxing on the deck overlooking Cruz Bay. The sun is setting in gaudy oranges, fuchsias, and shades of lavender. As Tom sips the owner's expensive single-malt scotch, the colors fade to darkness. My list of grievances is complete. Now I'll ask for amends, and Tom knows tonight's the night. The list is long. I clear my throat and begin. Again, it's hard not to sandwich these hurts with the good things, but I calmly proceed. Tom appears to be listening. When I finish, he says, "Many of the things you say are true. I understand what you're saying. All I can do is ask for your forgiveness. I can't take back my behavior early in the marriage. I shouldn't have remarried so quickly."

I wait. I guess I want him to say he's sorry for all the anguish he has caused me, even recently, but he doesn't say anything like that at all. Instead, he states his apology in a generic, tangential way that diminishes everything on my list. Oddly, this moment is like one of the grievances: the time on the sailboat when I was standing in the cockpit with another couple and Tom dropped the boom on my head. When it happened I was stunned. I gripped my head with both hands and immediately looked up at Tom on the deck, and I could tell he'd seen the event. While I know he didn't do it on purpose, he acted as if nothing had happened. Later when I asked him why he didn't say something, he said he was too embarrassed. And now, even though he has said he doesn't want to lose me, he refuses to step up to the plate and do or say anything to prevent it. I believe that if you have to ask for certain words or behaviors, they're not worth having. I'm watching Tom, thinking these things, aware that my head is tilted sideways the way dogs do when you say or do something they don't understand.

Tom breaks the spell. "Are you hungry?"

"A little," I say, my head still stuck in that befuddled sideways tilt.

"Well, then, let's go to Café Roma."

"Okay," I say. But it's hard for me to move, to change out of my mode of anticipation and drag myself upright. So Tom pulls me to my feet.

We walk down the steep hill in the dark. We cross the drainage gut at Mongoose Junction and walk past the closed doors of The Canvas Factory. We skirt Nature's Nook, Joe's BBQ and Caps before ascending the stairs to Café Roma. Tom's been going to this little restaurant and bar with his new friends. And now it's like we're on a date as we sit at the bar eating pizza while chatting with others. After eating, we stroll back toward my borrowed villa, and as we approach Caps the music draws us in. We dance a country and western swing to the music of the Dominican Republic, with Tom bouncing, his steps not in beat to the music, and both of us laughing like crazy people. The West Indian regulars watch us, an odd white couple dancing like honkies, the tall one dressed like a toucan getting all the attention. Too bad I'm not wearing my favorite shirt, the one that says *My Next Husband Will Be Normal.*

HALF PARADISE, HALF HELL

Sweetbottom shimmers with sensory possibilities, the way a quartz crystal amplifies radio waves. And I wonder this: if a heart holds both intelligence and memory, have I lived here in one of my previous lives?

Diddie, our landlady, tells us she named this piece of bottom land after the sweet scent of genip blossoms. In fact, one of the largest genip trees on the island stands its ground between her cottage and ours and its lollipop shape reaches upward over 80 feet to write on the tropical sky. The tree's massive, gnarled multiple trunks spread to nearly eight feet in diameter. I've read that slaves during the plantation era believed these were "spirit trees," and harbored jumbies. Genip trees are all over the three acres here, with several arching over the bedroom end of the cottage. This place is genip central.

Now in early October, the tree is decorated with edible, lime-colored fruits the size and shape of small chicken eggs. And on this, my first night at Sweetbottom, the fruits are dropping onto the thin metal roof above the new queen bed. Every few seconds another one will drop, like the other shoe. To amuse myself I picture Tom's size 12 ladies' sandals dropping one at a time onto the roof. Adding to the sound effects are ear-splitting thunder claps accompanied by lightning flashes—pyrotechnics rarely experienced on St. John. Other noises include the splash of heavy rainfall and the yowling of Inkie, locked in a bathroom to keep him from running away. While he's ripping up the floor tile and window screen, Lucky is caterwauling under the bed. Twodot, the GQ cat, is with *his* human on their last night at Woodbine. At least the new bed is comfortable. But starting tomorrow night, when Tom moves in, I'll be sleeping in the corner of the living room. We'll bring home a cot I found at the second hand store. It will be nice next to the two large screened windows, and no trees will be dropping fruits onto the roof above that end of the cottage.

At work in the morning I'm a sleep-deprived zombie. Too exhausted to change the thread on the sewing machine, I sew only black bags. Yesterday my housesitting gig ended, which is why I slept at Sweetbottom last night. Today we officially move out of Villa Debris. And tomorrow, Jan, the owner of Woodbine, returns. Just like last October, we've been playing musical villas.

Still, I keep thinking about leaving. However, Tom's daughter Melinda is getting married April 30 and wants her father to give her away, so I'll need to stay on island to work at the shop until next May.

Our new abode, with its two sleeping areas and two bathrooms, is perfect for a couple who now sleeps apart, eats meals separately, and no longer drives to work together.

With all of us under one roof again, our routine establishes itself quickly. Tom and Twodot sleep in the bedroom, while Lucky and I sleep in the living room. Inkie prowls in and out all night, seeking feral cat adventures. Tom is a sound sleeper, unbothered by the sound of hard fruits falling on the roof over his bed. Each morning he gets up first and makes his coffee. His towering ghost-like figure appears in the early morning darkness like one of those elusive spirits, the jumbies that some people believe wreak havoc here in the Caribbean. I watch from my cot as the apparition, wearing a diaphanous pink negligee, floats from the kitchen through the living room and into the screened porch. The theme song from *Ghostbusters* flits through my head. *Who you gonna call?*

The beating heart of our rustic West Indian cottage is a 10 ft. x 12 ft. porch with the walls on three sides made of screen. The floor boards are spaced about a quarter inch apart, inviting geckos, tree frogs and very large spiders to flow freely in and out. The roof leaks and rain blows in. It's a wonderful place for the two familiar strangers we've become to sit together in the predawn stillness, each on our own rickety director's chair. I hug my mug of coffee and listen to the birds, watch geckos, and pet Lucky as she rubs past my ankles. I'm biding my time until I can leave the island in six months. What a grand opportunity to practice grace and compassion. As usual, Tom is staring out into the branches of the giant spirit tree, integrating his second self.

This morning, we watch nature as a substitute for meaningful conversation, just like any couple who watches TV. A tiny hummingbird called the Little Green Flash sits on a branch of the tree, not far from the screen. This hummingbird is not to be confused with the green flash of color sailors occasionally see at sunset on the ocean horizon. Instead, it's the Antillean Crested Hummingbird, and it requires more food in relation to its size than does an elephant. While sitting on the porch thinking of hummingbirds and elephants, the ocean sighs in and out, a short distance away. Inkie walks to the screen door, opens it with a paw, and lets himself out. He looks all around at his options, and then walks on the pea gravel into the narrow, cleared patio area behind the cottage.

Diddie's screened porch, where she spends much of her time, faces away from our cottage, and I know she, too, enjoys her privacy. She does, however, welcome me whenever I approach her door. I call out "Hello!" in advance, to make certain she's decent. Her porch is about ten feet wide, and runs the length of her rectangular cottage. As the island eases into high season, this is where Diddie entertains old friends and new, dozens of people at a time, eat catered canapes and clink together glasses of rum and other adult beverages. Hundreds of people have celebrated life on her porch. During my first party at Diddie's place, I don't stay long but meet several people I've seen waiting in lines at the bank or post office. One of them, a long-time island resident, tells me, "Life is small on St. John. It's lucrative," she says, studying the contents of her glass, "but it's lacking in stimulation. I had pictured a life different from this one." I do not ask why she doesn't leave. My life is not the only one that's complicated.

On one of my morning visits with Diddie, she tells me she once partied with all the old white islanders, most of them now in ex-pat heaven. "One friend, Ethel McCauley, even wrote a book about building her house on the island," she says. "What's left of it is just up the hill, on the national park."

"I read that book before we moved here," I say. "*Grandma Raised The Roof.* It's a wonderful read."

"You know," she says, "her own title was *Grandma Did It With Donkeys*, but, of course, her publisher wouldn't let her keep that title. All she meant was that donkeys were the mode of transportation those days—donkeys and boats." She pauses then and looks out to the sweep of lawn and her flamboyant tree, shaking her head. "Oh, my, she was a character. I still miss her, and those wild parties. One thing Ethel liked to say was 'St. John is half paradise, half hell.' She said it fifty years ago, and nothing has changed."

Diddie is a character herself. At 80-something she works as a professional witness at beach weddings, and dresses for these occasions in Southern elegance: .flowing two-piece outfits, usually colorful, with bright red lipstick to match the hibiscus she always wears pinned in her upswept gray hair. Virginia-born, her overall appearance is that of being from "old money," and while she looks like she could have fit in at a party given by The Great Gatsby, I believe she's like many other island residents who are richer in land than in cash.

On days when she doesn't have a wedding, Diddie often dons her floral swimsuit and flip-flops, throws a beach towel over her shoulders, and strolls to Francis Bay with the help of her cane. She tells me that when she arrives at the beach, she chases "foreigners" away from her favorite spot and then works on her tan until she overheats. Leaving her cane behind, she wades into the ocean, where she stands waist-deep and splashes around to cool off before yelling for help. She says, "I can't negotiate the mound of sand at the water's edge by myself, but people always rush into the ocean to help me." She laughs and continues. "Sometimes it's the same foreigners I chased off my spot when I got there. It's a good way to meet new people. You may have met a couple of them at my party."

Tom has been staying out late with new friends, and tonight when he finally comes home, just after midnight, he roars up the driveway in the car, parks it below my window, slams the door, clomps up the wood steps in his women's hard-soled sandals, bumps into furniture, stomps into the kitchen, and bangs around in there for a while.

I yell, "Can you please be quieter? I have to work tomorrow."

"Oh, you're awake," he says. "I just had the most fun evening. I took Trudy to dinner at Rhumb Lines."

"This is getting too weird, even for me. For years I couldn't get you to go anywhere, and suddenly you're a social butterfly. And from now, on if you come home a minute after ten o'clock you have to park out by the road and walk in." It's my fishwife voice, a big dry growl filled with impatience. I hope I didn't wake Diddie.

In response he says, "Can I ask you a question?"

"Well, yes."

"Did the automatic lights come on by themselves when I drove up or did you leave them on?"

I can't believe he asked me this stupid question. "I left the light on for you."

He goes into his bedroom, puts on his negligee, comes out to my little bed in the living room, leans down to hug me, and says, "You're still my favorite."

Now I'm convinced. Tom isn't just a transgendered person; he's an alien from another planet. And I'm an animal with my foot caught in a trap. Maybe I should just chew off my foot and crawl away, into the muck over at the salt pond.

After his late night out, Tom is sleeping in. In the stillness before sunrise I'm pleased to be sitting alone on the porch in the calm. There's an energy shift that happens at sunrise. Geckos dart around on the screens, capturing insects surprised by the sudden light. Living at Sweetbottom makes me feel rich beyond measure, even as my personal life crumbles all around me. Half paradise, half hell, indeed.

A frangipani tree graces the entrance to the porch. I've already put sugar in the bird feeder hanging in the tree. More of a large, multi-trunked shrub than a tree, it is covered with six-inch long, strappy dark green leaves. And now, as daylight illuminates the tree, I'm surprised to see dozens of inch-long black and orange caterpillars all over the stems, branches and leaves. The bananaquits don't seem surprised. These sociable birds continue to take polite turns at the feeder. They wipe their sugary little beaks on the branches, right next to the caterpillars, and chirp up a low-decibel din.

Diddie's frangipani tree is holding its own near the bottom of the wood stairs leading up to our cottage. Thanks to Hurricanes Marilyn and Hugo, her tree features severely crippled limbs, bent over and growing toward the ground. The tree looks like an enormous green tarantula out of the film, *Jurassic Park,* whereas our frangipani is younger and more protected, with branches that reach upward. Diddie clearly dislikes the heathen caterpillars that are eating the leaves off her frangipani. One morning we witness her standing near her misshapen tree, wearing a white nightgown, her long gray hair taking flight as she strikes at the caterpillars with her cane. The next morning, when we're both at our respective cars ready to drive to the shop, she comes out of her porch to say she has hired someone to spray the trees and kill the caterpillars. We beg her to spare our tree, and she reluctantly agrees to leave it alone. While no one else knows it, and certainly not Diddie, our marriage is on the rocks; we don't want to lose our beautiful caterpillars, too.

With the need for some emotional chemo-therapy, I make an appointment with Lucy. She reminds me that we create our own realities. Ouch. While I can't yet believe I caused my own curious situation, I must acknowledge my role in the way it's playing out. Then, too, the question arises: what is real and what isn't, since we view everything that happens to us through filters of previous experience.

She tells me, "When you get a negative thought, just say to yourself, STOP! Think about what you want in your life, instead. Say it, state it clearly, and picture it. See yourself experiencing only what you want in your life."

She continues, saying how simple appreciation can help cancel negative thoughts and get the good vibrations flowing. Stop seeking (and finding) what is *wrong* in a situation, and then pondering it to death, but seek, find, and ponder what is *right* with a situation or a person. Also, when I lie in my bed hearing the ocean waves wash ashore, I'm to think of joy returning to my life. Lucy is quite the taskmaster, yet I believe what she says is true. Changes in life can be opportunities to evolve. I read online that this work to change one's thinking is called *self-directed neuroplasticity.* Knowing this, even *saying* it, becomes its own mantra, and makes me feel a little smug.

At one point she suggests, "Picture yourself as a butterfly in the pupal stage."

"Oh, well, in that case I'd like to become the butterfly of the frangipani caterpillar."

"Yes," she says, "picture that."

This seems like another good way to evolve. Easier, too, than all that other hard work. And when I do manage to struggle out of my cocoon, I'll be like the caterpillars I love. Yes, I'll emerge as a large, elegant, orange and black butterfly capable of long flights in first class.

At home alone in the evening I dial up the Internet and begin my research on the seasons of the frangipani caterpillar. I learn that these attractive members of the order Lepidoptera are not to be confused with the tent caterpillars on the mainland, those unattractive nuisances, even though they, too, eat leaves. These caterpillars on our frangipani tree will munch through all the leaves, growing bigger and fatter and furrier every day—as big around as a fat finger and up to six inches long. The sap from the leaves and stems of the tree are toxic, which makes the caterpillars safe from birds. When the leaves are all gone, the caterpillars simply drop to the ground, where they crawl underneath dead leaves and go into their pupal stages. So far so good. But then, to my horror, I learn that these caterpillars go on to become dull brown deltoid-shaped hawkmoths featuring six-inch wingspans, with thick, sturdy bodies, much like those of my peasant ancestors.

SQUEAK *THE* LIZARD

We all need a gimmick. A little kid leaves a bag of life-sized rubber lizards at the shop, the kind that squeak when you squeeze them. The kid doesn't come back, so I give a few away, but keep a green one that's eight inches long, nose to tail. At someone's suggestion, I put a sign near it that says, FOR HELP, SQUEAK LIZARD.

Barb and Jim squeak the lizard one day and invite us for a Thanksgiving dinner potluck. The night before, I make my signature rice vinaigrette salad. Tom makes fudge. We work until 4:00 p.m. as we have other Thanksgivings, and then drive separately to Jim and Barb's villa. They're always fun to be with. Tonight we meet two other guests, Livy and Tom, the new owners of Bajo el Sol Art Gallery in Mongoose Junction. A few years younger than we are, this couple is also fun, interesting and nice. Livy talks about her art and says she's doing a portrait of every child killed in the Columbine, Colorado, school shooting. She says, "It's my ministry."

Great. As soon as I decide to leave the island for good, new people arrive and want to be friends. Besides Livy and Tom, there's the beautiful young couple who just bought Hurricane Alley, the shop next to ours that sells beach wear and rents snorkel gear. Tina and James. Their six-year-old daughter, Maia, comes into the shop for canvas scraps and creates collages with them. Tina drops off little gifts for me, like a tiny marble turtle emerging from an egg. One day, Tina and I make plans to take a French secretary's lunch. We'll walk to Salomon Beach to sunbathe and swim topless. Knowing we might get caught is part of the adventure. Anyway, my breasts, my rollups, could use an airing.

"When are you going?" Tom asks.

"One day when you're working at the shop and can't see us."

"Too bad."

"'Course I don't have any bikini bottoms, so I'll have to wear a pair of shorts."

"I have a bikini set I got in a grab bag off eBay," Tom says. "You're welcome to it."

"You're kidding."

"Nope. It's a pink plaid affair."

But in the end, Tina and I become too busy to take our French secretary's lunch. Besides, Tom's grab bag bikini and I aren't really a good match.

Livy gives art lessons. I begin weekly two-hour sessions at the place she and Tom rent in Upper Carolina near Coral Bay. Livy is an excellent art teacher. The lessons go by way too fast. I paint a small pastel scene for Tom, from a photo taken on a sailing trip to the Broken Group Islands off Vancouver Island. It was on our way back from that trip, in the Strait of Juan de Fuca, when we got into that furious blow that ended my flirtation with sailing. More than once, since that episode, Tom has referred to the location as the Strait of Juan de Fuckit.

Now it's hard not to tell Livy the truth—that I'm leaving the island. I hate all the secrecy. But Tom doesn't want me to say anything yet about his gender issues or the divorce.

Livy and I work out a deal. I barter canvas bags and money for her to paint a pastel portrait of me at age five, from an old black and white photograph. I'm sitting in a little red wagon and I'm actually wearing a dress, although mostly I wore rompers in those days. A large cloth doll sits in the wagon with me, and I'm puzzled when Livy mentions that it has only stubs for arms. Someone else sees the photo and says the doll is ugly. I almost cry. I had loved the doll, and I'd never noticed its deformity. How many other things do I remember one way when they were something different altogether?

A niece told me once about a friend who released butterflies at her outdoor wedding in Wyoming. The butterflies arrived as cocoons, of course, and timing was everything. How lovely to release butterflies on such a special occasion, or at any ceremony representing a fresh start. So, trite as this may be, I ask Livy to paint a little blue butterfly on top of the doll's head.

Hermon drops by often. He has a radio at his place in the woods, and sometimes he tells me what he thinks about world affairs. He stores his heavy lignum vitae pieces in a corner of the shop and retrieves them as needed to carve his sculptures. During his many visits, I've learned that lignum vitae means "wood of life." These trees once covered large areas of the island, but were cut down to make room for sugar cane cultivation. Others were harvested for their valuable wood, and used for such things as propellers and gavels. A few trees are left, and you can see a magnificent specimen next to the old post office. Hermon and others have planted seedlings of this special tree all over the island. His carvings are made from the roots, and he sells them out of his knapsack or at various shops.

If I'm lucky at the end of a day, James will crouch down and sneak into the shop, reach up, and squeak the lizard. When I look up, no one is there, that is until he announces himself. Other times he'll crawl into the work area on his hands and knees. Out of the corner of my eye I'll notice something large down on the floor, and since I'm a nervous wreck anyway, this startles me. But it's James, not a giant iguana or worse. What a lovely way to suffer a fright. Today he stands up, dusts himself off, and says, "This morning while I was out at Peter Bay pruning a tree, I decided you should post a sign that says *BUY A HAT – GET A HUG.*"

"Good idea. Why didn't I think of it?"

His cell phone rings. It's the call of Tarzan of the Apes. "Gotta go," he says. "Tina needs my help next door."

He hugs me and leaves, and, as if on cue, in walks a tall man named Bill, a repeat customer from St. Paul, with his little sister, Nancy, from Boston. They're around my age, give or take. I help Bill try on our most expensive hat, an Ultimate, and he looks real good in it, too, but his sister says to him, "You look nerdy." She turns to me, wearing my oversized purple cowgirl shirt, and says, "You probably like that Cabela look."

"Oh, yeah!" I say, handing Bill a different hat, a high-performance floppy model that covers his neck and ears, one you'd wear riding a camel. And I'll be darned. Bill looks nerdy. But I want to sell a hat, so I just smile.

"You probably like *that* look, too," Nancy says.

"Oh, I'd chase after a guy wearing a hat like that."

"Well, close the door," Bill says. "And we'll see what happens."

Nancy says, "But he'd have to leave the hat on."

"Oh, of course," I say, "for the entire eight seconds."

And I think the wicked little sister might wet her pants, she laughs so hard. Their visit completes my day, and when they leave I hug them both goodbye, even though Bill doesn't buy a hat.

Tom comes in to work at noon one day, drenched in his new Gucci perfume.

"You're wearing so much perfume I can taste it."

He laughs.

I try to let it go, to be in the moment, but the air reeks. I've asked him several times to go lightly on the smells when I'm around. Finally I say, "Look. We have to get something cleared up. If you want me to work until after you go to Melinda's wedding, you have to stop wearing so much perfume when we work together."

"Okay." And within the hour he gets up, goes to the restroom and removes some of the perfume.

He's doing something right, because he's getting more attention and support now that he's different, shall we say, than he ever got before. For instance, one day when I'm home and he's at the shop, he calls to tell me about a man who came in. "The guy's a teacher," Tom says. "His students call him Cube-S, for silky, smooth and shiny."

"That's cool," I say. "Sounds like he gets along well with his students."

"That's the idea I got, but that's not the best part. Old Cube-S went gaga over my hair. He said, 'Man, if I had some hair, that's exactly how

I'd wear it.' A little while later he came back with a friend, and said to him, 'Isn't his hair just gorgeous?'"

"Really?" I'm puzzled. Tom recently started wearing his shoulder length platinum hair flipped out at the bottom, in the style of a court jester.

"He was a real nice guy," Tom says, a smile in his voice. "But I have to go. I'm sewing a cargo bag."

"Okay."

"Bye, Baby. Talk to you later."

And when I hang up I think, "Baby?" If we could conduct our relationship by phone, just maybe, baby, we wouldn't have so many problems. Odder yet is that Tom and I still hug once in a while. It just happens. Because as awkward and strange as everything is, I guess we feel a bit sorry for each other.

Some nights when I'm alone at Sweetbottom I think about the illegal immigrants that come ashore on St. John. There are several drop-off points, including Leinster, Brown, and Francis Bays. And Francis is only a short stroll from Sweetbottom. As illicit cargo on overloaded boats, these people risk their lives to get here. They're usually seeking asylum—and aren't we all, in one way or another? But when most of us come to St. John, we aren't escaping heinous political conditions and/or wretched poverty. If illegal immigrants do get caught, only people from Cuba and China get to stay, that is if they can get a foot on dry U.S. ground and have no criminal record. That's where the term, *wet foot, dry foot* comes from. Imagine being from Haiti and getting caught and repatriated, after using all the money you'd been able to cobble together over your entire lifetime to get here.

On full moon nights I lie awake on my cot, a little worried that a bunch of illegals might come ashore at Francis Bay, hungry and thirsty, half crazed from their ocean ordeal. We've heard they often arrive very early in the morning on nights like this. Our cottage is the first one they'd see after landing, and we don't even hook the screen doors because of Inkie, who lets himself in and out on his own.

Tonight I'm listening for the sound of footsteps. But the strange noises turn out to be tree frogs or cats, or weird voodoo bird sounds from the salt pond. Still, I'm all ears. Around midnight I hear a scuffle near the rear entrance. Fearing the worst, I reach for my flashlight and tiptoe toward the sound, which turns out to be all three cats taking turns leaping up onto the wall to reach a huge frog. The creature's eyes are bugged out in fear. I rescue him gently with a wet wash cloth, and carry him out to the bush.

When I try to go back to sleep, it occurs to me that if illegals were to sneak around the back of the cottage, they'd have to walk on the pea gravel. Even Tom would hear the loud crunching sound, the way sound carries near the ocean, and then all 6' 4" of him would come wandering out wearing his pink negligee. His long thin hair would be sticking out from his head like lightning bolts. They'd run, screaming. Having come up with my own little homeland security scenario, I sit up and take a last look at the moon. Lying back down, I imagine the moonlight threading through the tree branches, touching me with grace. Lucky leaps onto my bed to snuggle, and I drift off to sleep.

JUST CALL ME TIFF

*T*he first rays of morning sunshine are leaning in across the porch floor. From the salt pond across the road, bird song rises with the echoes of egrets, yellow-legs, and mangrove cuckoos. Mourning doves walk around on the rusting metal roof, like a convention of bird feet. Bananaquits twitter while eating raw sugar out of their coconut birdfeeder, hanging in the frangipani tree. And now, in the way that all geezers do in the morning, Tom clears his throat. "She looked like a man dressed like a woman." He seems puzzled. His mascara is smudged.

Feigning disinterest, I sit nearby in my own director's chair. If I let on that I'm eager to hear about his latest exploration of St. John's underbelly, he might withhold information. And for me these days, turned inward as I am, living vicariously is the next best thing to being there.

"Who?" I ask, playing with a newly discovered chin hair.

"Last night I sat next to this woman at the bar. In a man's voice, she said, 'My name's Tiffany, just call me Tiff.' Then I heard her say she used to play Little League, so I asked her, 'Are you a transgendered person?' and she looked puzzled and said, 'Whatever are you talking about?'"

"That's curious," I say, wanting him to keep talking. Something catches my eye on the frangipani—a sizeable brown lizard on a limb in the process of shedding a skin it has outgrown, the way Tom has shed his former self like a coat he removed and forgot on a long flight, a coat that never fit him anyway.

"When she left the bar, I asked the bartender if Tiff was a genetic female and he said, 'Oh, absolutely, and she's lived here for years.' I still can't believe I was so wrong about her."

I watch a gecko stalk a mosquito on the nearby screen and listen to the ocean, out of sight beyond the trees. The island is filled with strange sounds magnified by water vapors. This fact of the way sound carries on the island may have contributed to a belief in the presence of those jumbie spirits. It's also why the ocean, on a calm day, seems to be sighing as it washes in and out, like a living, breathing being, or a sleeping dragon.

"She and her friend Donna work at Shipwreck Landing," he says. "Why don't you go there for lunch tomorrow, tell me if *you* think they're for real."

"I might," I say.

But I'm thinking about the word *real*. In contrast to the strangeness of our lives, there's a magical quality to sitting here on the porch. From our little open-air theater, it's as if we're occupying another dimension.

Now I notice that the little tree near the entry has lost its leaves to the frangipani caterpillar, and new leaf buds are sprouting. Suddenly a kestrel hurls himself into the tree, talons extended to grab one of the bananaquits. In a flash of feathers, the kestrel fails to score a meal and disappears. All the little yellow birds are now hiding in a nearby grove of genip trees.

Tom stands up, his filmy pink negligee draping into place over his very tall, very lean, cellulite-free body, all the way down to his knees. "Well," he says, stretching, touching the rafters, "this girl's gotta shave."

It's my day off, and before I head out the door on my quest to discover whether or not Donna and Just-Call-Me-Tiff are for real, I stroll into Tom's bedroom to call him on the only phone in the house. Even though we continue to talk on the phone several times a day, his tone with me is cooler. He sounds distant, as if he's off in Kyoto. Inkie, the cat that goes anywhere he pleases, is asleep on Tom's blond wig in his open closet. Tom goes wherever he pleases, too, and he wore this wig on his solo outing to Maine, to The Big Closet, when he met that dominatrix. I think about how that outing changed him. I also believe he needed to take that trip.

Twenty minutes after leaving the house, remembering to keep left while driving to Coral Bay, dodging goats and water trucks, I arrive at Shipwreck Landing. Pretending to be a private investigator on assignment, I sit alone at my table for two, looking out at the ocean. I wait—an activity I'm good at these days. Trying not to stare, I glance at the woman behind the bar. Is that Just-Call-Me-Tiff?

A tall, mature woman is standing at the bar. She announces in a loud voice, "Yeah, I just retired from Homeland Security, and I can tell you one thing, that George Bush sure scares the hell outta me."

I love how people on vacation say what they think. Looking past her, I see the bartender taking the woman's order. If that is Tiff, she doesn't appear masculine. And although I don't hear what she says to the retired woman when she serves up her drink, her voice doesn't seem especially deep. The second bartender looks mannish, but like most women, they're both average-looking. Neither one of them has been to a make-up artist, and it's obvious they're both participating in that *going bra-less to pull the wrinkles out of your face* research project, sponsored by one island bar or another. They also have that Coral Bay attitude I envy that says, *Do not, under any circumstances, mess with me.* What would Tiff do if her husband realized out of the blue that *he* is really a *she*? Would his body be found washed ashore on a beach somewhere, after an unfortunate boating accident?

Ten minutes go by, and no one takes my order. That's the problem with being devastatingly average in height and weight, with a no-fuss short brown hairdo. Oh, and don't forget that I appear to be stable, trustworthy, and capable of multi-tasking. I look like most of the pushing-sixty white women in the world. Then, too, maybe undercover agents are invisible. Since I'm afraid to ask the two women behind the bar to wait on me, I take charge of the situation and leave.

When I arrive home I call Tom at the shop and report my findings, suggesting that he might have been projecting his own experiences onto others. As I listen to him reply that I probably observed the wrong bartenders, I notice that Inkie is still asleep in the closet on top of his wig.

After hanging up, I ponder my options for the rest of my day off. I could search through Tom's drawers and papers. But since he isn't secretive about what he does, that would be a waste of time. Maybe I'll raid his overflowing closet filled with feminine clothing, frilly items he got practically free off eBay.

I smile, remembering the morning he tried on his new 40AA padded bra, just in from London. He passed gas and said, "Guess my new bra is too tight." God, I'll miss stupid moments like that.

Yes, maybe I'll play dress-up, like little kids do. And while I'm at it, why not chase Inkie off the wig so I can put that on, too. I'll choose a lace slip and a slinky dress, and I'll don a pair of his size 12 heels. I'll apply some of his makeup. When my ensemble is complete, I'll top it all off with some Gucci perfume. And because he's so tall, I'll look like a little kid dressed up in her mom's clothing. Maybe I'll rip out a seam or two while I'm at it. No, slap my face. Months ago I decided that I'd at least pretend to be nice about all of this, that to fake it now would preserve the real for later, when I'll need it most, when it really matters. Anyway, it's too hot to play dress-up. Guess I'll walk to Francis Beach instead, maybe pretend I'm on vacation. I'll shed my messy life, step onto the sand, and stare mindlessly at the turquoise water. Maybe I'll sit down next to an unsuspecting tourist, and tell her about my strange life.

Tom's Saturday nights continue to start at 4:00 p.m. with his manicure appointment, and move on to a bar. Bars are where people socialize on the island, and I know that when you're drinking, people can seem awfully amusing.

This Saturday night, as usual, I stay home and watch a romantic comedy on my laptop, which distracts me from my own sit-com, one in which I play only a supporting role. Then I sit in the dark on the porch and listen to the tree frogs sing and, like a parent worried about her teenager, wonder what Tom is doing, who he's with, and when, when, WHEN will he ever get home? He needs to explore, to discover who he really is, which is why I've set him free to do just that. And I thought moving to paradise might help our troubled marriage. Hah! Maybe someday we'll be good friends. Maybe not.

Inkie is crunching dry cat food, the sound echoing in the moist night air. Lucky, who sleeps with me every night when she isn't out prowling around, is chewing a foot clean, and Twodot is asleep on top of the refrigerator. The cats and I have taken to calling Tom a new name: Daddy Girl, as in, "Daddy Girl's out tonight, going to the dogs."

As bedtime approaches, I go into my bathroom to brush my teeth and watch the family of daddy longlegs up in one corner of the mold-spotted white ceiling. Then, from the better viewing position of the toilet, I study the cluster of baby daddies to see if they've grown any bigger since the last time I peed.

From my cot I look out through the screens that serve as windows, listening to the gentle night sounds as the moon peeks through the branches of the ancient genip tree. Sometimes it feels as if the moon is my best friend, the way it loves without scorching. On the other hand, Tom has been like a campfire: a magical, warming experience, alternating with flames that flared up and get too hot. Yet now that I've gained some psychic distance from the fire, I feel a chill—even in the subtropical climate of St. John.

Finally I doze off, only to be awakened by the grind of the lawn-mower car as it makes its way up the driveway, lurching to a stop below my window screen. Oil fumes waft into the room as Tom clomps up the irregular wood steps.

As I sip my coffee in the early dawn light, waves crash ashore at Francis Bay. I'm waiting for Tom to speak. Suddenly all the banana-quits flee from the frangipani tree, as if blown away by a strong gust of wind.

"One of them farted," Tom announces.

And this is how I know he's in a good mood and will share his latest Saturday night adventure. He clears his throat and begins. He tells me that after dinner out with one of his new female friends, he ended up at a bar in Cruz Bay. "Two women tourists in their early fifties were there," he says, looking into his cup. "Darn. There's an ant floating in my coffee." He fishes it out and flicks it onto the porch floor. "Anyway, they were from Texas. I sat by one of them, and the next thing you know she was bragging about the boob job she got for her fiftieth birthday. And then to everyone's surprise, she took off her skimpy top and sat there pointing to her bare breasts, describing how the surgeon went in through the nipple to do the work. She said to me, 'See if *you* can find a scar.'"

He pauses then. I hold my breath, fearing that he won't finish this story.

"And no, I didn't stare," Tom says, smiling to himself, remembering the scene. "But I asked her if her nipples were still sensitive, and she said, 'Oh, yeah!' Then she took both of my hands and rubbed them on her nipples. She closed her eyes and said, 'Oh, yeah!' over and over, just like the woman in the porn movie we saw that time. I thought she'd never stop rubbing my hands on her nipples."

Tom holds up his right hand to admire his fresh manicure. He sips his coffee and gazes out into the giant genip tree, and I remember two things: that the bar tender at this particular watering hole is gay and collects pictures of erections. Knowledge like this helps me keep my situation in perspective. And now I hope Tom won't wander off to shave, leaving me hanging. It takes all of my self-control not to say, "So… what happened next?"

Finally, he continues. "Her eyes were closed, and she kept saying, 'Oh, yeah! I just *love* that.' After a while, she pushed my hands away, put on her top, and the two women left. Just like that. And everyone else left, too. End of party."

Suddenly all the bananaquits return to the frangipani tree near the door. Tom sits in his pink negligee, smiling. "Before the nipple incident, the other woman asked me if I was straight."

"So what did you tell her?"

"I said 'yes.'"

"You didn't mention that you're transgendered?"

"Oh, no. That topic is way too complicated for bar talk."

And a recurring thought pops into my head. Compared to the
people Tom's been hanging out with at the bars, I must seem awfully underwhelming. He's probably forgotten how conservative he was
when we met ten years ago, how I was the liberal one, the social one.
This was still the case four years ago when we moved to St. John and
bought The Canvas Factory. I also know that when he's with his new
women friends, he treats them with the utmost consideration and
charm. Because when he talks with them on the phone, his new, high-
er-octave voice goes all gooey. It's his transgendered-*Fargo*-car salesman voice.

DIALING FOR DOLLARS

On New Year's Eve I'm at Pastory Gardens with Livy and Tom, Barb and Jim. Tom stops by for one drink with us, on his migratory path from bar to bar this night of merry making. After dinner the two couples and I play miniature golf as the band plays a Garth Brooks song that goes, *I've got friends in low places, where the whiskey drowns and the beer chases the blues away.* It's one of my favorites, and I sing and dance around like a fool while golfing poorly, remembering the Montana cowboys and fishing guides I danced with to that song, before meeting Tom.

I arrive home first, and lie on my cot in the dark corner, awake, listening to the sighing of the ocean. I think about the mysteries of the quantum field. Were the past 11 years with Tom only an illusion?

Lord knows what time Tom finally straggles in, but on the morning of New Year's Day, we sit on the porch a little later than usual. The caterpillars have eaten all the leaves on the frangipani tree, growing long and fat and gorgeous in the process. Then poof, they disappeared. Now the tree's cane-sized branches are totally naked. Diddie's tarantula frangipani is also leafless, so I guess the spray did nothing to discourage the caterpillars.

Eager to hear more about Tom's adventures of the night before, I act nonchalant, not too eager. If he wants a witness to his most recent escapade, I'm available.

And Tom says, "Look how nice the birds are about taking turns at the birdfeeder."

I look toward the frangipani tree again. Now that the sunlight is shining more directly on the branches, I see that tiny new leaves are already beginning to sprout. During the tree's transition, the bananaquits went on about their business as if nothing was happening to the tree. These little yellow birds are gracious creatures, and they are regular in their habits. On the other hand, Tom is an exotic bird, an uncommon species. You just never *know* what he might say or do, or not. He doesn't even seem to know.

Tom stands up. "Well, time to go for a walk."

"Me, too," I say. "My cousin, Jimmy, and his wife, Lorna, are coming to visit in time to walk 8 Tuff Miles with me."

"Oh, really. Looks like we'll be sleeping together again."

"Yes, and the same rules will apply as before, when your kids were here." Tom's sons had visited in December and we'd had to sleep together then, too. I would not, however, let him wear his nightgown to bed. Or allow any groping.

There are numerous walking routes to choose from. I walk up the hill to Maho Bay Camp, down the goat trail to Big Maho Bay, then along the North Shore Road to Cinnamon Bay. Walking fast, I think about how good it will be to see my cousin again, with his outrageous sense of humor. We grew up in close proximity, but haven't seen each other much over the decades since. He and Lorna lived in Alaska for years, before retiring to Idaho, and I've moved around a bit, too.

As I walk home from Cinnamon Bay, I think about my situation with Tom. A familiar sadness sweeps over me like a tsunami. I realize why I've clung to the relationship all these years. Tom brought out my wildish wit, creativity, intelligence and latent voice. I was brighter and funnier with him than I've ever been with anyone else. In the film *Jane Eyre,* Jane tells a half-cousin, "Mr. Rochester was the first person who recognized me for who I really am and loved me for it." In spite of our problems, Tom was my Mr. Rochester, only with a better sense of humor—a Mr. R who was hiding a second self in the attic instead of a crazy wife. In some ways, it's as if our two personalities created a highly original and engaging third entity, one that was whole.

But I'd better step up the pace because I must get home so I can drive to the shop and open the doors at 9:30. With so many people on island over the holidays, it will be an especially hectic day at the shop.

And it is a busy day, with fun customers coming and going,

including a couple buying canvas bags for family members back home. As I run their credit card I say, the way I sometimes do, "I call this *Dialing for Dollars*."

The man says, "I directed that television show, years ago."

"You're pulling my leg."

"No. My name is Ralph Kuen."

"I used to love that show. How fun to meet you."

What I wish is that I could ask him to work out the terms of my divorce, because that, too, feels like dialing for dollars.

For the past few months, Tom has been practically bionic—full of energy, happy as a lark, staying out late, and getting up early. But this morning it's already 7:00 a.m. and he's still sleeping, so I tiptoe into his bedroom to make certain he's still breathing. He's also been pleasant and cooperative lately, even usually coming home right after work to cook and eat dinner with me, then going to bed early to read war books or books about the transgender experience. One day after work he invites me to go with him to the art reception at Bajo el Sol Gallery. It's fun to see Livy and Tom, happily hosting a gallery filled to overflowing with people who appreciate good art and free wine. Later, as we walk together toward our separate vehicles to drive home, I hang onto him when we walk past The Gecko Bar so he won't veer off and decide to stay there. We joke and laugh about this, with Tom pulling away toward the bar stools.

And he seems concerned about my welfare. One morning he asks, "Sleep all right?"

"Oh, off and on," I say. "Things kept waking me up. You know how sound carries. Someone burped up at Maho."

We're getting along so well that I hate to break the spell. But I had finally called the attorney, and she faxed me a list of documents and info she needs for a collaborative divorce. We will pay off all our debts and divide up our assets (except for inheritances and retirement funds) equally. I'm to bring the info along when I meet with her next week on St. Thomas. She'll help iron out a settlement, or separation agreement. Since Tom has been our business manager, I must get some of the required info from him, and this is awkward, especially since he still sometimes calls me *Baby*.

The counselor we both see on a separate basis tells me this is the hardest part, the way all our hopes and dreams and efforts come down to a division of property. She also doesn't think Tom consciously meant to harm me or drive me away, and that he doesn't want me to leave. She may be right, but for me a person's actions speak louder than a second-hand message from a counselor.

In Montana, if it's winter you connect an unused car battery to a trickle charger. The slow, steady charge this provides keeps the battery from freezing and going flat. Trustafarians, those lucky people who receive regular infusions of trust fund, must feel like one of those batteries. And if I can survive the next couple years until I reach green grass, at age 62, I'll start to receive a small trickle charge of social security and retirement. Just imagine. A fixed-income level of borderline poverty you can count on. In the meantime, I can access my 401K, now that I am 59-1/2 years old, and this will get me by until the lot sells and the provisions of the divorce are settled. My 401K, earned when I worked for the U.S. Forest Service, isn't exactly fat, and I hesitate to tap into it. What if it's like breaking a twenty dollar bill? The next thing you know, it's gone. The good news is that less than four years after we bought the lot at Fish Bay for $58,000, the realtor lists it at $179,000. This is a minor miracle, for someone who has, historically, bought high and sold low.

It's Saturday, Tom's day off, and he's sitting on the porch in his negligee, facing the genip tree and the sweeping lawn, integrating, drinking coffee. I'm heading out the door for an early morning walk to train for 8 Tuff Miles, aware that timing is everything. Tom knows I've been working on the draft separation agreement, a document we've come to refer to as our separation *dis*agreement. I've managed to pull together the needed information, including the exact date of my divorce from husband number two, back in the 1970s. I'd forgotten all about him. The attorney and I worked many expensive hours together crafting a settlement that she agreed was "more than fair and generous." And now I feel like I'm dropping a bomb on Tom. So I don't hand it to him on my way out the door. I chicken out again. Instead, I lay the proposal on his computer chair, and later when I leave for work, I mention it.

In the early afternoon when he calls me to chat, he doesn't say anything about the document. It's as if we're not getting a divorce. But then, he *is* required to respond to the agreement only in writing. Our counselor established this little protocol, after we failed to discuss the matter in a civil manner and requested her advice. Our early attempts at discussion went something like this:

"Can you just sit down and pretend to listen?" I ask.

"If you have any comments I can ignore, please speak up," Tom says.

Days go by with no response from Tom about the separation disagreement. He's more concerned with his manicure. One day I mention that my next appointment with the attorney is in three days. What about the document?

"I'm thinking about it," he says. "I'm completely overwhelmed by all that's happening. I'll miss our daily interaction terribly. I really do appreciate our time together."

I'm all stressed out, tearful, confused, and my head aches. Then I remember the pinched nerve in my neck. After a trip to see Bern, I feel much better physically and emotionally. How can I leave Bern? He knows how to fix me. But then, maybe I won't need to be fixed after I leave. Maybe my physical ailments are partly psychosomatic. And thank God I'm doing the 8 Tuff Miles race. The extra walking seems to alleviate some stress. I even decide to do one of the pre-race tune-ups, set up by race organizers to help island residents prepare for the big event.

This Saturday morning, the five and one-half mile tune-up for the race takes place on the Centerline Road. Participants will walk or run from Cruz Bay to Chateau Bordeaux Restaurant, almost to our former home at Villa Debris. The sky is clear and so far the temperature isn't too hot. As I walk, I decide to think only positive thoughts, like how grateful I am to be strong and healthy enough to walk this far, even if I am panting and bringing up the rear. Then I say all the affirmations I can remember, since I didn't bring my list. After about one and one-half hours of walking as fast as I can, mostly uphill, I'm finally on the steep climb to the topmost point of the route. Livy runs back to cheer me on and walk with me. She encourages me to go faster, to pass an elderly man who'd left his walker back in Cruz Bay. I don't want to let her down so I pour it on, practicing the race-walking technique, until I'm neck and neck with the old man, who is limping a little but is oh-so determined, and finally, finally I pass him by a hair just before reaching the finish line. I almost start to cry, like I just won a gold medal for my country, when all I did was pass an old guy so I wouldn't come in last.

After the event, Tom and I and Livy and Tom H. agree to meet in Cruz Bay for breakfast at the Inn at Tamarind Court. The shady, open air courtyard is pleasant, and the pace of the service allows the luxury of time to visit. I'm a little weak but happy, feeling expansive and free, so I tell everyone about the country and western song title I came across while doing some online research: "There Ain't Enough Room in my Fruit Of The Looms to Hold All My Lovin' for You."

Tom H. says, "Who sang that, I wonder?"

I say, "I think it was Charley Pride."

After our laughter subsides and we finish breakfast, I drive to Mongoose Junction, wash up in the restroom, throw on my goddess dress, open the shop by noon, and enjoy a record-breaking sales day.

Unable to hasten Tom along with the separation disagreement, I decide to wait until after Jimmy and Lorna's visit to meet with the attorney. I'll give the issue a rest, especially since our guests don't yet know about the divorce or Tom's gender dysphoria. There's plenty of time. Besides, Tom is acting all happy, and I don't want him to have a big fat Viking meltdown when we have company.

In the mornings and on my one day off a week, I train for the big race. On the spur of the moment, I decide to walk from Sweetbottom to Coral Bay for a massage with Cathy. This trek has to be close to five miles, one way. I set out walking east toward the early morning sun, first along Mary's Creek to Annaberg Plantation, continuing along Leinster Bay on the rock and dirt plantation road, then along the beach to the jump off point for snorkeling around Waterlemon Cay. From there I find a trail going into the sea grapes and a sign showing the start of the Johnny Horn Trail. Up the trail a little further I begin to scale new heights. In Montana we'd say this deeply rutted dirt road is "steeper than a cow's face." I stop often to catch my breath, but finally, after an hour and fifteen minutes I arrive at Cathy's massage studio in Coral Bay.

After a wonderful massage, Cathy and I eat breakfast at The Donkey Diner (Home of Some Kick-Ass Food). Then I walk home, most of the way at the speed of a crawl, retracing my route past the red-roofed Moravian Church, over the steep mountain trail past clothing strewn about by the illegal immigrants. It's roasting hot now, between 85 and 90 degrees, and I'm way too full. But I'm proud of my ten-mile walk. I'm taking care of myself. While I'm more optimistic than I've felt in a long time, I'm still a little paranoid about feeling too good for my plus-sized britches.

Back at home I decide to swim at Francis Bay, and when I reach for my black swimsuit, draped over a shutter on the back of the house next to the shower, two huge frogs leap out of the bra. What an honor.

Every two weeks I see Bern for a treatment. Today, a week before the big race, he tells me, "You're the third tall woman I've seen today." When I tell him I'm only 5' 7" he is surprised. He thought I was at least 5' 9". I have lost weight while training. And all the fuss about the separation disagreement has wrecked my appetite. I'm proud to say that anyone walking behind me on race day will notice that my jostling cheeks, once resembling the war of the worlds, are now more like a border skirmish.

Jimmy and Lorna arrive a few days before 8 Tuff Miles. During the day I show them around the island, and at night we all eat together, that is if Tom is home. On race day, as we drive into Cruz Bay where the race starts, Jimmy bites into an apple and a crown comes off an eye tooth. He says it doesn't hurt. "Oh, great," I tell him. "Now when I introduce you as my cousin from Idaho, you'll smile and be missing a front tooth."

"And they'll think I'm a hick from the sticks."

During the race, Jimmy, Lorna and I walk together most of the way. Soon Lorna decides she wants to walk a little slower, and tells us to go for it. Now I'm walking as fast as I can, while Jimmy walks as slowly as he can. At the first water station, Tina and James are handing out cups of water, cheering everyone on, and I do my race walking strut to show off. As we walk along, Jimmy and I talk and joke about our childhoods. His parents owned The Green Owl Tavern, and we recount some incidents that have become lore in northern Idaho. He's so funny and I laugh so hard, that I beg him to stop. I need to use the restroom and there isn't one.

On Bordeaux Mountain we walk through a cooling cloud of rain and wind. And before you know it, at a time of two hours and sixteen minutes, Jimmy graciously allows me to cross the finish line first. Five hundred and eighty-nine people finish the race, and, once again, Tom wins the trophy for his age class. We had negotiated a trade in work schedules. He will open the shop from 1:00 – 4:00. Later I learn that he missed the awards ceremony because of his manicure appointment.

After the race, Jimmy, Lorna, and I laze around Sweetbottom. Later, when we walk to Francis Bay to swim, I tell them about the pending divorce and explain that Tom is transgendered. They are, of course, sorry to hear about the divorce and totally surprised about the other news. While they'd noticed Tom's feminine appearance and manner of dress, they hadn't imagined what it meant. They enjoy Tom's company and want to be supportive.

"In Alaska and Idaho, there aren't any transgendered people," Jimmy says, smiling, exposing his missing tooth.

"That you know of," I say.

On the day before Jimmy and Lorna leave, we enjoy a lovely luncheon buffet at Caneel Bay Resort. Thanks to the camaraderie of their visit, along with the fun and successful race, I feel hopeful that someday everything will be all right. After they leave for Idaho, I'm back to moving the divorce proceedings along and sleeping alone on the cot in the living room. Tom is gleeful that he can resume sleeping in his negligee.

By now weeks have passed with no progress on the separation disagreement. The biggest obstacle is not having an appraisal of the business, and we can't get one easily without listing it for sale. But Tom wants to stay and operate the business by himself. It seems to me the business is worth more than it was in 2001. After all, real estate prices have escalated. But a business is worth only what someone will pay for it, and Glen doesn't believe the shop's value has increased. Since we both respect his opinion, we use the amount we paid for the business as the value. I only want what's fair. And I don't want to sever myself completely from St. John, my new friends, Sweetbottom, the cats or Tom. So I redo the agreement for the last time. As I hand him the revised document, I say, "I'll be lucky to escape with the clothes on my back."

Tom replies, "I might have a dress you can wear."

And after he signs the document, he says, "You know, you could crash here at Sweetbottom next winter in exchange for working weekends at the shop."

"By crash do you mean room and board?"

"Of course," Tom says. "You know I'm always willing to meet you a quarter of the way."

I don't make him say it twice. I'll leave my car over the summer and he'll drive it once in a while to keep it running, and he'll re-register it when the time comes. Lucky will stay, and be here when I return in early winter. I'm looking forward to cultivating a friendship with Tom that's more authentic, while keeping the good feelings we have for each other. It's a win-win situation. Tom gets the farm and I get free of the farm, yet retain visitation rights. I've decided to view this turn of events as one more way to build world peace—one ex-husband at a time. It will be a divorce with a happy ending.

CHICKSCHOOL.EDU

*T*he shop is a nuthouse, with both of us sewing on a new corporate order. One day Jan from Woodbine stops by. She jokes with me about how I work for food, clothing, shelter, and the big S = sex. We all have a great big wet-your-pants laugh over that one. And after she leaves, Tom and I continue to make jokes.

"Maybe I'm a candidate to be a dominatrix," I say. "Or wait, maybe *you* are. Maybe that's what this is all about."

Tom says, "I wonder if there's an online course you can take, maybe get a certificate. It would be a course like boat captains take to become certified as ministers so they can marry people and charge for it."

"What would they call a course that trains you to become a dominatrix?" I ask. "And what do you suppose the plural would be?"

"The word matrix becomes matrices," he said, suddenly professorial, "so it would be dominatrices. Of course."

I have to say this much for Tom: he does raise the IQ in a factory setting.

It's morning, again. My favorite time of day. Tom is sitting in his director's chair on the porch wearing his favorite nightgown, telling me about the previous night.

"I was sitting at a bar next to a hefty black woman. She leans over and says, 'You married?'"

"Not really."

"You lookin'?"

"No. I'm available, but I'm not really looking."

"You ever had you some black meat?"

"Excuse me?"

"I said, you ever been wit a black woman?"

"No, only white."

"You gotta try you some black meat. How 'bout it?"

"I sat up tall and straight and pointed to The Canvas Factory logo on my pink tank top, and said, 'Well, this is where I work.'"

She said, "'Okay, I'll bring a friend by to meet you.'"

"Be sure to practice safe sex," I say.

"Hah! Don't worry," he says. "There's nothing like taking estrogen with a testosterone blocker to wreck a man's libido."

Later I'm checking my email on the computer before I head to work, when Tom hands me a photo to look at. "Here's the official photo of the regulars at The Gecko Bar."

"Oh, it's your new tribe." He's in the picture, with a blond woman on either side, both sporting bodacious ta-tas and cleavage you cannot overlook. I blur my eyes and see a chihuahua peeking out from between a pair of boobs.

"And there you are," I say, pointing to Tom in the photo, next to the chihuahua.

That would be me," he says, actually looking at my face for the first time in quite a while. "And you need to remove your mustache."

There should be an online advice column or a website for people like Tom, something like www.chickschool.edu. And I'll be the webmaster. Because, it doesn't matter how pretty you make yourself or how feminine your voice sounds if you are a transgendered male-to-female (M2F) who lacks the feminine qualities of accommodation, caring, consideration, and thoughtfulness toward others. The term *post-macho dichotomy* might fit this syndrome. Think about it. Such an essential sea change of personality traits is a much bigger deal than changing the color of, say, your nail polish. It's probably more like learning to speak an entirely new language, one featuring a Cyrillic alphabet, knowing you will never again in good conscience speak the language of your homeland.

I find an article on the Internet by the wife of a transgendered man, discussing the choices a wife or significant other has. You can take on the role of his mother, believing that by doing so you can exercise some control over the situation. But it seems to me, this role would include imitating a golden retriever. You'd always be happy to see him (excuse me, her); be available to talk non-stop about his painful and difficult realization; be patient as he practices his feminine walk and arm gestures; and, in your spare time, you'd serve as his fashion and makeup consultant. You know, the partner as project program.

This witnessing of Tom's transformation has been a fascinating experience for me. And, of course, it's been painful. Of course, there are feelings of loss. I've tried to be big about it, and you might be thinking I'm pathetic in some way. But until such a thing happens to you, you can't know, really, how you'd respond. If you truly love someone, you can't help but feel compassion for the turmoil they're going through. If you're his wife, you'll probably also reach new heights of disappointment.

Then one day, when you hear him raise his voice an octave, when he uses *his* breath in a way you've never heard before, you'll catch yourself holding your own breath. For one thing, you've heard him make so many different sounds, before the two of you stopped making love. While still holding your breath, you'll listen intently, like cats do when a small branch touches the side of the house. And when he talks about how hard it is to be transgendered, using this higher octave voice when speaking, you'll take an inquisitive stance. For you are serving as a witness to his experience. If your own pesky feelings of betrayal erupt in sarcasm, well, shame on you. How is that helpful to someone going through so much inner turbulence? A bigger person, a more spiritually evolved woman than you, wouldn't have such feelings. And that would *not* be me. But I'm working on it. And, really, if you think about it, it really is funnier than hell.

And every couple is different, depending on the two individuals involved. Other factors include your cultural backgrounds, your political leanings, and your religion, or lack of it. I've decided that while Tom's discovery of who he really is changes our relationship, it also isn't the end of our world as friends.

On the other hand, there are ways the transgendered person can step up to the plate and make it easier on the spouse. It's called having grace, and grace works both ways. Frankly, Tom could have done better in this department. Important instructions along these lines would also appear on this website called www.chickschool.edu.

Other women will choose to abandon the S.O.B so he can discover who *he* really is as a *she,* without *her* interference. But for me, choosing something in between feels right. It isn't just love or loyalty. It's also selfish. Tom is a beautiful person, flaws and all, no matter what name or pronoun he goes by. Other than my parents and my son, he's been the most important person in my life to date. Some might compare my choice to the honking of a loud horn—out of sight but coming toward me. But that's the choice I'm making, no matter how large the risk.

My theory is that Tom wants to be free to discover who he is, at the same time as he wanted the security of having me close by. I believe that's why he alternately withdrew from me and then reconnected, only to push me away and then pull me back—for all those years. He's doing the best he can, all things considered. I mean, he is, after all, flying by the seat of his panties. And I admire him for negotiating these profound changes with so much intelligence and skill. After all, the suicide rate is high in the transgender community.

The learning curve is steep for anyone close to a transgendered person. It's taken a while for me, but I've come to my own realizations: that there are many kinds of love, and that loving someone at a soul level has absolutely nothing to do with gender.

THE KEEPER OF MEMORIES

When I tell my son on the phone that Tom is going to Bellingham for Melinda's wedding, he says, "Melinda will have one less bridesmaid to round up." Tom's response to this is, "I'd much rather dress like a bridesmaid than wear a tuxedo. And if I have to wear a penguin suit, I want it to be pink." Melinda considers his request. While it's none of my business, I think his appearance in a pink tuxedo would steal attention from the bride, on this important occasion. She decides on the black tuxedo.

After Tom leaves for the wedding, I sleep comfortably in the big bed. One night I awake just before 2:00 a.m. and can't go back to sleep. The full moon is lighting the island, so I walk to the salt pond overlook, where I sit on a bench. A feeling of infinite possibilities for the future comes over me. Below on the salt pond, birds make soft splashing noises and talk to each other, like benevolent spirits. Smiling, I amble home, drink warm milk with cardamom, and sleep like pond sediment until Lucky chews on my chin at 6:00 a.m.

For some reason, with Tom gone I feel more like going out on the island, and I make a date with Livy and Tom to meet them after work at Pastory Gardens for a drink. I'll probably drink cranberry juice with soda, which I call a Hibiscus Fizz. While waiting for them, I stand at the deck railing and watch the sky. Just before sunset a waitress distributes free rum punches and I take one, knowing I shouldn't, and as I sip, the sun eases itself below the horizon in a stunning profusion of oranges, pinks, fuchsias, purples. When I turn to the east to see what *those* clouds are doing, I see a perfectly full moon glowing in a lavender blue sky. I feel happy, and filled with hope that this moment symbolizes the rest of my life.

It's odd how some memories are doubled by the light of the moon. I think back to other evenings here, like the night Tom and I danced to the tune, *Man Smart, Woman Smarter,* a time when the marriage was already circling the drain. I drank rum that night, too. But tonight, after another half hour goes by, it becomes clear that Livy and Tom aren't coming, that we had a miscommunication. I'm glad for the time to savor my feelings of euphoria alone.

Driving home along the North Shore Road, I pass Easter Rock, that giant volcanic monument, and pass the trail that leads up to Peace Hill. During our second trip to St. John, in January, 2001, Tom and I were hitchhiking to Peace Hill and caught a ride with a nice man named, oddly enough, Bony Peace. I've since checked online, and the guy was for real. When I reach Cinnamon Bay, I pull off the road. The frogs are singing with so much gusto I feel sad and happy all at the same time, for I am, after all, hearing the frogs sing, and while I'm leaving St. John, I *am* coming back.

On my return from a morning walk, Diddie shows me the new flower buds on the genip tree. It's springtime on the island, and the buds are poised to burst into clusters of white, sweet-smelling flowers. Bees will swarm the centuries-old tree, and Sweetbottom will be infused with the smell of honeysuckle and vanilla. The frangipani, now covered with full-sized leaves, also reveals flower buds.

It's been hot lately. After my walk I feel the need for a meal featuring starchy carbs, and set about mixing up a batch of pancakes. I'm not totally naked, but I *am* topless, and this feels wonderfully freeing and risky, like that night Tom and I went skinny-dipping at Francis Bay. For me, lately, walking around the house without clothes defines living on the edge. While flipping a pancake, I notice a long cat hair, probably one of Twodot's, near my right nipple. I let go of the pancake turner and attempt to brush it off, taking care not to flick it onto my pancake, but the hair is attached. It's an inch-long nipple hair! I could give it new life, put some *product* on it, maybe train it. I'll bet little Miss Texas, with the boob job, doesn't sport a nipple whisker. I immediately leave to find a tweezers, and by the time I return to the kitchen, free of the offending whisker, my pancake is scorched.

After Tom has been gone for a week, I'm rudely reminded how fine it will be next winter when I only have to work two days a week at the shop instead of six or sometimes seven. My body needs attention. I go see Bern, and while he's taking my arm through the range-of-motion exercises, I tell him, "I think Tom is going to be my last, best husband." And Bern agrees that three marriages are probably enough. When I tell him that I want to be Tom's friend, he says, "As long as you spend time with someone because you really enjoy them and not because you invested twelve years on them and hate to give up."

That got my attention. Yes, once I leave I will need to place myself in a new context, to define my own culture. I'll even be free to date. Oh, dear God. I can only imagine the new batch of trouble I'll get into. This begs the question, *Is the devil you know worse than the devil you don't (yet) know?* When you're lonely and haven't had sex in a long time and you're me, you might be vulnerable. Yes, even at my age. What if some totally inappropriate man, let's say one just out of prison for killing his wife, makes eye contact with me? Let's say he's real good looking except for all those tattoos, and he's horny too, and then ... he winks at me. We know what *that* means. Okay, so he's interested in me and he's available immediately, no waiting. So what if he isn't the man of my dreams? He's not Russell Crow, Robert Duvall, or that handsome man from the Viagra ads. When he asks me to meet him in a dark alley, will I say, "Which one?"

I can't be trusted.

And then Tom returns. After only one day off in two weeks, I stay home two days in a row. I resume art lessons with Livy and finish a pastel painting of a huge tree with a strangler fig climbing all over it. I give the picture to James, who prunes and maintains trees on the island.

A friend with a cabin on a mountainside south of Helena, Montana, offers to rent me his cabin for the summer. My reply is a big fat yes. The log cabin has two small bedrooms, two big porches, a picture window that faces the Elkhorn Mountains, a wood-burning stove for heat and one for cooking, but only 12-volt power. In other words, no electricity. But I'll use batteries with my laptop. And I'll be only 45 minutes from Jeff, Lee and Madison. I'll finally get to be a real grandmother.

A mature couple comes into the shop, the man toting a knapsack with a Zermatt patch on it. Since I lived in Switzerland in my early 20s and want to go back, I ask about the patch. They tell me they've taken several guided hiking trips with a company out of Portland called Walking Softly Adventures. At home I look them up online and see that they aren't going to Switzerland this summer, but are offering other trips in Europe. One of them catches my attention, a hiking adventure over the Carpathian Mountains between Budapest and Krakow. I had thought Hungary was something like Kansas with big turnip farms, but they actually share a substantial mountain range with neighboring countries like Slovakia, a country I didn't even know existed. I make a reservation for August, the month I turn 60.

When I leave the end of May, I'll stop in New York City to see my friend, Carolyn, who worked here in 2003 as an interpretive specialist for the Virgin Islands National Park. When my son, Jeff, was here, she guided them on that hike down the Reef Bay Trail. After that it's on to Montana, where I'll move into the little cabin on the mountainside. During the month of September I'll be a resident at the Montana Artists' Refuge in Basin, and then I'll return to St. John to be Tom's roommate and part-time employee.

But now the shop is a nightmare. I continue to keep my head down and work hard, shaving seconds off every task, but there's simply too much to do. And Tom works hard as well, but he's much better at pacing himself than I am. How will he manage the shop all by himself? He's not terribly concerned, but he agrees to let me advertise for part-time help for him.

We hire a local woman who irons and trims pockets, cuts straps and zippers, and cleans, but she can't cut canvas because she's left handed and the shop and all the tools are tightly set up for right-handed people. She's good-natured, though, so I teach her how to sew mini bags. Soon she finds a full-time job and leaves. Since Angie left, we've tried off and on to hire part-time help. There was the woman unable to use the sewing machines. Another woman, when asked to cut ten-inch zippers for mini bags, using the tape measure glued to the cutting table, cut them all at nine and one-half inches instead, creating dozens of zippers that couldn't be used for anything at all.

A woman calls from St. Thomas, where I'd placed an ad in a newspaper. A quiet, pleasant West Indian woman, she knows how to sew and can work one day a week. And then another woman from St. Thomas appears in the shop. She's in her 40s, born on St. Kitts but has lived in New Jersey, where she designed and sewed bags. Engaging and talkative, she brags that she can sew anything, and we don't insult her by asking her to demonstrate. She begins working with Tom all day Wednesdays, my day off, and her only day free to work. She really can sew without too many mistakes, except during Carnival on St. Thomas, when she falls in love. That week we end up throwing several bags she makes in the Dumpster.

While packing a box of personal items to ship to Montana, I run across a photo of Tom and me on a backpacking trip in the Madison Range near West Yellowstone. We're sitting on top of a ridge, Tom with his crew-cut, me with longer hair blowing off sideways like a flag. We're smiling and holding onto each other so we won't blow away. Later in the day, when I tell a friend that Tom seems to have zero recollection of our good times together, she says, "So, you get to be the keeper of those memories for both of you." But part of me wonders, if your soon-to-be-ex doesn't treasure the good times, the very reasons you stayed married all those years, did those special moments even happen? It's the familiar tree falling in the woods question (if no one hears it, did it make a sound?). In ancient tribes, someone would be assigned the task of remembering the stories and events of the tribe, because there was no writing. I can do that. I can be the holder of memories for both of us. Does he not care to look back because at the time he wasn't being his true self? Or does he experience life in an episodic way rather than a more linear, chronological way. I've read that those individuals are good at living in the moment. Come to think of it, life would be simpler if I had amnesia. Forgetting and laughing seem better than remembering and being sad.

Then I remember the saying, *Don't cry when it's over—smile because it happened,* and this helps for a few minutes with some of the loss and disappointment.

When all six of my boxes are finally packed for Montana, I muscle them into my car and then double-park in front of the post office to unload them, fearing that Sgt. Adder will catch me. After moving my car, I wait in line, feeling lucky because Chester (The Mighty Groover) is working today. I stand, shifting my weight from one foot to the other, trying to think positive thoughts, when I overhear a woman say to the man behind her, "I have a crew of workers at my place, but the work is going so slow. And the men have gone to the bathroom all over my lot. The contractor didn't bother to rent a Porta-Potty. It is so disgusting. I can't wait for them to finish building the house."

"Go round up a bunch of soldier crabs," the man says. "They'll clean it all up for you."

Another man in line chips in, "Be sure to use soldier crabs and not land crabs."

In Montana, I won't hear conversations like this, but at least I'm hearing it now—and I can add it to my store of memories.

DADDY GIRL

"Do you have a minute?" Tom hollers from his bedroom. And I know this does not mean, "Do you have time for a quickie."

At this exact minute, I'm sitting in the living room on the couch, hunched over my laptop, head phones on. I look up from an episode of the TV show, "Grey's Anatomy." When I take a deep breath, I smell the vanilla and honeysuckle scent of genip blossoms wafting into the room through the window screens. On one of my last nights at Sweetbottom before leaving for Montana, I'm already dressed for bed. Tom might let me wear one of his pink nighties, but I prefer to sleep in more basic attire on warm subtropical nights—a wife-beater under shirt and a pair of granny panties.

So often during our marriage when Tom would ask, "Do you have a minute?" I wanted to say, "No, I'm sorry, I don't." I've learned to con-sider this question of his with caution. For instance, during our sail-ing adventures, he might have meant, "Can you take the helm? I have to use the head." And at that exact *minute* we'd be barreling along in a gale with all sails up toward one lost continent or another in the San Juan Islands. The wind would be screaming through the rigging, with waves kicked up to the height you'd expect in a perfect storm. And in some ways, that image could represent our entire 12-year marriage. And that's exciting, if you live through it.

"Sure, I have a minute," I say, stealing one last glance at the comput-er screen, at my new best friends, the interns at Seattle Grace Hospital. It's true that at my age I could be the mother of every one of these young doctors, but their lives are so wonderfully screwed up, some even worse than mine. And I need friends. It gets a little lonely being the roommate and soon-to-be ex-wife of a man who now has every intention of becoming a woman.

When I remove my head phones, night music floods the room. Thanks to a late afternoon storm, the tree frogs are performing in surround sound, yet I can still make out the whoosh and sigh of ocean waves—the calming white noise that helps me get to sleep most nights.

"I have a new outfit," Tom calls. "Can I model it for you?"

"This had better be good," I yell above the tree frogs. "There'd better be some cleavage."

Tom laughs his hearty male laugh. He still thinks I'm funny, a quality I find endearing in another human being. He's funny, too, which is one of the reasons I'll be returning to St. John this coming winter. There's the great scenery and climate, of course. And it's good to be here as a friend, during Tom's transition from babe magnet to babe.

And soon all 6' 4" of him, mostly legs, enters the living room, practicing his best runway strut. He's wearing a new top with a very short, white knit skirt. The camisole top hugging his chest is a lightweight knit with cap sleeves in an elegant taupe color. The V-neck is beaded with flat, shiny sequins and the color is surprisingly lovely against his tanned, hair-free arms and chest. Lord, yes, his chest. The chest I fell in love with was never all that hairy, but I can recall the exact minute of that early spring day in a remote cabin near Polebridge, Montana, when I first thought of Tom's chest, with its two tiny pink birds in little nests, as a haven on which to lay my head and my future.

Here are a few details regarding the anatomy of the person standing before me: his legs are very long, lean, tan and ultra-smooth. There isn't a hint of cellulite, and I hate him for this. His former silver crew-cut has been replaced by shoulder-length platinum blond tresses which he wears flipped up at the bottom. His manicurist and new best friend keeps the nails on his fingers and toes polished to a high sheen in the color called Chiffon, a sparkly pink confection containing actual diamond dust particles.

He's waiting, watching me, poised like a mannequin. I have found new usefulness as a fashion consultant—me, who hasn't worn lipstick in over a year and whose favorite dress-up attire is a pair of rompers in a color called mango peach. All I can say is, "Wow!" You might lose your vocabulary, too, if the 62-year-old man you'd been married to for over a decade was suddenly prettier than you while still, technically, being a man.

"Do you like it?" he asks. "The whole outfit, top and bottom, cost me less than $10 on eBay."

Inkie, our bad-ass cat, saunters into the room and stops to consider Tom. We watch as he pops a squat on the throw rug. He's usually sleeping on the top shelf of Tom's closet, on the platinum wig that saw service before his own hair grew long. Twodot is observing us from the top of a bookshelf. Over in the corner, Lucky sits on the end of my bed in the corner, licking her herself.

"Inkie," I say. "Do you like Daddy Girl's new outfit?"

This cat can usually be counted on to express some kind of opinion about our lives, and provide relief from the strangeness of our situation. And now, as if on cue, he sits, lifts his hind legs in the air in front of him, and scoots along the rug on his butt. I call this performance "sailing," which makes me smile. When he gets back up on all fours, he resumes his stroll into the screened porch room, where he opens the screen door with a paw. The door bumps shut behind him as he lets himself out into the night.

My attention returns to Tom. The little bird nests on his chest disappeared months ago, along with his daddy longlegs eyebrows. And thanks to the estrogen pills he's been taking, he has successfully grown small breasts. If he were a teenage girl, he'd be ready to wear a size 40 AA padded training bra, and he owns one, but doesn't feel the need to wear it. And, to his credit, he doesn't think it's necessary to have large breasts in order to feel feminine. Oddly, though, he now hangs out with women friends with pasts more interesting than mine, women who sport oversized breasts and have hair the color of a yellow jacket trap.

"Wow," I say again. "That top really is a lovely color for you."

He smiles coyly, brings his upper arm inward against his left breast. "See, I have a little cleavage, and the gathers here on the top do emphasize my booblets."

"That outfit might actually look better on me," I say, to offset his preening.

"Hah! Nice try."

But I know he'll let me try on his new clothes. He always does. Sometimes they even fit me and not him, and in this way I have ended up with a sexy sleeveless, teal and green Jam's World dress and a windfall of lacy pastel panties from Victoria's Secret.

Tom doesn't yet wear his women's clothing in Cruz Bay. While the other merchants at Mongoose Junction might wonder about his change in appearance from crew-cut to long, flowing platinum tresses, no one yet knows that he's transgendered. For now he dresses in an ambiguous style of presentation he calls *gender queer*, which is to say he wears floral shorts in soft fabrics, pastel tank tops, earrings, necklaces, bracelets on ankles and wrists, pale lipstick and, of course, Gucci perfume.

Close friends who know about Tom's metamorphosis have asked, "Didn't you see this coming?"

I've thought about this a lot and the answer is, "Nope, and I still can't quite believe it." I did finally have to give up the notion that this was a temporary obsession.

By the time I met Tom in the early 1990s, he had reinvented himself many times as he changed locations and careers. And during our marriage there had been that sudden switch from landlubber to being, quite exclusively, a man of the sea. In a matter of weeks I found myself married to Captain Ahab. And now I wonder if his new identity as a woman may be what he was searching for all along.

Tom takes a couple more steps in his low-heeled, white, size 12 ladies' sandals and turns in that jaunty way tall slender models have of showing off their wares. As I watch him walk back into his bedroom, I place my hand on my heart, take a deep breath, and listen over the night music for the abiding, constant whoosh and sigh of ocean waves.

ABOUT RAINBOWS

(dedicated to James Ginther)

On the days I work alone, James sometimes creeps into the shop, startles me, and then helps do various tasks requiring muscle, like installing heavy rolls of canvas on the rack. If customers wander in while he's here, he always makes them laugh. When James is in the shop, sales of bags and hats skyrocket. And so does my mood.

One afternoon James and I are standing together out in front of the shop, watching a huge cloud in the western sky, backlit from behind. The edges all around the cloud are glowing. He's a skydiver, and he tells me that he once dropped through a cloud just like that one. "When you're falling at 120 mph you can sometimes see your shadow on the cloud below you. If you're lucky, your shadow will be outlined by a rainbow. And then you fall into your shadow, into the cloud, and everything goes all gray and moist for a while until suddenly you drop out the bottom of the cloud and keep floating down toward the ground, until you land and return to reality."

"Wow! That is one of the most beautiful stories I have ever heard."

"Skydiving's awesome," he says. "Landings are something else, though. You gotta let go. And when you hit the ground, you have to be sure to roll and not bounce. You should try it sometime. Why don't you come with us to Puerto Rico. You can jump tandem with me."

"Thanks, but living here is extreme sport enough for me. I'll just picture you skydiving, outlined by a rainbow."

I'm packing my suitcase to leave, when I decide to take a long walk in the sunshine. On my way out the door, I smell the waxy white flowers now gracing the frangipani tree. Legend has it the sweet scent is capable of restoring peace and harmony to whoever smells it, so I've been breathing in the smell as if it's medication.

While I know I'll go for walks every day wherever I am, and I'll be hiking over the Carpathian Mountains in that new-old country called Slovakia, there's simply no place like St. John. I'm already looking forward to coming back. In the meantime, I've been looking at every scene as if I'm a camcorder, so after I leave I'll be able to close my eyes and *see* myself walking my favorite routes on the island. Now, after a long loop route, I'm heading west on the paved road next to Mary's Bay, between Annaberg and Francis Bay. In front of me are the dark clouds of a storm, and a complete rainbow on the ocean horizon. I stop. The pavement in front of me is wet with rain. The early morning sun is warm on my back, and behind me, where I've been walking, the pavement is completely dry. Here, caught in a moment of timelessness, are both sides of my life. As I make my future alone, I hope to find treasure in the form of freedom from emotional turmoil. I'll search for community among the loose fragments of past relationships. I know one must reach for a destination in order to arrive at it, of course, but there are so many questions and mysteries. Can I make a clean sweep in a tidy and exuberant manner? Will I find a storybook tale in my future? Will I be safe, now that I'm honoring a promise to take care of myself? Will this transition I'm undergoing allow me to reconcile the past with the present? And when I land, will I bounce or will I roll?

A mangrove cuckoo takes flight from one tree to the next on the side of the road next to the bay, its feathers flashing the iridescent blue of the rainbow. This sight gives me a feeling of bounty, of enough for all of us, and reminds me that it is safe to trust the present and accept the future. If every person and experience is to be ephemeral like a rainbow, I want to be grateful for them, nonetheless. This is a weightless, hopeful moment, poised as I am on the edge of the sunlight while facing a rainbow.

THE END

THE OLD COUNTRY

An Epilogue

After a grand hiking adventure over the Carpathian Mountains in August 2005, I returned to St. John to work for Tom at the shop in exchange for room and board. We never once dialed 911 because of a fight. Finally, though, I realized it was time to leave the island for good, and I returned to live in Bellingham, Washington. I now hike with a kindly man named Don, his black lab, Gracie, and my blond doodle named Sudsie. My smart and funny granddaughter lives in Montana, and our time together is most precious.

In August 2007, after 30 years at Mongoose Junction, The Canvas Factory, one of the last artisan shops on the island, closed its doors. Various reasons figured into the decision, including an economic downturn. The Friends of the Virgin Island National Park now operate a gift shop in the space once occupied by The Canvas Factory.

Tom left the flamboyant theater of St. John and also returned to Bellingham, sometimes referred to as The City of Subdued Excitement. He's even hiked with me again, up near Mt. Baker, and on the hike I wore the shirt he bought me on Jost Van Dyke bearing the slogan *MY NEXT HUSBAND WILL BE NORMAL*. Then, in December 2007, I accompanied Tom, the person I now call my *wasband*, to the Whatcom County Courthouse—and I left the judge's courtroom with a woman named Rebekah Jane Lee. She has since become immersed in politics as a Democrat, and promotes civil rights for everyone who differs from that big bell curve called *normal*. She's also a co-ed studying nursing, and is, of course, an honor student. Now more like sisters, we live separately but continue to make fun of life, and she still reminds me when it's time to remove my mustache. She has read this memoir and approves of it. Neither of us is embarrassed by the secrets I shared.

I'd like to add that people who live in the Caribbean tend to be open-minded and accepting. Differentness is embraced, especially when it doesn't actually hurt anyone else. A long-time resident of St. John told me, "This island is a crucible. People come here and get changed. They stay or they leave. The crucible itself does not change. Not really."

But there *have* been physical changes to St. John. There are new buildings, many of them over-priced, oversized and impotently placed. There's a new power station, making power outages less frequent. Shops have changed hands or disappeared. Roads have been improved. And St. John and St. Thomas now have new ferry terminals, so that trips off island have lost much of their flavor, drama, and chaos.

I've come to believe that St. John is an undiscovered vortex site, one of those locations with an energy flow that exists on multiple dimensions. The vibrations of these sites supposedly interact with a person's inner self, enhancing one's spiritual and psychic powers. All I know for certain is that the island, the friends I made there, the customers of The Canvas Factory, and the person who was Tom Lee, all live on—safe in my heart where absolute truths get collected and stored forever.

ACKNOWLEDGMENTS

First, I want to thank the Jentel Artist Residency Program in Banner, Wyoming. They gifted me with one of the best months of my life in the form of a writing residency, and it was there along Big Piney Creek, in the spring of 2007, that I began writing this memoir.

Special thanks to fellow members of the GBTC, The Growing Brainless Together Club—Sherry Gohr, Kathryn Hamshar, and Penny Bews—for reading an early draft, and for their continuing love and encouragement. I'd also like to thank Ken Speer, who warned us before going to the island, "Never squat in the woods, because there are land crabs as big as dogs." Now, if you've consumed sufficient rum, this warning could work as a metaphor for life on the island.

When St. John resident, Lucy Portlock, first read the manuscript, she said, "This is better than *Don't Stop the Carnival.*" I love her for saying that. Bellingham writing groups have had their way with portions of the narrative, and I am grateful for their attention and help. These fine individuals include Sue Erickson, Nancy Canyon, Carol Austin, Barb Crowley, C. J. Prince, Dawn Landau, Lynn McKinster, Nancy Minter, Mike McQuaide, Sara Stamey, and Kirk Smith. Laura Kalpakian, novelist and memoir-writing instructor, wisely guided me to focus on the funny side of events. My heartfelt thanks go to my book designer, Kate Weisel, who is truly a magician.

Other readers offered valuable comments and inspiration, including Bobbie Ryder Johansen, Tina Pettito, Radha Speer, Angie Hart, Walt Maloff, Patsy Lee Moore, and, of course, Rebekah Jane Lee. Christine Nunamaker, Marian Exall, Kenton Allen, and Jan Willing read later drafts of the manuscript and each made startling comments that changed the manuscript for the better. Thanks, also, to best-selling author, Pamela Beason, for her generous help in wading the deep waters of "indie" publishing, for astute editing, and tips on social networking. Special thanks to Don George, for his kindness, his careful readings of the manuscript, and for taking care of Sudsie in my absence.

There are many characters on St. John who brightened my days. In addition to Tina and Radha, mentioned above, there was Glen Speer, Hermon Smith, Capt. Phil Chalker, Jan Frey, Jim and Barb Nelson, Livy and Tom Hitchcock, James Ginther, Maia Ginther, and of course, Denis Hart, and our dear Angie Hart. To name only a few. And I'd love to hug all the customers who came into The Canvas Factory during our tenure there, because they helped make it all worthwhile.

Lastly, I want to thank Alex Politus, who often visited The Canvas Factory. After reading my first memoir, *If* The Shoe *Fits*, (now titled *I Only Cuss When I'm Sailing)*, he suggested I write a memoir about coming to live on St. John, in the same style as the first book. His comment reminded me to keep a journal handy and write down the details of events as they happened.

ABOUT THE AUTHOR

Rae Ellen Lee grew up on a stump ranch in northern Idaho. She worked for the U.S. State Dept. in Washington, D.C., Switzerland, and (then) Yugoslavia before attending the Univ. of Idaho, where she earned a degree in Landscape Architecture. Employment with the U.S. Forest Service in Idaho and Montana followed, until 1997, when she resigned and moved to the sailboat, *The Shoe*. She wrote about that experience, in *I Only Cuss When I'm Sailing* (first published as *If The Shoe Fits*).

Her first novel, *The Bluebird House*, is a paranormal, historical, romance-adventure novel with a mystery and some mountain man recipes, set in and around that old Montana mining camp brothel she lived in and renovated.

She has also published *Powder Monkey Tales—A Portrait in Stories*, by Wesley Moore alias Post Hole Augerson, a geezer of some renown in northern Idaho. A farm boy from Illinois who headed west in 1941, Wes became a woods worker and powder monkey, who used dynamite to help build roads for the logging industry in the 1940s and 1950s. This booklet captures the history and humor of her father, in his own words.

Rae Ellen now lives and writes in Bellingham, WA, in the company of her doodle dog, Sudsie, and as often as possible, she hikes, bikes, and sketches with her Montana granddaughter, Madison. She welcomes your email: rae@raeellenlee.com.

For additional information, please visit her at http://www.raeellenlee.com, and on Facebook, or give her a tweet @raeellenlee.

I hope you enjoyed *My Next Husband Will Be Normal – A St. John Adventure.*

Please read the following two chapters from my novel, *The Bluebird House,* a paranormal, historical, romance-adventure novel with a mystery and some mountain man recipes, set in and around an old Montana mining camp brothel I lived in and renovated. Look for this book on the Internet and at my website.

Excerpt from

THE BLUEBIRD HOUSE

by Rae Ellen Lee

CHAPTER I

Two weeks after my accident, I am released. Even with good insurance, the hospital has its limits. A steady stream of patients had arrived with various illnesses, not one of them as bizarre as my reason for being hospitalized.

Alone now in our cavernous house with my pets, I move slowly and only when I must. My body's bruised condition and the stiffness in my joints control my movements. I rest. I read. I watch *Days of Our Lives.* At other times I stare out the picture window in the living room over the Prickly Pear Valley. I sit silently, watching the afternoon light change on the Big Belt Mountains. When the moon rises you cannot see it move unless you look away and then look back again. That's the way the light changes on the mountains, except, when the cloud shadows gallop soundlessly across the rock on their ghost legs. When the cloud shadows race along the face of the steep mountains I always think of immense dark leaves let loose, fleeing ahead of a storm—until they reach an unseen line of fences and the outer limits of their freedom.

I study the horizon to the north, with its odd, shallow dip like an antique wash basin. The Missouri River once passed through that basin, until the mountains lifted and the river took an elbow turn to the east toward the Great Plains. When the uplift occurred, I suppose that, too, was nearly imperceptible.

I've read there are no accidents in life, that things happen for a reason. My accident must mean something, and that is what I ponder while I rest and stare out the window. Maybe I'm being reminded that *I* have never been the dominant creature, not once, not in any situation. A heavy, oddly-centered anger sometimes seethes and roils in my chest underneath the faded purple hoof print, and it isn't anger at the animal. Instead I've been thinking about love, about how I don't really love Bradley, and how by staying with him all these years I haven't loved myself. Like some slow geologic event, I had barely noticed it happening.

I can recall no joy in our marriage that was unbearably good, the way I've heard other women, like Myra, talk about their relationships. Years ago I read *Total Woman*. Other women were reading it, too, but we never talked about what the book did or didn't do for us. I even wore *Wind Song* perfume for a while, but nothing I tried seemed to make me more of a woman, or Bradley more of a man, or our marriage any more like the song of the wind.

We've been married twenty-six years. I remember the night I met him at a dance at the University of Montana, where he was taking business management and I was studying biology. I loved to dance. He knew the steps and danced smoothly, confidently. But we only danced one other time after that—at our wedding reception. Mom and Dwight were pleased that I'd done so well at college, landing a man with a secure future in business. Boy, was I surprised that first year of marriage, and bewildered, too, at how little there actually *was* to being married. But then my two beautiful boys came along and kept me busy. When they went off to grade school I got a job as a biological technician at the state water quality lab and found that my college studies were good for something besides landing a husband.

When Bradley's in town and at home in the evenings, he reads war stories, works on the computer, talks on the phone or plays golf with his associates. I've heard his subtle reprimands about my cooking and housekeeping so often I no longer listen. He says, "Molly, if you'd get rid of the dog and cat the house wouldn't need to be cleaned so often." But the house is never what I'd call dirty, even though I no longer spend all my free time cleaning. I do love my pets. He's probably jealous. I find it curious how pets can take the place of one's significant other, especially when he proves to be other than significant.

Years ago I began to notice that after Bradley was home a few days from his business trips I'd develop flu-like symptoms. When he'd leave again I'd recover. In case my symptoms meant something besides an allergy to Bradley, I went to my doctor. After several tests he found nothing wrong with me physically. Then he asked if I'd ever considered counseling. Later that week I arranged free sessions with a counselor through the employee assistance program at work. It didn't take the counselor long to tell me, rather bluntly, "You're a caretaker and it's making you sick." She didn't say I should leave my husband, but I figured that's what she meant. The weird part was, I couldn't do it. Bradley needed me. He still needs me.

But how important will the words loyalty and faithfulness be when I'm in a rest home someday? I don't think they'll matter much. What I'll want when I'm old is a deep well of memories to drink from. Yet who am I without Bradley?

And then, without bidding, I relive the details of my afternoon in the woods, and once again I hear the sound of my bones snapping like twigs under the weight of the wild animal. He was the dominant creature, in control and forceful. I was his prey. After he charged, after time had stopped, I was left behind, abandoned to my silence and pain. My helplessness swims over me, pulling me under.

CHAPTER 2

What can it hurt if I rob the food chain of a few stems and shoots? Pushing my way through willows and alders, I take care to step over the occasional mound of frozen moose droppings. Chickadees flit from branch to branch, chittering like Gregorian crickets, as my boots chuff along the frosty ground. *Chick-a-dee-dee-dee.* Occasionally I hear a bird's faraway clear whistle—*fee-bee.* It's a perfect Montana spring day—just right for hunting and gathering—and I'm determined to take a little wilderness home with me to our modern, oversized house in Helena, the house that Bradley built.

A clump of red-osier dogwood bushes stops me. A long wine-colored branch, straight and round as a fishing pole, will give me two or three pieces for the face of my window shutters. The frames are built. Now is the best time to gather the stems, before the bushes sprout leaves. At midday, the air is chilly in the shade of the firs and pines where the dogwood branches grow long and straight. The pruning shears snap cleanly through a stem, and I add it to the growing bundle on the ground near my feet, pleased that soon I'll be able to replace one boring set of beige, pleated drapes with a bit of color from the wild. Cascading all around me is the chatter of birds, like the sound of a stream filled with miniature waterfalls. At home, when I look at my finished shutters, I'll think of today and of chickadees.

I wipe my wet, cold nose on a sleeve then reach up for a perfect branch. Suddenly the woods fall silent. A slight breeze stirs the tips of fir branches, otherwise no bird sounds, no movement. Nothing. Curious about this strange hush, I turn my head.

At first only a puff of breath, behind me and off to my right. Then a small cloud, like steam from a radiator and a loud snort, an announcement. I hold my breath, my heartbeat. When I turn my head further, I see a looming dark form, too close and slightly out of focus. Where did he come from? Another grunt, this one louder, angrier. A hoof strikes frozen snow. I must keep calm. I've seen bigger. I will put something between myself and the beast. The bush in front of me doesn't offer much of a barrier, but moose don't see well. If I move slowly, he might not notice me. I step sideways with the right foot, and gradually bring the left foot along. I do this again, and then sink down, moving under the branches, around to the other side. Maybe the moose will get confused and think he's seeing things. I take another slow step. I'm almost there. The bush is now between me and the moose.

I don't know if I hear a pause before the moose lunges, or how I know he's coming at me through the bushes. Dropping to my knees with a lurch, my glasses fly off my face and catch in a low, red stem—a stem just right for twig shutters. Now crouching to shelter my internal organs, I clasp my hands over the back of my neck to protect my spinal cord. Or is this what you're supposed to do when you meet a grizzly? Oh, God. Please help me.

It happens so quickly, so inevitably—the furious snorting, the pawing, the crashing of brush over my head and the one step, heavy as a logging truck, onto my back, crushing me into the ground. I hear bones break with a dull, muffled snap, and my ears are filled with the thundering vibration of hooves pounding frozen ground. In the seconds before I pass out, I smell the musty, acrid exhaust of the large, unwashed animal.

When I come to, the pain in my back bites like the jagged, rusty teeth of an old crosscut saw. I must cough, but when I do the pain surges. The ground spins me around. Bushes blur. I wipe my mouth and see blood on a sleeve, a sleeve on an arm that I am barely able to move.

My car is somewhere out near the gravel road. But which way is it to the road? I pass out again. The cold wakes me up. The road. I must reach the road. I can hear Bradley, if I live to hear him again, saying, "What in the world were you doing out in the woods alone?"

As I drag myself onto all fours, a few broken branches fall away from me while others cling to my clothing like claws, or fish hooks. The relentless pain in my back and chest sears like hot coals, and I am dizzy again. Not far away, the creek trickles past between ice-bound banks. If I listen carefully maybe I can hear the direction the creek is moving. The loudest trickles should come from downstream, not upstream, and the creek flows downstream toward the road. But the slope of the ground appears level, except for patches of snow, broken branches, and the mounds of frozen moose shit I now see everywhere.

Groaning, I drag my pain, as if it is contained in a basket, forward on arms so weak they feel as if they belong to a stranger in a dream. Pieces of branches, now like broken wings, dangle from my jacket. Other branches hide the creek from me, but I believe I'm crawling toward the road. Every time I move the pain strikes, hot and forked as a lightning bolt. My legs trail along behind me. Moving ahead is too painful. Oh God, please don't let me die out here. Cold and numb, I inch my way forward, my hands freezing.

Wait … a sound … a car on the road. Without my glasses, I reach toward the invisible noise, toward a blur of brush. Moving forward again, slow as a glacier, I realize it will take hours, days, for me to reach the road. I will die from my wounds. I'll freeze to death tonight a short distance from help. Using my elbows I crawl toward a slant of afternoon sunlight in a clearing. Finally, finally, I flop a leaden arm over a bank of snow. But is it the edge of the road?

"Wake up, wake up," a man yells. "Jesus, what happened to you?

I open my eyes to a gray wool hat and a face so near that I can see individual wiry hairs in his brushy, walrus mustache. I close my eyes and groan. My teeth rattle against each other. "Moose … help."

"Hold on. I never found a half-dead person before. Gotta get you into the truck."

With more gratitude than I have ever known, I give in again and let the darkness reclaim me.

Curled in the fetal position on the seat of an old pickup truck, I am wrapped in a dirty blue blanket smelling of stale beer. The pain, like knives, stabs at me, over and over and over. My head rests against the man's thigh that smells of oil and sawdust. My feet bump against the door handle. During the few moments I am conscious, the truck rattles and shakes and hammers the bumpy, icy road. I doze and, moaning, wake up to the engine roaring in my ears. Now white snowy silence. Then I hear a growling rumble as the man shifts down, and the jarring clatter of loose tools and beer cans on the floor. *Am I worse off now than when I lay in the woods?* But I don't care. All I want is to stay alive, to sit on a mountaintop one more time with the sun on my face, to hear birds singing. Drifting off again, I dream that Bradley cannot find me, that this strange mountain man takes me to a deserted old building in a long-ago place in another century, and hides me there.

END OF EXCERPT

To purchase books please visit
www.raeellenlee.com

Made in the USA
Middletown, DE
30 May 2019